EVE *and* ADAM

EVE *and* ADAM

DISCOVERING THE BEAUTIFUL BALANCE

MELINDA WHEELWRIGHT BROWN

DESERET BOOK

SALT LAKE CITY, UTAH

Visit us at deseretbook.com

Library of Congress Cataloging-in-Publication Data

Names: Brown, Melinda Wheelwright, 1970– author.
Title: Eve and Adam : discovering the beautiful balance / Melinda Wheelwright Brown.
Description: Salt Lake City, Utah : Deseret Book, [2020] | Includes bibliographical references and index. | Summary: "A doctrinal explication of the Fall of Eve and Adam, with a particular emphasis on how the traditional telling misunderstands the reasons for the Fall and both Eve and Adam's roles in it"— Provided by publisher.
Identifiers: LCCN 2019054640 | ISBN 9781629727288 (hardcover)
Subjects: LCSH: Eve (Biblical figure) | Adam (Biblical figure) | Plan of salvation (Mormon theology) | Fall of man.
Classification: LCC BX8643.S25 B765 2020 | DDC 222/.1106—dc23
LC record available at https://lccn.loc.gov/2019054640

Printed in the United States of America
Publishers Printing, Salt Lake City, UT

10 9 8 7 6 5 4 3 2 1

For my brothers and sisters,
all of them.

I remembered that the real world was wide,
and that a varied field of hopes and fears,
of sensations and excitements,
awaited those who had the courage
to go forth into its expanse,
to seek real knowledge of life amidst its perils.

—Charlotte Brontë, *Jane Eyre*

CONTENTS

Author's Note xi

Introduction: **ETERNAL PROGRESSION** 1

Chapter 1: **THE POWER OF A STORY** 8

Chapter 2: **FRUIT** 20

Chapter 3: **PLAN A** 28

Chapter 4: **THE MEASURE OF OUR CREATION** 42

Chapter 5: **SIDE BY SIDE** 54

Chapter 6: **THE GARDEN OF GOD** 74

Chapter 7: **THE CRUCIAL CONFLICT** 82

Chapter 8: **NAKEDNESS** 98

Chapter 9: **THORNS AND THISTLES** 118

Chapter 10: **ACCORDING TO THE FLESH** 128

Chapter 11: **COMPLEMENTARY NATURE** 136

Chapter 12: **DIVINE COLLABORATION** 146

Epilogue: **EMBRACING LIFE WITH COURAGE** 158

Acknowledgments 161

Appendix A: **GENESIS 1:1–3:24** 163

Appendix B: **MOSES 2:1–5:16** 169

Appendix C: **ABRAHAM 4:1–5:21** 179

Bibliography 185

Index 197

AUTHOR'S NOTE

It was Eve who first transgressed the limits of Eden
in order to initiate the conditions of mortality.
Her act, whatever its nature, was formally a transgression
but eternally a glorious necessity to open the doorway toward eternal life.
Adam showed his wisdom by doing the same.
And thus Eve and "Adam fell that men might be."

—President Dallin H. Oaks[1]

This book began with a painting. In January 2016, I found myself navigating rough and uncharted waters related to some family challenges—difficult choices with no obvious, ideal, or easy answers. For Christmas the previous month, my husband had given me a beautiful portrait of Eve, which now hung in my office and had become the regular object of my drifting gaze during moments of contemplation. One particular day, as I sat puzzling over our predicament, I *really* studied Eve's image, and it occurred to me that perhaps her story could *truly* matter to mine.

With my interest piqued, I began to read and research and dig, and I soon discovered that Eve's experiences not only held answers to my tough questions but also demonstrated the trusting perspective I'd been lacking. Her faithful courage to do the hard thing for life, love, and family was precisely the example I needed.

As I read and studied everything I could find about her, my searching yielded many insights but also raised many questions and concerns. Across religions, cultures, and philosophies, there is a broad range of ideas and attitudes regarding Eve. Tragically, many of those ideas are damaging, not only to Eve's reputation and honor but to women's in general. The gross discrepancies between so many women's reality and what God intends for them hurts my heart. As one concerned Christian minister observed, "The history of our world—all periods of history, all continents, all cultural traditions—is rampant with damage, oppression, diminishment, contempt, and hostility aimed at women."[2] Attempting to capture the gravity of this reality, given what scripture teaches us, she went on to assert: "God's image is only fully reflected in both man and woman. When we exclude women, we exclude part of God. When we put women down, we tarnish the image of God."[3] Though these issues are hugely complex, at least a small piece of the puzzle can be traced back to pervasive and persisting ancient misconceptions and misapplications of the biblical record of Eve.

In Tad R. Callister's comprehensive work *The Infinite Atonement*, he examines some of history's "misunderstandings, confusion, and doctrinal heresies" associated with the story of Eve and Adam and the Fall, summarizing them into a simple list of five fundamentally false ideas:

1. Adam and Eve would have had children in the Garden of Eden if they had been allowed to remain.
2. Adam and Eve were not in a state of innocence in the garden, but rather were experiencing unparalleled joy.
3. The Fall was not part of God's master plan, but rather a tragic step backwards. It was a stumbling block, not a stepping stone in [humankind's] eternal journey.
4. If [they] had not fallen, all of [their] children would have been born in a state of bliss, to live "happily ever after" in Edenic conditions.
5. Because of the Fall, all infants are tainted with original sin.[4]

While each of these deep-rooted misunderstandings has had serious repercussions, my research has led me to feel that perhaps the most prevalent *modern* misconception is that the story of Adam and Eve is merely legend, an ancient myth. At one point in my ongoing studies, I must confess that I wondered if the distinction between fact and fiction even mattered, but I came to agree wholeheartedly with this statement from Elder Jeffrey R. Holland: "We *cannot* fully comprehend the Atonement and Resurrection of Christ and we *will not* adequately appreciate the unique purpose of His birth or His death . . . without understanding that there was an actual Adam and Eve who fell from an actual Eden, with all the consequences that fall carried with it."[5]

Even to those discounting Adam and Eve's historicity, those "consequences" are widely believed to have doomed us all to a life of misery and hardship; Eve's choice to first partake of the fruit has led to her disgrace and dishonor. Unfortunately, as Dr. Camille Fronk Olson, BYU professor of ancient scripture, has surmised, "Our interpretation of Eve's role in the Fall likely influences the manner in which we regard women in general."[6] So unfairly degrading Eve has tragically influenced the degradation of all women.

There seems to be good evidence for that hypothesis. Dr. Nehama Aschkenasy, professor and director of the Center for Judaic and Middle Eastern Studies at the University of Connecticut at Stamford, has watched an interesting pattern repeat itself among her students over the past thirty years. Before taking her class on images of women in world literature, most of her pupils have never actually read the Genesis account of Eve and Adam, yet they arrive with strong, preconceived notions that "the biblical story pronounces female inferiority and advocates the subjugation of women." Under Dr. Aschkenasy's careful tutelage, the students are consistently surprised to discover that, on close examination, the scriptural text professes nothing of the sort.[7] Rather, Dr. Aschkenasy extols Eve by helping them see her as "epitomizing the human predicament in her wish to transcend her limitations and expand her horizons."[8]

Dr. Carol Meyers, professor of biblical studies and archaeology at Duke University, shares Dr. Aschkenasy's belief that the general public tends to misjudge Eve based on a serious misunderstanding of the biblical record. She recommends examining "the pristine Eve" of ancient scripture—her noble character and symbolic significance—rather than embracing tradition's distorted Eve.[9]

Though much of the world feels that Eve disastrously introduced death and sin into the world, I believe she bravely introduced life and hope; I believe the scriptural record plus the teachings of living prophets and apostles strongly support that interpretation. As President Dallin H. Oaks has declared, "Some Christians condemn Eve for her act, concluding that she and her daughters are somehow flawed by it. Not the Latter-day Saints! Informed by revelation, we celebrate Eve's act and honor her wisdom and courage in the great episode called the Fall."[10]

However, perhaps you are one who is trying so hard to believe this, but nonetheless you are wrestling with some uncomfortable discrepancies between what is preached and what is practiced, both throughout broad Christendom and within personal experience. To you who are struggling, I hope to share my witness that there is no reason to fear the wrestle. If we will ask and search and plead and work and then ask again, our Father in Heaven *will* answer our sincere questions, and those answers will be awesome, not awful. The past several years of searching for answers have taught me that Doctrine and Covenants 42:61 teaches a profound truth: "If thou shalt ask, thou shalt receive revelation upon revelation, knowledge upon knowledge, that thou mayest know the mysteries and peaceable things."

I've come to believe that when I have a problem with some aspect of life or the gospel, including women's issues and gender relations, it is a challenge of the fallen world, not a problem with God's plan for happiness, salvation, and exaltation. I've learned firsthand that it takes work to understand how the pieces of the puzzle fit together, but I believe they do fit, and the finished product they form is beautiful.

And now, three caveats before you delve into the following pages. First, though a desire to better understand Eve has driven my research, I've gained a strong testimony that her experiences cannot be separated from Adam's any more than Adam's can be separated from hers. They are the quintessential couple. Even so, I examine their story with the specific intent to shed light on the roots and results of history's broad misunderstandings regarding Eve. My sincere desire is to inform misperceptions of the scriptural account and provide evidence of Eve's noble position beside Adam. One cannot recognize their beautiful, balanced interdependence without first restoring her to her proper place.

Second, I'd like to state unequivocally from the outset that I recognize that there are many missing pieces in the scriptural accounts of this story. The following pages include several of my own ideas and thoughts, which fill in some of those unknowns, helping me feel increased hope and understanding regarding my place in the kingdom. Though faithfully sought—the product of much prayerful study and contemplation—they are still my own and are not meant to contradict or undermine our trusted authorities or divine doctrine in any way.

And finally, some information about the book's structure. I begin with a few introductory thoughts regarding the overarching theme of Eve and Adam's story: eternal progression. Chapters 1 and 2 lay important groundwork for examining their tale through a cultural and literary lens. Though somewhat academic in nature, these ideas provide a helpful scaffolding to support the analysis and application that follow. Chapters 3 and 4 examine premortality and Creation, two often overlooked but critical pieces of the puzzle. The drama of the Garden of Eden unfolds in chapters 5 through 8. The final section, chapters 9 through 12, takes a close look at mortality and its attendant challenges and blessings, both theirs and ours.

Please note the three appendices at the back of the book; rather than including extensive scriptural passages within the text, I have placed the core scriptural accounts of Eve and Adam's story there. Unless otherwise noted, I draw passages from the King James Version of the Bible. When quoting early Church leaders, I retain original punctuation and spelling as far as is reasonable. Finally, I include rather extensive chapter endnotes throughout in hopes of encouraging further study of and deeper reflection upon this beautiful story that is so fundamental to our faith.

Ultimately, I hope to add my testimony to that of the many others I have tried to respectfully represent in this work. I believe Eve exemplifies faithful courage at its finest, maintaining an eternal perspective demonstrated through obedience, sacrifice, and consecration, in spite of *and because of* the daunting challenges of mortality, as President Henry B. Eyring has noted. "You have her example to follow. By revelation, Eve recognized the way home to God. She knew that the Atonement of Jesus Christ made eternal life possible in families. She was sure, as you can be, that as she kept her covenants with her Heavenly Father, the Redeemer and the Holy Ghost would see her and her family through whatever sorrows and disappointments would come. She knew she could trust in Them." He then added this powerful prophetic promise: "I leave you my blessing that, like Eve, you may feel the same joy that she felt as you journey back home."[11]

So, at the outset, I add my witness to President Eyring's. Eve deserves our highest esteem and sincerest emulation. Since redemption's prerequisite was the Fall, God's great plan hinged on her heroism.

NOTES

1. Oaks, "The Great Plan of Happiness."
2. Caine, *Unashamed*, 72–74. See also Genesis 1:27; 5:2; Moses 6:9; Abraham 4:27; D&C 20:18–19. Christine Caine is the founder of Propel Women, an organization designed to help women "fulfill their God-given passion, purpose, and potential." She is also cofounder of The A21 Campaign, a global anti–human trafficking organization working to abolish slavery in the twenty-first century. She is the author of several Christian-themed inspirational books.
3. Caine, *Unashamed*, 72–74.
4. Callister, *The Infinite Atonement*, 13. Brother Callister includes the following corresponding scripture references to clarify these five misunderstandings: 2 Nephi 2:23 and Moses 5:11; 2 Nephi 2:22–23; 2 Nephi 2 and Alma 42; 2 Nephi 2:22–23; and Moroni 8.
5. Holland, "Where Justice, Love, and Mercy Meet"; emphasis in original.
6. Olson, *Women of the Old Testament*, 7.
7. Aschkenasy, *Eve's Journey*, xiv.
8. Aschkenasy, *Eve's Journey*, 45.
9. Meyers, *Discovering Eve*, 77, 196.
10. Oaks, "The Great Plan of Happiness."
11. Eyring, "Daughters in the Covenant."

INTRODUCTION

ETERNAL PROGRESSION

Eve set the pattern. . . .
She made the most courageous decision any woman has ever made
and with Adam opened the way for us to progress.

—Sister Sheri L. Dew[1]

In the fourth century BC, Aristotle sought to understand the laws of physics at work in a water pump. His observations led him to postulate that because of pressure differences, a void will be filled by surrounding material, an idea he termed *horror vacui,* or "fear of empty space."[2] In the sixteenth century AD, French humanist Rabelais rephrased that notion as *natura abhorret vacuum,* inspiring the expression "nature abhors a vacuum."[3] Though physicists have debated the scientific accuracy of Aristotle's postulate, philosophers have embraced Rabelais's idiom and its implications.

Empty space is quickly filled. Personal experience demonstrates this is true. For example, children frequently, and often humorously, fill gaps in their language recognition with similar-sounding familiar words, like the child in church singing, "Dearest Children, God Is Near You." "Cherries hurt you, cherries hurt you," she sang with feeling, just like the rest of her family. Well, almost; they were actually singing, "Cherish virtue, cherish virtue."[4]

Like that well-intentioned child's linguistic confusion, holes in our doctrinal understanding may also be erroneously filled, though with results more damaging than darling. Unfortunately, if nature abhors a vacuum, Satan *adores* a vacuum—where there is a gap, he is standing by, eager and ready to commandeer that empty space. The adversary's falsehoods are often popular, compelling, and even attractive, but they are poor alternatives to true doctrine, having no power to exalt or save.

There's no room for apathy; effectively countering Satan's strategies requires our undivided attention. "In our mortal existence there is no place for an uncertain, indifferent awareness of our responsibility and obligation to decide whom we should follow," taught Elder F. Enzio Busche. "Either we must attain a knowledge of our Creator and God, who loves us, who wants to bring peace, dignity, light, and happiness into our lives, or by and by we will forget our divine origin and remain in the foggy mists of the deceiver." He further explained, "The half-truths of men, often mingled with scripture, are sometimes strong enough to fulfill the expectations of the people for a season or for a generation, but they can neither bring them along the path of exaltation and eternal life nor bring satisfying answers to the demanding problems of mankind in these days."[5] There comes a point when we must do the hard work of digging deep enough to make sense of the *whole* truth, not just the simple parts that are easily understood. Otherwise, Satan stands by, watching impatiently for gaps in our individual and collective understanding, ready to fill those voids with harmful lies, effectively preventing our eternal progression.

In my estimation, this is the precarious state of many regarding their foundational understanding of the doctrine of the Fall and the experiences and stewardships of Adam and particularly Eve.[6] This is a challenging position, since there are many pieces of their story missing from the biblical account. The following pages include several of my *personal,* though faithfully researched, thoughts regarding those unknowns. I share my feelings because I believe the cumulative effects of long-term misunderstandings and superficial faith regarding these particular points are reaching a tipping point; it's in our best interest to restore stability through a thorough examination of doctrinal truth.

To do that, we must be able to articulate our doctrine. In 2009, while serving as Relief Society General President, Sister Julie B. Beck concisely declared that "without the family, there is no plan; there is no reason for mortal life."[7] She then clearly delineated our three-part "theology of the family" based on the Creation, the Fall, and the Atonement. First, "the Creation of the earth provided a place where families could live." Second, "the Fall provided a way for the family to grow." And third, the Atonement "allows for families to have eternal growth and perfection."[8] A spotty sense of this doctrine or a vague view of its significance is insufficient to provide satisfying solutions for modern humanity's demanding problems.

Since the family is key to eternal progress, and men and women are key to the family, this is logically what the adversary chooses to target. As President Dallin H. Oaks has taught, "Satan's most strenuous opposition is directed at whatever is most important to God's plan."[9] We know firsthand that the family, marriage, and relationships between men and women are under attack—they always have been, but the adversary's weapons are deadlier than ever.

Unfortunately, because of the interdependent nature of male-female relationships, an assault on either men or women will damage both. Furthermore, any successful strike simultaneously hurts children and harms generations. If Satan can disrupt the intended balance between the sexes, innate equality is quickly replaced by unjust dominance and belittling subservience. The adversary targets man's and woman's stewardships and then twists them to expose weaknesses—since man tends toward independence, a nudge there might tempt him to neglect his duties to protect and provide for his family; since woman typically values camaraderie, a jab there might induce her to relinquish her rights in order to keep the peace necessary for a nurturing environment.

Satan would have us believe the lie that male-female relationships are like a zero-sum game—that if one wins, the other loses; if one is built up, the other must necessarily be torn down.[10] His evil meddling and manipulation result in a syndrome of serious societal ills that disproportionately target and harm women. These include sexual harassment, domestic violence, and rape; physical objectification, dehumanization, and pornography; female infanticide, child marriage, and human trafficking; not to mention the more "commonplace" problems of poverty, single-parent families, and abortion.[11] In her fascinating research regarding the safety of women, internationally recognized academic and gospel scholar Dr. Valerie M. Hudson, along with her colleagues at Texas A&M University, has studied the "societal devaluation of female life," noting anecdotally that "more lives are lost through violence against women . . . than were lost during all the wars and civil strife of the twentieth century."[12] This fact leads to her well-documented conclusion that "the greatest [international] security dilemma is, then, the systemic insecurity of women—half of the world's population."[13]

But imagine if humankind truly understood God's perfect plan: the gift of agency and the opportunity to choose to collaborate with Divinity; a physical body that makes learning by experience possible and impactful; and countless opportunities to exercise faithful courage, supported by repentance—all made possible by a loving Savior and His Atonement. Now add to that the difference it would make if society embraced God's divine design for balanced interdependence between men and women. Wouldn't life be vastly different? Spectacular possibilities exist for those willing to adopt this exalting perspective, as Dr. Hudson describes:

> *We were meant to win together. As the two halves of humanity forge a truly equal partnership at all levels of society, female contributions will not only be valued equally with men's but will be honored as the necessary counterpart to men's thinking without distorting that which is unique to each. Neither will think to operate without the other—not the man without the woman nor the woman without the man—in all human societies throughout the world. The synergy that would emerge from such partnership would generate an unprecedented human wisdom that would propel the accomplishments of the human race and more than double again the human potential not only to solve the problems of the world but to prepare the world for true peace, a peace that extends from the home to the community to the nation and to the international system.*[14]

Such a transformative approach must begin at the most basic level, with the individual, and then spread outward, from home to neighborhood, nation, and beyond. As one internationally respected anthropologist recently noted, "Since the family is the basic unit of society, only if there is justice and democracy within the family can you possibly have justice and democracy in the wider society."[15] Surely there is no better place for this enlightened mindset to be rooted than in the hearts and homes of the members of The Church of Jesus Christ of Latter-day Saints, but gaining this perspective requires that we *clearly* understand the doctrine and then align our attitudes and actions accordingly. At that point, the power of our beliefs will have the power to change the world.

For millennia, the world has dismissed the story of Adam and Eve as simply a choice between good and evil, with the obvious conclusion that Eve chose evil. But on much closer inspection, we can discover, and lead *others* to discover, that the choice was in fact between certainty and uncertainty, security and risk, fear and faith. Eve's most remarkable choice had everything to do with stagnation versus progress. Hers was a decision to trust God.

In a profound way, Eve represents all of us. On close examination, we see ourselves reflected in her faith. We each chose mortality, even knowing it would be hard and often painful, because we trusted that Divine Council who assured us we could learn and progress, ultimately not only *returning to* Them but *becoming like* Them. Exaltation isn't just a destination, a grand event that happens once we finally cross the finish line; it's also a journey, a sanctifying process that happens gradually, line upon line, all along the way.

This enlightened view reveals a better way to navigate our lives—not as one long, black-and-white, true-or-false test but as an experiential obstacle course through challenges, detours, and difficulties, with plenty of opportunities for practice. Such an approach necessitates an expanded understanding of the Atonement of Jesus Christ. With a broader perspective, we no longer see His Atonement as merely providing repentance for our unfortunate mistakes; instead we recognize it as a gracious gift clearing a path for growth, learning, and progress, as our Savior lovingly guides us home. *Allowing* Christ to assist us doesn't remove the obstacles along our path, but it repurposes them. Once stumbling blocks, they become stepping-stones, transforming us, even exalting us, each step of the way, refining our divine natures until we eventually become like Him.

NOTES

1. Dew, "Are We Not All Mothers?" Sister Dew went on to say, "She set an example of womanhood for men to respect and women to follow, modeling the characteristics with which . . . women have been endowed: heroic faith, a keen sensitivity to the Spirit, an abhorrence of evil, and complete selflessness. Like the Savior, 'who for the joy that was set before him endured the cross,' Eve, for the joy of helping initiate the human family, endured the Fall."
2. Aristotle, *Physics*. See Book IV.
3. Rabelais, *Gargantua and Pantagruel*, 20.

4. Wagner, "Hilarious Misheard Hymn Lyrics That Will Make You Laugh Out Loud." Such misunderstandings are referred to as malapropisms, from the French phrase *mal a propos*, meaning "inappropriate."
5. Busche, "Do We All Believe in the Same God?"
6. Author Neylan McBaine has made a detailed study of how some women experience the alignment between doctrine and its implementation. Expressing her concern for the well-being of all members of the Church, she writes, "We currently have one of the most progressive gender doctrines among any Western religion—an acknowledged female deity, a 'fortunate fall' which lifts Eve from condemnation, a doctrine of divine love despite gender, and an endowment of divine power for women in the temple—and yet even these revolutionary beliefs have not inoculated us from gender challenges in our culture." See McBaine, *Women at Church*, xvii.
7. Beck, "Teaching the Doctrine of the Family." Sister Beck also stated, "The plan of happiness . . . was a plan created for families. . . . When we speak of qualifying for the blessings of eternal life, we mean qualifying for the blessings of eternal families."
8. Beck, "Teaching the Doctrine of the Family."
9. Oaks, "Truth and the Plan." See also Dew, "It Is Not Good for Man or Woman to Be Alone."
10. I am indebted to Dr. Valerie M. Hudson for her extensive and spiritually informed research on gender relations. Before joining the faculty of Texas A&M, Dr. Hudson was a professor of political science at Brigham Young University for twenty-four years. In her religious writing, she typically uses her married name, Valerie Hudson Cassler.
11. This disproportionate harm to women was memorably summarized by Barber B. Conable, former president of the World Bank, who reportedly noted that while women comprise half the population, they perform two-thirds of the world's work, receive one-tenth of the world's wages, and own one-hundredth of the world's property.
12. Hudson et al., *Sex and World Peace*, 4. Specifically, Dr. Hudson is referring to such violence as "sex-selective abortion, female infanticide, suicide, egregious maternal mortality, and other sex-linked causes."
13. Hudson et al., *Sex and World Peace*, 4.
14. Hudson et al., *Sex and World Peace*, 200.
15. "Understanding Islamic Feminism: An Interview with Ziba Mir-Hosseini," February 7, 2010. In Hudson et al., *Sex and World Peace*, 127–28. Dr. Mir-Hosseini has a PhD in anthropology from Cambridge University and has authored several books on Islam, gender, and the family.

CHAPTER 1

THE POWER OF A STORY

The gospel story is a family story. . . .
It begins with heavenly parents,
and it ends with children making their way through the
sometimes exhilarating, sometimes overwhelming
challenges of mortality and back to their heavenly home,
having received all of the essential ordinances of eternal exaltation.
That's the story of our lives. . . .
There is an extraordinarily happy ending in store for all who desire it.

—President M. Russell Ballard[1]

Stories are one of the most fundamental ways we communicate; as we relate our experiences to each other, our sharing often takes the shape of a story. Stories are also one of the most fundamental ways we learn—they convey morals, values, principles, and beliefs, as well as attitudes and social norms, all of which influence our perception of the world.

Powerful stories engage us such that we are inclined, even compelled, to puzzle through a character's actions and the resulting consequences while remaining detached enough to reflect with objectivity and honesty. We examine cause, effect, and rationale through countless examples and non-examples, allowing us to process and connect these lessons to our personal experiences and to others'. As a result, stories can change us—shaping how we behave, think, and act, thanks to the characters we meet.

Simply put, stories allow for interpretation, internalization, and application. As such, a great story's influence lies in its ability to move us from "a position of powerlessness to a position of possibility."[2]

One of history's most prevalent type of story is the origin story. Found in virtually every culture, past and present, origin myths emerge and take root because groups, and the individuals who comprise them, long to make sense of how they arrived at where they are, collectively hoping that telling stories to memorialize their past will also enlighten their future. Such composite reminiscences can't help but become mythic, not only because historical accuracy fades over time but because their very purpose is to be a widely applicable guide for well-being. As one biblical commentator and writer explained, "Over the years, [origin stories] morph into a colorful amalgam of truth and myth, nostalgia and cautionary tale, the shades of their significance brought out by the particular light of a particular moment."[3]

Arguably humanity's most foundational and enduring account, that of our noble First Parents, has undergone such reshaping, retelling, and reiterations, several of which are recorded in holy scripture and sacred text. Those various accounts share a noble purpose: to illuminate our collective path—past, present, and future.

Despite such potential for good, any story—including an origin story—can prove perilous when misinterpreted and misapplied. As we all know, Eve and Adam's story hasn't always blessed lives the way it was intended. Gospel scholar Joseph Fielding McConkie observed that "from Genesis to Revelation, no story in scripture has been the source of more theological mischief than the story of Eden. It is the prime example of scriptural misuse and abuse. The errors that have come from the perversions of this story have given birth in turn to a thousand more."[4]

The roots of these errors are not necessarily malicious, though certainly some of the results have caused pain. Bible stories, and especially *this* Bible story, can prove tricky for several significant reasons that are worth briefly considering.[5] First, employing historical characters figuratively can blur the distinction between fact and fiction. Second, the limitations of language, especially translated across cultures and stripped of context, can wreak havoc on our understanding of important truths. Third, multiple versions of an account, with their inevitable variations, can cause a reader to hear dissonance in differences.

FIGURATIVE NONFICTION

Applying a literary perspective to a historic episode like Adam and Eve's can cause confusion because fact can so easily be interpreted as fiction. Nearly everyone, regardless of religious affiliation and even among the areligious, is familiar with Eve and Adam's story. Asked to categorize its genre, though, most would choose fiction rather than nonfiction, biography, or self-help. Despite this mythical mindset, the restored gospel of Jesus Christ unequivocally establishes, and even hinges on, the actuality of this real-life duo, notwithstanding their legendary status.

Yet even while affirming their actual existence, we must also embrace symbolic interpretations. In Adam and Eve's case, much of their relatively brief biblical account resembles a double-sided puzzle with both literal and figurative images, so it can be quite challenging to discern which are which and how they each fit.[6]

Furthermore, since Eve and Adam's story is brief yet full of unanswered questions, it long ago opened the door for extensive speculation and what we would today consider creative "spin-offs." Writers and storytellers through the ages have enjoyed filling in the blanks, providing fictional backstories and follow-ups.

Some of these fictional retellings have taken deep root, the most noteworthy being John Milton's *Paradise Lost*. First published in 1667, this enormous work chronicles in elaborate and imaginative detail the Creation, Adam and Eve's experiences in the Garden of Eden, and their life in the fallen world. With such scope paired with Milton's artistry, it didn't take long for *Paradise Lost* to be considered the greatest epic poem written in the English language.[7]

Though Milton writes with the tone and grandeur of scripture, he authored what we would today call historical fiction, superimposing and embedding his own ideas and opinions over and among the biblical basics.[8] Most notably, his depiction of the nature of God, the relationship between Eve and Adam, and the significance of the Fall is often contrary to revealed doctrinal truth, though arguably dramatic and intriguing. Despite these inaccuracies, such a highly acclaimed and prominent work has had significant effects on our opinions of Adam and Eve.[9]

Because the story of Adam and Eve is so fundamental to our faith, it is important that we examine their experiences and impact based on our doctrinal canon, both ancient scripture and modern revelation, while refraining from embracing secular authors' imagination and speculation.

LANGUAGE LIMITATIONS

Such a careful doctrinal examination requires a means of communication—a medium, if you will—and that medium is language. Unfortunately, language is imperfect. In fact, more often than not, language is the very source of misunderstanding. Even the Prophet Joseph Smith expressed frustration over the limitations of language, writing, "Oh Lord God deliver us in thy due time from the little narrow prison almost as it were total darkness of paper pen and ink and a crooked broken scattered and imperfect language."[10] Such challenges are particularly evident in the case of ancient scripture, where translation, interpretation, redaction, and cultural biases all weave together over time, influencing our understanding of sacred writ. The complicated tapestry that results may ultimately manifest itself as misinterpretation; and, once misinterpreted, the resulting misapplication is often far reaching and long lasting, as has been the case with the story of our First Parents.[11]

Translation

The Prophet Joseph's desire to break free from some of language's limitations led him to study Hebrew, Egyptian, and German, in the hopes that a broader understanding of language would help him be a better translator. For him, translation was neither simple nor straightforward, but required prayerful work. He openly acknowledged that not all translators of scripture had been so conscientious, conceding that "many things in the bible . . . do not, as they now stand, accord with the revelation of the holy Ghost to me."[12] He elaborated by explaining that "ignorant translators, careless transcribers, or designing and corrupt priests have committed many errors."[13]

Because of the inherent challenges of enlightened translation, many biblical scholars, both amateur and revered, consult multiple versions of the Bible to find the most accurate meaning. Though the King James Version of the Bible is The Church of Jesus Christ of Latter-day Saints' official authorized translation, consulting other versions is certainly not only acceptable but often useful, as demonstrated recently by Elder Dieter F. Uchtdorf. In his April 2017 general conference talk, "The Greatest Among You," Elder Uchtdorf quoted Mark 10:35–40 using the New International Version, and, later in that same talk, he used the New English Translation's wording of Philippians 2:3. Clearly, Elder Uchtdorf finds value in examining multiple translations as part of his in-depth scripture study, which suggests that we might do the same.[14]

Interpretation

If we think of translation as the warp threads of our tapestry, interpretation might be considered the weft threads, which effectively lock the translation in place.[15] When subjective opinions are boldly declared, they can prove quite sticky and may result in lasting consequences.[16]

An example of preserving an unfortunate interpretation can be found in the writing of the revered Jewish scribe and scholar Ben Sira, who lived two centuries before Christ. He made the first recorded negative statements regarding Eve's choice to partake of the fruit of the tree of knowledge of good and evil, declaring that "through her we all die."[17] This was an interpretive statement, since it's not explicitly stated anywhere in the ancient text itself. However, Ben Sira's respected opinion served to narrow and bias his followers' perspective regarding Eve. That narrowed mindset likely influenced other commentators, solidifying tragically degrading attitudes toward the Mother of All Living.

Redaction

Yet another complicating factor of the translation process is the possibility that pieces of the text may be inadvertently or purposely removed, a process known as redaction. While there are often valid reasons for the deletion of text from a secular document (such as to protect someone's privacy or to correct misinformation), as far as scripture is concerned, there is often less valid justification. Thanks to Joseph Smith's work on his inspired translation of the Bible (now known as the Joseph Smith Translation, or JST), we are able to see clearly where many "plain and precious" truths have been removed.[18] As he explained, "many important points, touching the salvation of man, [have] been taken from the Bible, or lost before it was compiled."[19]

Perhaps nowhere are lost truths more troubling than throughout the account of Eve's life story because of the damaging effects they have had on women's well-being. Members of the Church are richly blessed by having access to the Pearl of Great Price (parts of which are a portion of the Joseph Smith Translation), as well as our sacred temple liturgy. This latter-day revelation allows us to gain a far greater understanding of the noble characteristics and roles of Eve.

Cultural Biases

Cultural biases are one of humanity's great manipulators. We process practically everything through the culture-tinted spectacles we wear. Every time we read something written in a different time and place, we have to cross multiple cultural bridges in order to apply it to ourselves. Biblical scholars E. Randolph Richards and Brandon J. O'Brien have written extensively about this challenge. They've observed that "we tend to read Scripture in our own *when* and *where*, in a way that makes sense on our terms"; they note that "when a passage of Scripture appears to leave out a piece of the puzzle because something went without being said, we instinctively fill in the gap with a piece from our own culture—usually a piece that goes without being said."[20]

One simple example of cultural bias occurs in connotations. Beyond their basic definitions, some words convey a subtle feeling or emotion, such as *bossy* versus *assertive*, or *lazy* versus *laid-back*. Connotations are highly culture specific, which is why someone learning a new language often inadvertently provides amusement to a native speaker. Similarly, when we filter scripture's words and phrases through our modern English connotations, we may take offense when none was intended.

Navigating around translation issues, wading through assorted interpretations, and seeing beyond our assumptions—all these tasks demand insightful selectivity and introspective objectivity; both are vital if we are to understand, extract, and apply timeless truths accurately.

MULTIPLE ACCOUNTS

Beyond the subtle dangers of fictionalizing nonfiction and the all-pervasive limitations of language, members of The Church of Jesus Christ of Latter-day Saints face the additional interpretive challenge of having multiple accounts of our First Parents' story—those found in Genesis, Moses, Abraham, and our sacred temple liturgy. These four accounts provide plenty of room for comparative analysis, which can lead to questions and even concerns.

The same tale may be told in various ways to highlight certain themes or appeal to unique audiences. Most are comfortable with the four New Testament Gospels doing exactly that. Matthew, Mark, Luke, and John all recount the story of Christ's life and mortal ministry, but each does so differently from the others. Coming from different backgrounds and writing for different populations, the writers emphasize different elements, as individual authors always do. Likewise, we can appreciate the harmonies among the various accounts of Adam and Eve.[21]

Additionally, we have priceless commentary throughout the Book of Mormon to enhance our understanding. As we apply that to the accounts, it's helpful to remember that ancient America's prophets were writing for *us* in the latter days.[22] Ancient Israel's scribes, however, were recording formerly oral traditions in order to preserve their religion and influence their contemporaries. Recognizing authors' unique intentions frees us to find meaning in differences rather than to condemn discrepancies.

Finally, we are blessed with the teachings of modern-day prophets and apostles to help us apply doctrine and principles effectively in our lives. Occasionally, leaders may seem to contradict each other as they offer their personal understanding of the gospel. Elder D. Todd Christofferson elaborated on how inspiration is received, even for prophets and apostles, explaining that spiritual communication is expressed "in words or in feelings that convey understanding *beyond words.*"[23] Verbalizing spiritual impressions that are "beyond words" requires us to process sacred feelings through culture, traditions, and life experiences, all while using limited language. The resulting choice of words may not always resonate identically with every listener. As Sister Sheri Dew conceded, "*We are imperfect people trying to understand and communicate a perfect message.* Therein lies the source of many challenges."[24]

In spite of the challenges inherent in fitting together our multiple accounts of Eve and Adam, imagine having only one narrow view of this integral episode of human history, seen only through ancient eyes and intended solely for ancient people. Thanks to the harmony of inspired, divine voices, the restored gospel offers us a multifaceted and timeless perspective.

A FRESH PERSPECTIVE

With this helpful groundwork now in place, let's take a fresh, objective, and mature look at the story of Adam and Eve, with the benefit of the inspired and expanded insight provided by the restored gospel of Jesus Christ. Such a perspective will require that we clean our lenses, sharpen our focus, and examine this powerful true story carefully and prayerfully, willing to let go of former assumptions. Doing so will allow us to embrace new understanding and apply doctrinal truth in potentially life-altering and world-changing ways.

NOTES

1. Ballard, "Women of Dedication, Faith, Determination, and Action."
2. Short, "Children Taking Action within Global Inquiries," 50–59.
3. Evans, *Inspired*, 9. Rachel Held Evans was a popular Christian journalist and a *New York Times* best-selling author.
4. McConkie, "The Mystery of Eden," 34.
5. Sister Sharon Eubank has urged us to be *articulate* in defending our faith—to courageously step forward and clearly express how we feel and *why* ("Turn On Your Light"). Attitudes and understanding can change over time only to the degree that

we share new ways of looking at ingrained ideas. Though some may feel familiar with the issues enumerated in this chapter, I believe their examination here is helpful in order to equip us with added insight so that we might feel comfortable articulating our understanding of this fundamental story.

6. See Lyon, *Understanding Temple Symbols*, for an excellent section on ten keys to help us understand sacred symbolism. It is also helpful to remember this wise advice from the Prophet Joseph Smith: "The things of God are of deep import, and time and experience, and careful and ponderous and solemn thoughts can only find them out" (https://www.josephsmithpapers.org/paper-summary/history-1838-1856-volume-c-1-2-november-1838-31-july-1842/86#historical-intro).
7. Samuel Johnson, the renowned literary critic of the eighteenth century, considered *Paradise Lost* (with its 11,000+ lines of blank verse) a masterpiece and ranked it among the greatest "productions of the human mind." Modern critics, as well, widely regard it as "a monumental pillar of the literary canon." See Tonkin, "Why Milton Still Matters."
8. Milton wrote in what has become known as "Miltonic grand style" because he did not want any sense of triviality belittling his prose. He relied heavily on Latin-based words, even coining some original Latin-derived English words, such as "terrific" and "jubilant," to "impart a classical gravity and authority, shifting the style away from the commonplace." He believed his work was inspired, even dictated by a heavenly muse, and therefore possessed with *nearly* biblical authority. It is also of note that Milton had lost his eyesight completely when *Paradise Lost* was authored; he spoke his lines of prose to a scribe who then recorded them, checking with him for accuracy. See Carey, *The Essential Paradise Lost*, 11–16.
9. Gospel scholar, English professor, and current president of BYU–Hawaii John Tanner notes that *Paradise Lost* "helped shape some such popular traditions in the New England mind, since the poem was enormously popular in early America. . . . Thus, although Joseph [Smith] likely never read the poem, its ideas may have filtered into even the unlettered culture of rural upstate New York." See Tanner, "Making a Mormon of Milton," 201.
10. Joseph Smith to William W. Phelps, Nov. 27, 1832, in *Personal Writings of Joseph Smith*, 287.
11. Perhaps this explains why several Book of Mormon prophets wisely refrain from recording their most sacred experiences and teachings. For example, see 2 Nephi 33:1; Alma 8:1; Helaman 8:3; 14:1; 3 Nephi 7:17; 17:15; 19:32, 34; 26:6; Mormon 8:23; Ether 12:25; Moroni 9:19.
12. Smith, *The Words of Joseph Smith*, 211.
13. https://www.josephsmithpapers.org/paper-summary/history-1838-1856-volume-e-1-1-july-1843-30-april-1844/127.
14. By way of further example, in 1992, Elder Neal A. Maxwell, speaking at BYU's Education Week on the topic of "The Inexhaustible Gospel," expounded on

Colossians 1:17 using the Revised Standard Version's wording. Rather than choosing the King James Version, "And he [Christ] is before all things, and by him all things consist," Elder Maxwell chose this alternate translation as his prominent theme: "in [Christ] all things hold together." Throughout this marvelous talk, Elder Maxwell illustrated the divine doctrine that Christ brings meaning and value to all things, a concept that is difficult to grasp through the word choice of the King James Version but is straightforward in the Revised Standard Version translation.

15. In weaving, the warp threads or yarn extend the length of the loom and are crossed by the weft (or filling) threads or yarn. By interlocking perpendicularly, they effectively form the structure of a length of fabric. See *Merriam-Webster Online.*
16. Because of the risk of preserving misunderstanding, biblical interpretation has become a careful science. The process involves both *exegesis* (discovering a passage's original intended meaning) and *hermeneutics* (how one interprets and applies a text's present meaning).
17. Ecclesiasticus 25, particularly 25:24. Ecclesiasticus is a book of the Apocrypha and is also known as The Wisdom of Jesus Son of Sirach; it is generally believed to have been written by Ben Sira.
18. The loss of "plain and precious things" is described in both 1 Nephi 13:20–39 and Moses 1:40–41. One prime example of such redaction is found in the story of the Exodus from Egypt, in which the King James Version describes the Lord repeatedly "harden[ing] the heart of Pharaoh," portraying a conniving God with little concern for agency. The Prophet Joseph's inspired translation changes this phrase to "and *Pharaoh* hardened *his* heart," depicting a significantly different source of Pharaoh's stubborn attitude (JST, Exodus 7:13; emphasis added; see also JST, Exodus 7:3; 9:12; 10:1, 20, 27; 11:10). In other instances, redaction may allow for rather dreadful repercussions, as was the case in the King James Version's word choice for Exodus 22:18, which commands, "Thou shalt not suffer a witch to live." The JST corrects this to accurately state, "Thou shalt not suffer a *murderer* to live," a potentially lifesaving difference to many falsely accused women, such as those living in the Puritan town of Salem, Massachusetts, in the seventeenth century.
19. https://www.josephsmithpapers.org/paper-summary/history-1838-1856-volume-a-1-23-december-1805-30-august-1834/189#source-note.
20. Richards and O'Brien, *Misreading Scripture with Western Eyes,* 11–17. Dr. Richards is provost and professor of biblical studies in the School of Ministry at Palm Beach Atlantic University. His coauthor, Dr. O'Brien, earned his PhD from Trinity Evangelical Divinity School.
21. See Meservy, "The Four Accounts of the Creation," where he writes: "In one sense, the harmony of the four accounts of the Creation could be compared to the harmony of the four gospels of the New Testament. They complement one

another. Details from one embellish those of the others, ultimately giving us a fuller picture, a broader understanding, and a deeper appreciation."

22. Mormon 8:35.
23. Christofferson, "The Doctrine of Christ"; emphasis added.
24. Dew, *Worth the Wrestle*, 43; emphasis in original.

CHAPTER 2

FRUIT

Either make the tree good, and his fruit good;
or else make the tree corrupt, and his fruit corrupt:
for the tree is known by his fruit.

—Matthew 12:33

With the preliminary scaffolding of chapter 1 in place, one additional aspect of groundwork needs to be laid because of some pervasive yet problematic cultural connotations. Let's briefly examine the deceptively simple but significant element at the core of this story: fruit.

One of the reasons Eve has been so punished by the world over time is that the nature of the fruit she ate has been misunderstood. When we hear the name "Eve," the image of an apple often accompanies it. This is a prime example of a facet of human nature the Enlightenment thinker John Locke recognized back in the 1600s, a phenomenon that has come to be known as word associations.[1] He recognized that when we retrieve one thought or concept from memory, a second often gets pulled up with it, as if our brain has filed the two close by and they've grown together. Finding the rationale behind word associations can provide insight into conditioned connections, both individually and collectively. In the case of Eve, fruit has become a powerful symbol of her story, at least in part, because it's familiar, tangible, and involves other senses, like taste and smell, all of which reinforce mental pairings.

Symbols can pack a punch, wrapping deep ideas and complex connotations into a simple, yet thought-provoking, form. In order to tease out the metaphoric elements of this symbol, we have to ask the question, why an apple? The biblical narrative never mentions an apple, yet there it is, in paintings, sermons, and commentaries. Why not an orange or a pear or a fig? Figs actually do get mentioned in the story, so that would make sense. But the likely reason for the ubiquitous apple is both clever and slanderous: the Latin word for *apple* is *malum,*[2] the same word used for *evil*. So, for centuries, this enduring symbol, originating in a Latin pun, has subtly been reinforcing Eve's most unfortunate stereotype.

Understanding the likely source and strength behind the pervasive apple nudges us toward more objectively examining why *fruit,* in general, may have been chosen to represent the doorway to mortality. Looking at three of fruit's general characteristics gives us a clue: it's sweet, it's healthy, and it's a good source of energy.

Our tongue's taste buds are designed to discern five types of taste: sweet, salty, bitter, sour, and umami. The molecular form of a food is like a chemical key that unlocks specific taste-bud receptors, opening the door for a message to be sent to the brain regarding taste. When something mentally registers as tasting sweet, we are instinctively inclined to eat more of that food—effective, since naturally occurring sweetness closely correlates with high health benefits. Fruit contains many essential vitamins and minerals, like potassium to regulate blood pressure, vitamin C to heal wounds, and vitamin K to strengthen bones. And fructose, the carbohydrate or sugar found in fruit, is an efficient source of immediate energy without unnecessary calories. So fruit's naturally occurring sweetness is intended to be a reward, encouraging healthy consumption.[3]

As further evidence of this figurative significance, consider the word *vitamin*. It's a combination of two words, *vita*, from the Latin for life, and *amine*, relating to amino acids.[4] A vitamin, by definition, is an organic compound, essential for normal growth and nutrition, which cannot be synthesized naturally in the body, and so it is required to be ingested. With that elementary understanding, we see Eve's consideration of the fruit in a new light. That fruit, whether literal or figurative or some blend of the two, contained certain elements *essential* for growth and development, elements that could not be acquired in any way other than the conscious choice to partake.[5]

Before we examine that literally life-altering choice, let's pause to consider trees. Throughout scripture, we repeatedly read of living things being created "after their kind"[6]; this holds true for plants, animals, and humanity alike. For example, Moses specifically mentions "the fruit tree yielding fruit, after his kind,"[7] and Luke understands "a good tree bringeth not forth corrupt fruit; neither doth a corrupt tree bring forth good fruit."[8] Characteristics of the fruit should reveal much about the tree and vice versa, but in the case of the garden story, we sometimes neglect to integrate our understanding of the trees with that of their fruit.

With more than 60,000 species of trees on earth, it makes sense that we assign names to differentiate between them. We assume the Garden of Eden had a vast assortment of trees, but we learn the names of only two—the tree of life and the tree of knowledge of good and evil.[9] These names don't follow our typical English pattern for naming trees. We call a tree that produces cherries a cherry tree; a tree that grows pears is a pear tree. Perhaps a closer look at these two trees' unique names will help us better understand their unique place of honor within the garden.

Let's start with the tree of life. Depictions, tales, and representations of the tree of life are countless and widespread among religions, across cultures, and throughout time. Historically, a monarch's "royal scepter represented a life-giving branch of the tree of life."[10] In the Middle Ages, Christ's cross was often depicted as being made from the tree of life.[11] The sacred menorah, with its seven branches, brings light like the tree of life.[12] Even our genealogical depictions, "family trees," symbolize the tree of life. The tree of life seems to be everywhere! But biblically it receives very little attention; there are only three brief mentions of the tree of life in the Genesis narrative.[13] Later, in Proverbs, it's referred to metaphorically on four fleeting occasions.[14] But in the final chapter of the New Testament, almost 2,000 pages later, in nearly the last verse of the entire Bible, the tree returns for the denouement. Perhaps it is the combination of the bookended imagery of Genesis and Revelation that has led to the tree's widespread and long-lasting cultural influence. Here, in John the Revelator's final plea, we have three powerful verses that highlight the eternal significance of the tree of life:

> *And, behold, I come quickly; and my reward is with me, to give every man according as his work shall be.*
>
> *I am Alpha and Omega, the beginning and the end, the first and the last.*
>
> *Blessed are they that do his commandments, that they may have right to the* tree of life, *and may enter in through the gates into the city. (Revelation 22:12–14; emphasis added)*

In these verses, I hear powerful prophetic echoes reminiscent of "The Living Christ: The Testimony of the Apostles." That beautiful document uses similar wording as it encapsulates the mission of "the Great Jehovah of the Old Testament, the Messiah of the New":

- "Each of us will stand to be judged of Him according to our works and the desires of our hearts."

- "I am the first and the last; I am he who liveth, I am he who was slain" (D&C 110:3–4).
- "His way is the path that leads to happiness in this life and eternal life in the world to come."

These verses and phrases, added to our comfortable familiarity with Lehi's vision of the tree of life in the Book of Mormon, as well as many other references in our Restoration scriptures and sacred temple liturgy, make it clear that the tree of life could more accurately be considered the tree of *eternal* life. Or, to rephrase by applying basic botanical nomenclature, we might call it "the eternity tree."

Since the laws of nature dictate that fruit is directly related to the tree from which it comes—in other words, "after its kind"—the fruit of "the eternity tree" would be expected to have eternal qualities and characteristics. None of our various garden accounts detail Adam and Eve's experience eating this fruit, but Lehi describes in detail what he tasted in his vision. He called it the sweetest fruit he had ever eaten, the whitest thing he had ever seen. It was "desirable to make one happy," and "it filled [his] soul with exceedingly great joy."[15] For further emphasis, Nephi later explained, it was "desirable above all other fruits" and "the greatest of all the gifts of God,"[16] just as we would expect the "eternity tree's" fruit to be. Lehi and Nephi wanted nothing more than to share it with their family because "eternal life with our loved ones is sweeter and more desirable than any other thing."[17]

Now, let's turn our attention to the other tree, the tree of knowledge of good and evil. We've already determined that its fruit needed to be eaten to enable growth and development, and that it was divinely designed to taste delicious. Like the "eternity tree's" fruit, it was desirable. Yet, like Eve's so-called apple, this tree has historically been unfairly maligned.

When we are presented with pairs, like these two trees, our minds often slot them into a dualistic structure, taking a mental shortcut to make sense of their relationship. We dichotomize them, even if applying a complementary framework might prove a better fit. This seems to have been the sad fate of the tree of knowledge of good and evil. When seen as the *opposite* of the marvelous tree of life, the tree of knowledge of good and evil looks like the dreadful tree of death. But it doesn't make sense that delicious, desirable, essential fruit would come from a terrible tree. A closer look at its name helps restore respect to this equally precious tree.

With a good understanding of English syntax, specifically prepositions and prepositional phrases, we can thoughtfully reorder the words and call this "the good-and-evil knowledge tree." The descriptor, "good-and-evil," used to describe the kind of knowledge this tree gives, employs a literary device intended to designate a spectrum. By definitively noting the two extremes, a creative storyteller paints a picture of the *full range* of options. So "good-and-evil knowledge" describes *all* knowledge—the full range of moral distinctions—black and white *and* all the grays in between.[18] President Wilford Woodruff stated that this tree's fruit was ordained to be eaten, "in order that [humanity] might know both good and evil by passing through this school of experience which this life affords us."[19] How sensible that eating this tree's fruit provided entrance to mortality,[20] since the tree itself represented mortality's precious learning experience. "The fruit tree yielding fruit, after [its] kind."[21] This is no terrible tree, just as mortality is no terrible punishment. This leads us to the same conclusion Elder B. H. Roberts makes in his book *The Truth, the Way, the Life:* "Let it be observed that the Tree of Knowledge, even though the Tree of Death, is nowhere called an 'Evil Tree,' or its fruit bad. . . . Rather to the contrary: it is included among the 'trees pleasant to the sight, and good for food,' in the same verse in which it is named (Genesis 2:9)."[22]

This makes logical sense, since we have been taught repeatedly that mortality is a necessary phase of life on our journey toward salvation and exaltation. Elder Jeffrey R. Holland recognized that necessity when he stated that "inherent in the fruit of the tree of knowledge of good and evil" is "the path toward growth and godhood."[23]

Thinking of the tree of knowledge of good and evil as the "mortality tree" makes it easy to recognize it as the "eternity tree's" divine complement, instead of its destructive opponent, since the best proof of complementarity between two things is when neither matters without the other, when the absence of one renders both meaningless. This is precisely the relationship between mortality and eternal life, the relationship that set up the perfect conditions for the plan of salvation to proceed.

NOTES

1. Locke, *An Essay Concerning Human Understanding*, Vol. I.
2. *Pocket Oxford Latin Dictionary*, "apple."
3. Wadyka, "Get the Health Benefits of Fruit."
4. *Oxford English Dictionary Online*, "vitamin."
5. Some wrongly equate the eating of the fruit with some act of unchastity or immorality. Prophets and apostles have strongly and repeatedly spoken against this false notion, perhaps most vehemently Elder James E. Talmage, who addressed these false ideas pointedly in *Jesus the Christ*, writing, "Such a doctrine is an abomination. . . . The human race is not born of fornication. These bodies that are given unto us are given in the way that God has provided. . . . Our first parents were pure and noble, and when we pass behind the veil we shall perhaps learn something of their high estate." See Talmage, *Jesus the Christ*, 29.
6. See Genesis 1; Moses 2; Abraham 4.
7. Moses 2:11.
8. Luke 6:43.
9. Genesis 2:9; Moses 3:9; Abraham 5:9. Note that the tree of knowledge of good and evil is occasionally referred to as the tree of *the* knowledge of good and evil; see Genesis 2:17 and Moses 3:17.
10. Peterson, "The Qur'anic Tree of Life," 198.
11. In his essay "The Tree of Life in the New Testament and Christian Tradition," BYU professor and biblical scholar John W. Welch writes: "The tree of life in the Garden of Eden possessed the regenerative power to allow Adam and Eve to live forever. Drawing on this imagery, Christians readily saw in the resurrection of Jesus Christ the culmination of this same saving and immortalizing power. Thus, the symbolism of the tree fit snugly together with the gospel message of

the earliest Christian writers. . . . The cross itself was soon interpreted and represented as the tree of life in Christian texts and art." His essay includes several excellent photographed examples of medieval European artwork depicting Christ's cross as the tree of life (Welch, "The Tree of Life in the New Testament and Christian Tradition," 82–83, 95).

12. Yarden, *The Tree of Light*, 35–40.
13. Genesis 2:9; 3:22, 24.
14. Proverbs 3:18; 11:30; 13:12; 15:4.
15. 1 Nephi 8:10–12.
16. 1 Nephi 15:36.
17. Pearson, "Stay by the Tree."
18. This is one of those cases, considered in chapter 1, where employing literary tactics in the retelling of a story can both simplify and complicate the details, altering the meaning if one isn't careful. Still, the Prophet Joseph Smith recognized the usefulness of such dichotomizing, stating, "By proving contraries, truth is made manifest" (http://www.josephsmithpapers.org/paper-summary/history-1838-1856-volume-f-1-1-may-1844-8-august-1844/1#full-transcript). While dualism can be a useful teaching tool, such oversimplification may have gone too far in Adam and Eve's case, since Parley P. Pratt referred to the watered-down version as a "childish tale" (Pratt, *Spirituality: The Key to the Science of Theology*, 33–34), and Brigham Young called the simplified Bible story a baby story (in *Journal of Discourses*, 2:6–7).
19. Wilford Woodruff, in *Journal of Discourses*, 23:125.
20. Elder Bruce R. McConkie explained: "What is meant by partaking of the fruit of the tree of the knowledge of good and evil is that our first parents complied with whatever laws were involved so that their bodies would change from their state of paradisiacal immortality to a state of natural mortality" (McConkie, "Christ and the Creation").
21. Moses 2:11.
22. Roberts, *The Truth, the Way, the Life*, 387.
23. Holland, *Christ and the New Covenant*, 203. The following similar statements have been made: President Joseph Fielding Smith made clear the absolute necessity of mortality, explaining that "through the various vicissitudes [we have] to pass, [we] receive a knowledge of both good and evil, without which it would be impossible . . . to gain the exaltation prepared for [us]" (Smith, *Doctrines of Salvation*, 1:121). Elder James E. Talmage called mortality "the means of winning . . . glory, exaltation, and eternal lives" (Talmage, *The Articles of Faith*, 63). Elder Dallin H. Oaks declared that eating this tree's fruit was "a glorious necessity to open the doorway toward eternal life" (Oaks, "The Great Plan of Happiness").

CHAPTER 3

PLAN A

If salvation means only erasing our mistakes and sins,
then salvation—as wonderful as it is—
does not fulfill the Father's aspirations for us.
His aim is much higher:
He wants His sons and daughters to become like Him.

—Elder Dieter F. Uchtdorf[1]

In the spring of 2005, our family relocated to a new state. Feeling adventurous, we purchased a new home that was at the framing stage of construction. This was our first home-building experience, so perhaps we weren't as concerned as we should have been when the builder issued a curious caveat. The plans for this house had been designed by a draftsman, not an architect. The difference meant less education, less experience, and less stringent standards for the draftsman, but our builder had used several of his designs before and was confident things would work out. He said, "Just know, some of the things he's designed might not come together quite like he's drawn them, so we may have a few surprises, but nothing we can't fix. We'll just figure it out as we go along. We may need to come up with a Plan B in a few spots."

Sure enough, improvisation became the name of the game. As the framing was wrapping up and the roof trusses were being placed, our first Plan B had us moving a bathroom because there wasn't room to stand in the shower. A bigger surprise came a bit later with the heating, ventilation, and air conditioning. Apparently, the draftsman had neglected to leave any room for cold-air returns through the center of the house. This time, we got all the way to Plan E before agreeing on a satisfactory solution. That memorable construction project taught me the value of employing skilled architects and *starting* with the best plan.

THE MASTER ARCHITECT

Our Heavenly Father is the Master Architect, and He *started* with a perfect plan. The Book of Mormon describes that plan as a "plan of redemption,"[2] a "plan of deliverance,"[3] a "plan of mercy,"[4] a "plan of restoration,"[5] truly, a "great plan of happiness,"[6] and it specifies that it was formed from the very "foundation of the world."[7] One of the blessings of the Restoration is the clarification that not only *was* there a plan but that it was prepared, presented, and accepted in the premortal realm. In other words, it was the plan from the start—it was never a haphazard improvisation; it was never a backup plan. "This wasn't an experiment. He knew what he was doing," President Spencer W. Kimball explained. "There were no guesses here, no trial and error."[8]

Modern-day prophets frequently articulate and elaborate on the plan and its many details. One of my favorite descriptions was given by Elder Bruce R. McConkie at a BYU devotional delivered in 1984. He defined the plan of salvation quite simply as "the system ordained by the Father to enable his spirit children to advance and progress and become like him."[9]

This definition is packed with powerful significance. First, it addresses our divine identity as children of Heavenly Parents. Second, it establishes emulating God's divine character as our ultimate goal. And third, it acknowledges our divine potential for growth and transformation.

OUR DIVINE IDENTITY

All of us are beloved spirit sons or daughters of Heavenly Parents. This foundational truth, proclaimed by prophets and sung by Primary children, forms a bedrock of love on which we can build our lives using the Master Architect's perfect plan. Understanding our eternal identity highlights a crucial distinction: we are His children, not His creations. As children, we are like apprentices in His architecture school; we are *not* His architecture. Rather, the entirety of Creation serves the purpose of providing us a place and an experience that allows us to progress to become like Him.[10]

Brother Tad R. Callister has examined and elaborated on this doctrinal distinction of child versus creation, noting that the difference is "monumental in its consequence because our identity determines in large measure our destiny."[11] To make his point, he asked, "Can a mere creation ever become like its creator? Can a building ever become an architect? A painting a painter? Or an invention an inventor?" And then he offered this philosophical response: "If not, then those who believe we are *creations* of God, rather than His spirit *offspring*, reach the inevitable conclusion that we do not have the capacity to become like our creator."[12]

Mortality's family structure wisely provides valuable insight into our divine identity and our Heavenly Parents' divine love for us. Like any devoted earthly parent, They love *all* of Their children; They are no respecters of persons. "Anyone who claims superiority under the Father's plan because of characteristics like race, sex, nationality, language, or economic circumstances is morally wrong and does not understand the Lord's true purpose," said Elder Quentin L. Cook.[13] Restoration scripture makes it abundantly clear that *all of His children*—rich and poor, bond and free, male and female—can be "partakers of the heavenly gift" of God's great love.[14] Echoing Nephi, we may not yet understand all life's mysteries, but we know that God loves us, and that knowledge sustains us.[15]

GOD'S DIVINE CHARACTER

In addition to understanding our divine identity, understanding God's divine character also adds clarity to our mortal journey.[16] At the very core of God's nature is His commitment to truth and goodness; this reality fixes the parameters within which true happiness may be found.[17] Because God is God, unchanging and immutable, the same yesterday, today, and forever, when He declares His commitment to truth and goodness, it follows that He will *always* speak truth and He will *always* pursue goodness. He *cannot* lie or deceive. He *cannot* support evil or condone wickedness. It simply is not His nature.

This truth is found repeatedly in the scriptures, especially throughout the Book of Mormon. The brother of Jared, in his singular experience conversing directly with the Lord, declared, "Thou art a God of truth, and canst not lie."[18] And while teaching the people of Gideon, Alma testified that God "cannot walk in crooked paths; neither doth he vary from that which he hath said; neither hath he a shadow of turning from the right to the left, or from that which is right to that which is wrong."[19]

This eternal law, that God is infinitely committed to truth and goodness, coupled with His perfect love for His children, has significant implications when we consider commandments, sin, and suffering. When God issues counsel or warnings, the basis will always be truth and goodness and love. Always. As we are counseled to do a certain thing or live a certain way, and that way or that thing proves uncomfortable or hard, perhaps even painful, we can make a conscious choice to trust God *because* of His commitment to truth and goodness.

OUR DIVINE POTENTIAL

That conscious choice to trust God is at the crux of reaching our divine potential. Elder Jeffrey R. Holland testified of the connection between who we are, how God loves us, and who we can become. He declared, "Just because God is God, just because Christ is Christ, they cannot do other than care for us and bless us and help us if we will but come unto them, approaching their throne of grace in meekness and lowliness of heart. They can't help but bless us. They have to. It is their nature."[20]

"*If we will but come unto them.*" Therein lies one of life's great secrets: reaching our divine potential is all about agency. And the wise exercise of agency is best accomplished by remembering that God loves us and that we can trust Him.

As I strive to become my best self, it helps me to recall that "all these things shall give [me] experience, and shall be for [my] good."[21] This simple couplet defines my faith because of the implications of God's love for me as His daughter, as well as His infinite commitment to truth and goodness. To live in faith is to demonstrate confidence in the Master Architect and His perfect plan. However, this is no guarantee of smooth progress.

AGENCY

Life often feels like a schoolyard three-legged race, where my agency is tied up awkwardly to my playmate's. I attempt to use *my* agency to actively progress along my personal path, but meanwhile, those I'm connected to are using *their* agency to pursue their own agendas and pioneer their own way. Their choices don't always align with mine, making for halting, tripping, even painful progress. Sometimes, it doesn't feel like a very fun game. Agency can be downright difficult. I value mine, of course, but how other people choose to exercise theirs can be extremely frustrating. In my experience, that clashing of agency, rather than any divine manipulation, is at the root of most mortal challenges. Recognizing that distinction helps me pace myself while managing my experiences *and* my expectations.

The fact is, agency is an absolutely critical part of the plan; one could say that agency *is* the plan. It's been called "the preeminent law of the universe"[22] and "the very essence of our existence."[23] President David O. McKay said, "Next to the bestowal of life itself, the right to direct that life is God's greatest gift to man."[24] But it doesn't always feel like a gift, especially when we are faced with a difficult choice or when we are suffering the effects of someone else's difficult choice.

The blessing of agency is that it requires us to actively assume personal responsibility, and that leads to growth. When we use agency well, it allows the Lord to bless us with righteous rewards; when we use it poorly, it allows us to learn from our mistakes through the uncomfortable consequences of our choices.[25] "The gospel of Jesus Christ is not just a gospel of belief; it is *a plan of action,*" explained President Howard W. Hunter. "[Christ] did not say 'observe' my gospel; he said 'live' it! He did not say, 'Note its beautiful structure and imagery'; he said, 'Go, do, see, feel, give, believe!'"[26] The purpose of life is not just to *have* experiences; rather, the purpose of life is for us to be *transformed by* our experiences. Positive transformation, growth, and change happen when we allow the Spirit to teach us through our adventures. "Action is one of the chief foundations of personal testimony. The surest witness is that which comes firsthand out of personal experience."[27] As we shall see throughout the course of this book, there is no substitute for *learning by doing.*

ACCEPTING THE PLAN

God's perfectly designed plan requires each of His children individually to choose whether or not he or she will participate. Unfortunately, even premortally, the inherent challenges of agency meant that not everyone *wanted* to participate. I often reflect on the great debate in the Council in Heaven, when we almost certainly discussed the merits and costs of the plan. We were all there. I imagine listening to both sides being presented; I picture what must have been lively discussion and critical questioning amid passionate persuading. We were already familiar with agency to a certain extent, since we had been making choices throughout our premortal progression.[28] But now mortality and, by extension, exaltation hung in the balance, and we each had an extremely important decision to make.

I envision what must have been a tense turning point when someone particularly insightful realized the ramifications of what mortal agency *for everyone* could mean. Such unchecked freedom would allow for abuse at the hands of one another, possibly even heinous, devastating, large-scale abuse. We were familiar, even then, with so many different personalities that we must have recognized that some might exploit and misuse this expanded power, especially when paired with the capability of a physical body. As we came to realize what this might look like away from the safety of our heavenly home, it must have been frightening. It isn't surprising that some just weren't willing to risk such abuse. I imagine our suspicions were confirmed by those presenting the plan: yes, agency for all would mean varying degrees of suffering and pain, even for the innocent. That Divine Council wanted us to know what we were agreeing to; surely, They hid nothing from us.

Yet even with our worst fears confirmed, we chose it. We even *celebrated* it.[29] *Why? How?* There can be only one answer: trust. We must have known our Heavenly Parents, our Elder Brother, and the Holy Ghost so incredibly well, loved them so profoundly and so devotedly, as to know that They *could* and They *would* do what They said They would do, that the plan was perfect, and that it would work perfectly, though painfully. Mortality would pave the way for our returning to our heavenly home, for our gradually becoming like our Heavenly Parents. Our Savior, recognized and revered as such even then, would be able to make everything work together for our good. And the Comforter would be with us to guide and direct us throughout the journey. This was no tacit agreement—it was a *covenant*, which They may have made between Themselves in our presence.[30] And we then joined the covenant as well when we *chose* this mortal life as the pathway to godliness. That choice was based on trust then, just as it is best based on trust now.

With our decision to participate made, we were nearly ready to proceed. But first, the Divine Council would need to designate two individuals perfectly suited to initiate our mortal adventure.

A PURE AND NOBLE PAIR

Gratefully, we have a few key pieces of Eve and Adam's premortal story, thanks to the latter-day Restoration of the gospel of Jesus Christ. In particular, some priceless prophetic insights significantly enlighten our understanding of Adam and Eve's qualifications for the privilege and responsibility of leading the way into mortality.

Elder James E. Talmage succinctly described our First Parents as "pure and noble,"[31] which is what one might expect, given the magnitude of their responsibilities. Elder Bruce R. McConkie elaborated, stating, "Adam, a male spirit, then called Michael, stood next in power, might, and dominion to the Lord Jehovah. Eve, a female spirit, whose premortal name has not been revealed, was of like stature, capacity, and intelligence."[32]

"Of like stature, capacity, and intelligence." In a world culture, both ancient and contemporary, that often details, records, and honors men's achievements more prominently than women's, this understated yet significant phrase, "*of like stature, capacity, and intelligence,*" speaks volumes. It's the verbal equivalent of arithmetic's transitive property of equality: if a=b and b=c, then a=c. The statement, "*of like stature, capacity, and intelligence,*" helps us recognize Eve's capability and competence as being equivalent to Adam's. Though we may not know many particulars about Eve, we do know much about Adam (premortally known as Michael[33]). Trusting that premortal Eve was equivalent to Michael/Adam in "stature, capacity, and intelligence" therefore teaches us as much about her as we've been taught about him, though without some of the specifics for which we yearn.

The name *Michael* means "he who is like God,"[34] and both scripture and revelation affirm that this is a fitting moniker for premortal Adam. In the New Testament, Luke refers to him as "the son of God,"[35] the only person besides Jesus to receive this great honor. Similarly, the Prophet Joseph Smith declared, "Christ is the great High Priest. Adam next."[36] In the Old Testament, the prophet Daniel designated him "the great prince."[37] Adding some explanation for such supernal recognition, President Joseph Fielding Smith stated that Michael/Adam "had reached great distinction and power before he ever came to this earth" and "was one of the greatest of the intelligences."[38]

Furthermore, his proven capacity for leadership earned him the title *archangel.*[39] The prefix *arch-*, in this case, means "quintessential" or "most fully embodying the qualities of [his] kind"; *arch* is also used within a word to represent a ruler, as in *monarchy* ("one ruler") or *anarchy* ("without a ruler").[40] In other words, Michael is the chief angel, as Joseph Smith asserted when considering his status among his fellow angels: "[They] are under the direction of Michael or Adam, who acts under the direction of the Lord."[41]

Though biblical angels are typically described as messengers, Michael is repeatedly portrayed more specifically as a warrior—leading the charge to contend, fight, and stand against evil. Renaissance artwork commonly depicts him wearing armor and wielding a sword, sometimes with the scales of justice in his other hand—all symbols of his great integrity, courage, and strength.

Likewise, we can deduce that Eve was similarly heroic and brave, and that has been prophetically confirmed as well.

In Abraham 3:22, we read: "Now the Lord had shown unto me, Abraham, the intelligences that were organized before the world was; and among all these there were many of the noble and great ones."

Referring to this Divine Council, Elder McConkie identified Eve and several other women as being among "the noble and great ones." He then added treasured insight by describing Eve and the other women as fearless and faithful warriors: "Certainly these sisters labored as diligently then, and fought as valiantly in the war in heaven, as did the brethren, even as they in like manner stand firm today, in mortality, in the cause of truth and righteousness."[42]

This statement about Eve, coupled with the broader background we have of Michael, highlights our First Parents' stellar "stature, capacity, and intelligence," which qualified them each to play such a pivotal role in God's great plan of salvation and happiness.

BECOMING LIKE GOD

As we conclude our examination of God's perfect plan, let's recall Elder McConkie's defining description of the plan as "the system ordained by the Father to enable his spirit children to advance and progress and become like him."[43] This master plan was never just about saving souls; it was always about something even greater—*becoming like God.*[44]

Surely this doctrine is among the most precious of those truths lost from sacred writ. In the absence of such clarity, the Bible leaves many readers confused about the meaning of life because the missing pieces of premortality and the plan are so crucial for understanding the big picture.[45]

President Boyd K. Packer stated that understanding this doctrine "is so essential a part of the equation of life that, left out, life just cannot add up, it remains a mystery."[46] With that in mind, this is the rightful beginning of Adam and Eve's story, though much of Christianity inadvertently skips right over it.

By starting with premortality and the plan—and what they teach us of our divine identity, God's divine character, and our divine potential—Adam and Eve's story becomes a profound model centered on the importance of agency in our personal eternal progression. BYU English professor Francine R. Bennion summarized this connection beautifully in a talk delivered in 1986 at BYU Women's Conference. She said:

> *We are here not just because God decided it would be a good idea and made it happen, not just because Adam and Eve fell and we automatically followed, but because* we chose to come. *However essential what God or Eve or Adam did to make it possible, we believe the decision to be born was our own. Our very brief accounts of life before this earth suggest that we chose as Eve chose, and we defended that choice in whatever kind of war can take place among spirits. Our birth is evidence of courage and faith, not helplessness, shame, and disobedience.*[47]

This core understanding of not only Eve's faithfully courageous choice to embrace mortality, but each of ours, is fundamental to our religion. We acknowledge that initiating mortality required a unique transgression of a commandment in order to fully respect agency, and that that transgression had serious repercussions—even the Fall—yet we believe our First Parents' individual reasons for choosing to transgress were noble ones. In addition to the desire to become more like God, as Elder Jeffrey R. Holland has declared, "They did it for the one overriding and commanding reason basic to the entire plan of salvation and all the discussions ever held in all the councils of heaven. They did it 'that men might be.'"[48] This belief sets us apart from the rest of Christianity, who typically consider Eve to be helpless, shameful, and disobedient. Our enlightened understanding links us to Eve because premortally we each made a similarly brave choice. And as with her, our courage and faith before we came to earth can continue to inform our actions and attitudes here in mortality.

NOTES

1. Uchtdorf, "The Gift of Grace."
2. Alma 12:25–26, 30, 32–33; 17:16; 18:39; 22:13–14; 29:2; 39:18; 42:11, 13.
3. 2 Nephi 11:5.
4. Alma 42:15, 31.
5. Alma 41:2.
6. Alma 42:8.
7. 1 Nephi 10:18; 2 Nephi 9:18; Mosiah 4:6–7; 15:19; Alma 13:7; 3 Nephi 11:11; Ether 3:14, 4:14–15.
8. Kimball, "The Blessings and Responsibilities of Womanhood."
9. McConkie, "What Think Ye of Salvation by Grace?" Elder McConkie added, "It consists of three great and eternal verities—the Creation, the Fall, and the Atonement—without any of which there could be no salvation."
10. President Russell M. Nelson declared, "Grand as it is, planet Earth is part of something even grander—that great plan of God" (Nelson, "The Creation").
11. Callister, "Our Identity and Our Destiny."
12. Callister, "Our Identity and Our Destiny"; emphasis added.
13. Cook, "The Eternal Everyday."
14. Ether 12:8; 4 Nephi 1:3.
15. 1 Nephi 11:17.
16. Elder Brian K. Ashton said, "A correct understanding of Heavenly Father's character can change how we see ourselves and others and help us to understand God's tremendous love for His children and His great desire to help us become like Him" (Ashton, "The Father").
17. It is worth noting that there is a difference between *God's* nature and *human* nature, even though we are His children. I may be committed to truth and goodness, but human nature dictates that, at some point, I will inevitably tell a lie or do something bad. President Russell M. Nelson has taught, "Eternal perfection is reserved for those who overcome all things and inherit the fulness of the Father in his heavenly mansions. Perfection consists in gaining eternal life—the kind of life that God lives" (Nelson, "Perfection Pending").
18. Ether 3:6–16.

19. Alma 7:20. Similarly, in the New Testament, John declared, "God is light, and in him is no darkness at all" (1 John 1:5).
20. Holland, *Trusting Jesus*, 68. Elder George Q. Cannon made a similarly powerful statement a century earlier: "No matter how serious the trial, how deep the distress, how great the affliction, [God] will never desert us. He never has, and He never will. He cannot do it. It is [against] His character [to do so]. He is an unchangeable being. . . . He will stand by us" (Cannon, "Freedom of the Saints," 228).
21. D&C 122:7.
22. Campbell, *Eve and the Choice Made in Eden*, 37.
23. Morris, in Conference Report, April 1958, 38.
24. McKay, in Conference Report, April 1950, 32.
25. President Joseph Fielding Smith explained that agency is "the only principle upon which exaltation can come" because "it is the only principle upon which rewards can be given in righteousness" (Smith, *Doctrines of Salvation*, 1:70). And Elder D. Todd Christofferson taught that "we cannot realize our full potential as daughters and sons of God" without agency's "opportunity to assume personal responsibility" (Christofferson, "Free Forever, to Act for Themselves"). For these reasons, among others, the Apostle James called agency "the perfect law of liberty" (James 1:25).
26. Hunter, in Conference Report, April 1967; emphasis added.
27. Hunter, in Conference Report, April 1967.
28. Elder Jörg Klebingat explained it this way: "In the premortal existence we possessed agency, reasoning powers, and intelligence. . . . Opportunities for growth and learning were widely available. However, equal access to the teachings of a loving heavenly home did not produce a uniform desire among us—Heavenly Father's spirit children—to listen, learn, and obey. Exercising our agency, as we do today, we listened with varying degrees of interest and intent. Some of us eagerly sought to learn and obey. With war in heaven on the horizon, we prepared for graduation from our premortal home. Truth was taught and challenged; testimonies were borne and ridiculed, with each premortal spirit making the choice to either defend or defect from the Father's plan" (Klebingat, "Defending the Faith").
29. Regarding this celebration, Joseph Fielding Smith explained: "The thought of passing through mortality and partaking of all the vicissitudes of earth life in which they would gain experiences through suffering, pain, sorrow, temptation and affliction, as well as the pleasures of life in this mundane existence, and then, if faithful, passing on through the resurrection to eternal life in the kingdom of God, to be like him, filled them with the spirit of rejoicing, and they 'shouted for joy'" (Smith, *Doctrines of Salvation*, 1:58).
30. Joseph Smith reportedly taught that "everlasting covenant was made between three personages before the organizations of the earth, and relates to their dispensation of things to men on the earth, these personages according to Abraham's

record, are called God the first, the Creator; God the second, the Redeemer, and God the third, the witness or Testator" (https://www.josephsmithpapers.org/paper-summary/discourse-circa-may-1841-as-reported-by-unknown-scribe-a/1).

31. Talmage, *Jesus the Christ*, 29.
32. McConkie, "Eve and the Fall," 58.
33. It may be helpful to be aware and remember that other religions do not recognize the archangel Michael as Adam, though they understand the high and noble stature of Michael; as far as my research has determined, Adam's premortal identity is openly discussed solely within The Church of Jesus Christ of Latter-day Saints.
34. Youngberg, *Sacred Baby Names*, 115.
35. Luke 3:38.
36. https://www.josephsmithpapers.org/paper-summary/history-1838-1856-volume-c-1-2-november-1838-31-july-1842/546.
37. Daniel 12:1.
38. Smith, *Doctrines of Salvation*, 1:90.
39. Jude 1:9; D&C 29:26; 88:112; 107:54; 128:21; see also 1 Thessalonians 4:16.
40. *Merriam-Webster Online Dictionary*, "arch."
41. https://www.josephsmithpapers.org/paper-summary/history-1838-1856-volume-c-1-2-november-1838-31-july-1842/551.
42. McConkie, "Eve and the Fall," 59.
43. McConkie, "What Think Ye of Salvation by Grace?"
44. President Kimball insisted that "the whole intent" of the plan of salvation is about reaching our "fullest potential, which is eternal progression and the possibility of godhood" (Kimball, "Privileges and Responsibilities of Sisters").
45. Robert J. Matthews insightfully noted: "While there is not enough in the Bible alone to learn that God does indeed have such a plan, after learning about the plan from latter-day scriptures one can then discern traces of it in the Bible" (Matthews, "The Fall of Man," 39). See also Ecclesiastes 12:7; Jeremiah 1:5; Ephesians 1:4–5; 2 Timothy 1:9.
46. Packer, "The Mystery of Life." Interestingly, in this same talk, President Packer noted that "this doctrine of premortal life was known to ancient Christians. For nearly five hundred years the doctrine was taught, but it was then rejected as a heresy by a clergy that had slipped into the Dark Ages of apostasy." Also worth noting, Elder Neal A. Maxwell taught that "most human misery represents ignorance of or noncompliance with the plan. A cessation of such mortal suffering will not come without compliance to it" (Maxwell, "The Great Plan of the Eternal God").
47. Bennion, "A Latter-day Saint Theology of Suffering," 223; emphasis in original. In addition to teaching, Sister Bennion worked on the Church's instructional development committee and served on both the Young Women and Relief Society General Boards.
48. Holland, *Christ and the New Covenant*, 204. See also 2 Nephi 2:25.

CHAPTER 4

THE MEASURE OF OUR CREATION

Earth's crammed with heaven,
And every common bush afire with God;
But only he who sees, takes off his shoes,
The rest sit round it and pluck blackberries,
And daub their natural faces unaware.

—Elizabeth Barrett Browning[1]

If you're like me, a handful of powerful spiritual experiences stand out in your memory. Those pivotal events—when you've felt the Spirit enlarging your heart and enlightening your mind to a whole new degree—can change the course of your life.

One of my earliest spiritual pivot points occurred on a Sunday in a Young Women class when I was twelve or thirteen years old. I can still picture the classroom and where I was sitting. Our teacher, an angelic woman who intrigued me because of the thoughtful way she experienced the world, was telling us about a scientist who had recently passed away. This man had been the world's leading expert on butterflies. According to an article she had read, he had spent his entire professional career learning everything he possibly could about butterflies. She showed us beautiful pictures of colorful butterflies as she explained some of the discoveries this scientist had made about this lovely, gentle creature. And then she asked us to imagine the scene of this man, newly arrived in heaven, having his first interaction with our Father there, humbly and earnestly saying, "I have spent my entire life learning everything I possibly could about your magnificent creation, the butterfly." And then, almost begging, "Please, now tell me everything else there is to know!"

Picturing that man's interview with God—his gratitude and anticipation—captured my spiritual senses completely. To that moody, pubescent teen, those feelings that rushed over me evoked complete awe at the magnitude and magnificence of God's creations. That moment was a life changer: it permanently altered the way I appreciated and interacted with the natural world.

I'm reminded of that experience and those feelings each time I read section 59 of the Doctrine and Covenants. Here, the Lord details some of the reasons He created such a magnificent earth:

> *Yea, all things which come of the earth, in the season thereof, are made for the benefit and the use of man, both to please the eye and to gladden the heart;*
>
> *Yea, for food and for raiment, for taste and for smell, to strengthen the body and to enliven the soul.*
>
> *And it pleaseth God that he hath given all these things unto man; for unto this end were they made.*[2]

"For unto this end were they made." President Russell M. Nelson elaborated on this significant phrase, stating, "The very purpose of creation was to provide bodies, to enable [us] *to enjoy mortal life and experiences.*"[3] Those mortal experiences, made possible thanks to physical bodies and this physical realm in which we currently live, are meant to teach us, gradually exalting us, "line upon line, precept upon precept."[4] The Restoration's expanded explanation of both *how* the world was created and *why* the world was created enlarges our perspective and alters the way we experience, appreciate, and interact with the natural world. Restored truth provides the information we need to figure the measure of earth's creation, as well as the measure of *our* creation.

CREATION

The first sentence of the Old Testament reads: "In the beginning God *created* the heaven and the earth."[5] With the support of Abraham's account, latter-day prophets encourage a broader interpretation of *creating*, suggesting a process of *organizing*, since something cannot be made from nothing.[6] The Prophet Joseph likened this expanded view of creating to building a ship, wherein the worker manipulates preexisting materials, increasing their usefulness through ingenuity and creativity.[7] In his great vision of Creation, Abraham referred specifically to preexisting materials, detailing how the Lord stood with many "noble and great ones," inviting them to join Him in taking "these materials" to organize and "make an earth" where God's children could dwell.[8]

Recognizing that the earth was created, or organized, *ex materia* (from preexisting matter)—as opposed to *ex nihilo* (from nothing), as some believe—enhances our understanding, particularly relating to our identity as children of Heavenly Parents, as discussed in chapter 3.[9] This understanding reminds us that the purpose of the earth is to allow for the experiences and training necessary to prepare us for godliness.

Before rushing ahead to the culmination of Creation—the introduction of earth's first man and woman—briefly considering the phases of Creation, as well as two of its important facets, will lay some important groundwork for the further examination of our story.

Comparing the similarities and differences between Genesis 2:5 and

Moses 3:5 reveals that the Bible has lost a precious detail of doctrinal truth regarding the *phases* of Creation.

Genesis 2:5	**Moses 3:5**
"And every plant of the field before it was in the earth, and every herb of the field before it grew: for the Lord God had not caused it to rain upon the earth, and there was not a man to till the ground."	"And every plant of the field before it was in the earth, and every herb of the field before it grew. For I, the Lord God, created all things, of which I have spoken, spiritually, before they were naturally upon the face of the earth. For I, the Lord God, had not caused it to rain upon the face of the earth. And I, the Lord God, had created all the children of men; and not yet a man to till the ground; for in heaven created I them; and there was not yet flesh upon the earth, neither in the water, neither in the air."

As we can see, the Moses account includes a critically important idea: "I, the Lord God, created all things . . . spiritually, before they were naturally upon the face of the earth. . . . For in heaven created I them."

Restoration scriptures clarify that there was a *spiritual* Creation before the *physical* Creation. Thanks to modern-day prophets, we've also been told of a *third* phase of creation—a *paradisiacal Creation.* President Russell M. Nelson called the creation of Adam and Eve "a *paradisiacal creation,* one that required a significant change before they could fulfill the commandment to have children and thus provide earthly bodies for premortal spirit sons and daughters of God."[10] This paradisiacal period of Creation describes

Edenic earth—the place and time in which Adam and Eve's garden story takes place.

Before delving into that unparalleled paradisiacal setting, let's first consider two powerful principles of creation that have important implications for Eve and Adam, and for each of us: order and differentiation.

ORDER

Heavenly Father is a God of law, working within such frameworks as the basics of cause and effect, as well as the complexities of divine design and eternal purpose. President Nelson has taught, "Whether in the predictability of the tides, the phases of the moon, or the location of stars in the sky . . . law and order undergird all creation."[11] Organizing the elements was, is, and will continue to be accomplished in a highly structured fashion, based on natural laws designed, implemented, and adhered to by God.

As Alma testified to Korihor, "All things denote there is a God,"[12] whether or not we fully understand the natural principles and systems governing His creations. Even a lepidopterist who spends his entire professional career studying butterflies has more to learn. Still, noticing and appreciating the divinity of the natural world doesn't require an advanced degree. Nature's patterns are everywhere, and each is a manifestation and reminder of the underlying order in God's creations.

Consider the concentric growth rings visible in a felled tree or the predictable five-petal motif on every sand dollar. More "advanced" patterns, like the helix of a giant sunflower or a chambered nautilus, impress even the most apathetic student of nature. And the self-similar symmetry of fractals is awesome. Found in such diverse and wide-ranging natural applications as mountain ranges, cottonwood trees, and broccoli florets, fractals demonstrate spectacular scaling, reminding the observer that, even in nature, the steady repetition and expansion of small and simple things eventually grows greatness. Indeed, "all things bear record of [Him]."[13]

Learning to maneuver within the parameters of natural law is a crucial part of the mortal experience because it allows for relatively predictable outcomes as we exercise agency. Much of the fun of spending time with a toddler lies in watching him or her figure out how the world works, experimenting with the orderliness of physical laws and their consequences. For example, gravity provides seemingly endless entertainment for baby, dropping her toy to the ground and watching Dad or Mom retrieve it repeatedly. The fun turns to frustration, though, when Mom and Dad quit playing and the toy is out of reach. At that point, the lack of intervention promotes powerful learning, and baby decides to hold on to the toy. The sooner her parents step back and let nature take its course, the more quickly she learns. Natural consequences are some of the most efficient and effective teachers, thanks to their predictability and consistency. When a child sees everyone, including her or his parents, living with the same rules and the same results, fighting fades to acceptance and acceptance fosters ingenuity. What a brilliant system!

DIFFERENTIATION

Like natural law and order, differentiation is another meaningful and applicable principle of creation. Creating implies designing, differentiating, and separating, which fits nicely within the basics of Organizing 101. Even amateur organizers know you begin work on a drawer or closet by first making categorized piles of its contents, then winnowing each pile, and finally finding the ideal spot for the remaining smaller piles. A place for everything and everything in its place.

On a much grander scale, the Creation of the earth involved separating and setting bounds as well, echoed throughout the various accounts of the

Creation story in words like "divided" and "gathered," and ideas like "after their kind" and "in our own image." The light was separated from the darkness, the dry land from the wet, the atmospheric water from the surface water. And the distinctions were accompanied by naming: day and night, ground and sea, heaven and earth. Plant life was similarly created with labeled distinctions—grasses, herbs, trees—and the types would remain categorized "after their kind." Animal life followed suit, with specific names and groupings like swimmers, flyers, creepers, and crawlers, each meant to reproduce "after their kind." And each differentiation, each separation, each new boundary was declared *good* by a loving God who clearly celebrates variety and distinction.

Why, exactly, is differentiation *good?* Same is easy, but same is boring and same is stagnant. Different is dynamic, interesting, and challenging. Variety and contrast are two pieces of differentiation that are essential for learning through living.

The beauty of variety is one of the first things we learn as children. Parents happily provide opportunities to expose their children to diversity. We visit the zoo, not to see one kind of animal but to see an assortment of animals in a wide range of colors, shapes, and sizes with different habitats, diets, and skills. We visit the aquarium, not to see one kind of fish but to see a vast array of water-loving creatures, each individually unique and fascinating. Slightly less exciting to kids, parents even drag them to botanical gardens and national parks, not to see just one kind of flower or one kind of landscape but to see the vast diversity of nature. Variety is *good*, even glorious! The sooner we can extrapolate this lesson and recognize how beautiful the diversity among humanity is, the sooner our appreciation for unique gifts, talents, and interests grows. If heaven is the "prototype" for this beautiful earth,[14] surely diversity is divine.

Also inherent in differentiation is contrast. Contrast invites comparison, and comparison allows for analysis, preference, and choice. Since agency is the preeminent law of heaven, a place where analysis, preference, and choice can be practiced constantly is the perfect environment for learning through mortal experiences. For a young child, the world's variety, coupled with exposure to alternatives, prompts simple, individualized, but relatively insignificant preferences, like the emergence of a favorite color, a favorite food, or a favorite animal. As we grow and mature, and our experiences expand and diverge, we begin to recognize more nuanced contrasts. We gradually learn to distinguish the subtle differences between fun and satisfying, pleasant and peaceful, leading to more conscious decision making.

Inevitably, we come up against tough choices, since some options are mutually exclusive, even oppositional, forcing us to exercise discernment and then choose between good and better, better and best.[15] Comparison, made possible by differentiation, is the very thing that allows us to feel and experience joy.[16] Ideally, each step of this line-upon-line learning equips us to embrace our God-given agency and strive to use it to faithfully return to His presence.

PARTICIPATION

Elder Dieter F. Uchtdorf has declared the desire to create "one of the deepest yearnings of the human soul" and one of the most direct routes to "experiencing a fulness of joy."[17] This makes sense, given that we are children of an infinitely creative God and are made in His likeness and image. We too are creative beings. And since God's purpose is "to enable his spirit children to advance and progress and become like him,"[18] then we are meant to play an active role in the ongoing Creation.

Expanding on this idea, BYU professor of comparative literature Dr. George S. Tate explained: "The creation is not complete, it does not reach its plenitude without our collaboration, our laboring with the Lord in his work, without what we do and what we create." Then Dr. Tate added something each of us occasionally needs to be reminded of: "This includes not only the great works of the past like the tragedies of Sophocles, the Cathedral of Chartres, and Bach's Mass in B Minor, but also all the products of *our* minds and hands, from the lowliest to the best: the gardens we plant, the trees we prune, the meals we prepare . . . to say nothing of the hypotheses we prove or the poems or pottery we shape."[19]

Could it be that this divine desire to create, not just to create *children* but to create *anything*, had something to do with Heavenly Father's directive to Adam and Eve to be *fruitful*, as well as something to do with Eve's decision to partake? After all, the vast majority of times we read of scriptural fruit, it is in relationship to action, deeds, and doings. "By their fruits ye shall know them."[20] When we consider the paradisiacal yet static state that Eve and Adam found themselves in as they resided in the garden, with all creation waiting on their grand step into mortality that would finally allow for progress,[21] there likely wasn't much *to do* there. I can't help but imagine that Eve perhaps became a bit restless and felt ready to get to work and make something happen.

We too must take action in order to make progress, especially grace-guided progress. As Elder D. Todd Christofferson has explained, we can't just *want* God's help; we must actually *choose* God's help—through *doing*—in order to honor agency. "My plea is simply to take responsibility and go to work so that there is something for God to help us with."[22] And there are literally countless ways for us to go to work. Whether we find joy in cooking or composing, painting or producing, dancing or designing, that desire to create is divine. And if we will put forth sincere effort, God will help us give our unique gift to the world.

But what if we feel incapable or inept, untalented or unskilled, as we all occasionally do? Our brave First Parents must have felt the same as they ventured into the vast unknown of mortality, but they undoubtedly possessed some of the helpful characteristics of those striving to channel their creativity: "curiosity, eagerness to learn, courage to be innovative, willingness to work hard, a desire to be a problem solver, and the ability to learn from mistakes."[23] None of these markers require innate talent, expensive lessons, or hours in a studio. In fact, they are each more related to attitude than to ability. Each calls for engagement and effort—in short, putting our agency to work. Additionally, these characteristics can be fueled by exercising faith and following the Spirit. In the creative realm, faith is most often demonstrated by continuing to show up and put in the work, pushing through or maneuvering around the mental blocks, frustrations, and discouragement that hound all artists.[24] And following the Spirit calls for patience and practice, since creative inspiration is like a holy dance of back and forth, give and take, listen and try.

As Sister Patricia T. Holland advised, we can each fill the measure of our creation "by thrusting in a sickle and reaping with all our strength—and by rejoicing in our uniqueness and our difference. To be all that you can be, your only assignment is . . . to cherish your course and savor your own distinctiveness."[25] Since fruitfulness is the conduit to growth, let's get to work. Our participation in Creation, guided by our individual interests and passions and helped along by our unique skills and talents, however humble and modest, allows each of us to participate with Divinity, becoming like God as we fill the measure of *our* creation and find joy in doing so.[26]

NOTES

1. Browning, *Aurora Leigh*, 246.
2. D&C 59:18–20.
3. Nelson, "Lessons from Eve"; emphasis added.
4. 2 Nephi 28:30.
5. Genesis 1:1; emphasis added. See also Moses 2:1; Abraham 4:1.
6. Joseph Smith taught, "God did not make the earth out of nothing; for it is contrary

to a rational mind and reason that a something could be brought from a nothing; also it is contrary to the principle and means by which God does work" (Smith, *The Words of Joseph Smith*, 61).

President Russell M. Nelson stated, "I testify that the earth and all life upon it are of divine origin. The Creation did not happen by chance. It did not come *ex nihilo* (out of nothing)" (Nelson, "The Creation").

Elder Bruce R. McConkie declared: "The Creation is an organized venture. . . . And the earth is created from matter that already exists. Truly the elements are eternal, and to create is to organize" (McConkie, "Christ and the Creation).

7. In what is known as the King Follett Discourse, Joseph reportedly said: "The word create came from the word *baurau*; it does not mean so; it means to organize; the same as a man would organize a ship. Hence we infer that God had materials to organize the world out of chaos; chaotic matter, which is element, and in which dwells all the glory" (https://www.josephsmithpapers.org/paper-summary/discourse-7-april-1844-as-reported-by-times-and-seasons/4). See also Walton, *Ancient Near Eastern Thought and the Old Testament*, 152–53. Walton offers an extremely enlightening comparative analysis of the Hebrew *bara'* ("create").
8. Abraham 3:22, 24.
9. The Doctrine and Covenants expands on the distinction and significance of organizing *ex materia*: "Intelligence, or the light of truth, was not created or made, neither indeed can be. . . . The elements are eternal, and spirit and element, inseparably connected, receive a fulness of joy" (D&C 93:29, 33). The two fundamental building blocks used in earth's construction are intelligence and element, what Lehi called "things to act and things to be acted upon," respectively (2 Nephi 2:13–14).
10. Nelson, "The Atonement"; emphasis in original. Similarly, Elder Bruce R. McConkie referred to their Edenic state as "paradisiacal immortality" (McConkie, "Christ and the Creation").
11. Nelson, "Faith in Jesus Christ." See also D&C 88:42–43, 47.
12. Alma 30:44.
13. Moses 6:63.
14. In *Journal of Discourses*, 23:175.
15. Oaks, "Good, Better, Best."
16. There's a hint of irony here, as any of us familiar with social media knows—comparing ourselves to others can be downright depressing. Teddy Roosevelt wasn't all wrong when he reportedly said that "comparison is the thief of joy," but he was referring to rejecting our individuality in favor of competitive sameness. Recognizing the difference between damaging comparisons and enlightened discernment is part of growing up successfully.
17. Uchtdorf, "Happiness, Your Heritage."
18. McConkie, "What Think Ye of Salvation by Grace?"

19. Tate, "Obedience, Creation, and Freedom."
20. Matthew 7:20; 3 Nephi 14:20. Sister Sharon Eubank mused to a packed auditorium at BYU Women's Conference, "Creation isn't only about children. . . . There are many ways for women to multiply, replenish, and create in the world" (Eubank, "Eyes to See, Discipline to Create, Glue to Bind—Converted unto the Lord").
21. See 2 Nephi 2:22.
22. Christofferson, "Free Forever, to Act for Themselves."
23. Bigelow, "Creativity." Dr. Bigelow is head of viola studies at BYU. In this excellent BYU devotional, she described many divine aspects of individual creativity.
24. Sister Eubank suggested we remind ourselves of the following when we're feeling frustrated with our creative abilities: "I have been a being with creative gifts for millennia. There are laws on this earth that help me discipline my body and my will so I can create even more powerfully in the future. Every day I am creating influence, compassion, love, and grace that did not previously exist" (Eubank, "Eyes to See").
25. Holland, "Filling the Measure of Your Creation."
26. The Jesuit theologian Pierre Teilhard de Chardin described how, ultimately, the value and meaning of our personal creativity, no matter how modest, is to assist in completing Creation, which makes our humble, human efforts divine (see Teilhard de Chardin, *The Divine Milieu*, 34–37).

CHAPTER 5

SIDE BY SIDE

[God] made men and women for happiness,
to share their journey with someone who complements them,
to live the wondrous experience of love.

—Pope Francis [1]

Great art radiates *balance*—complementary elements beautifully combined to create a sum greater than their unique parts. Harmony is widely recognized and appreciated in the musical realm, but duets are far more prevalent than that. On the theater's stage, speech and movement work together to transport the audience to a new time and place. In the gourmet's kitchen, distinct flavors combine to tantalize the taste buds in satisfying ways. On the painter's canvas, colors reinforce and intensify each other, bypassing the viewer's mind and speaking directly to the heart. The list could go on and on—evidence that artistry almost demands interdependence.

Not only do Eve and Adam share such beautifully interwoven balance, but their story is told in several artistically creative ways to specifically highlight each element of their complementarity. However, historically, nearly every aspect of that telling has been misinterpreted, both individually and institutionally, and hence misunderstood and misapplied for centuries. Recounting the specific and literal details of each of their births is not the goal of any of the scriptural accounts; establishing them as man and woman's ultimate model of relational interdependence is.

Given the complexities of male-female relationships, such a lofty undertaking benefits from a multidimensional approach. Examined both separately and side by side, the various narratives of Eve and Adam's story provide a far more complete and meaningful model of ideal partnership than one straightforward report ever could.

TWO COUPLED VERSIONS

The three recorded scriptural texts—found in Genesis, Moses, and Abraham—have distinct differences, but as they apply to the introduction of Adam and Eve, they share one significant similarity: each introduces our First Parents twice, in close succession, the first occasion brief, and the second occasion extended. Even allowing for the obvious variations in length, the two coupled accounts are quite different from each other, and those peculiarities are consistent across the various versions of the story. The following chart detailing the verses of each version's two accounts is helpful. Please refer to the appendices for the full text of each of these accounts.

	Account A	**Account B**
Genesis	Genesis 1:26–31	Genesis 2:4–25
Moses	Moses 2:26–31	Moses 3:4–25
Abraham	Abraham 4:26–31	Abraham 5:4–21

To keep things relatively simple, I'll refer primarily to the Genesis version of Account A and Account B since the other versions each follow the same general pattern and include the same pertinent details. Additionally, the Genesis version benefits from extensive research by biblical scholars, linguists, anthropologists, and a host of other respected thinkers who have contributed meaningful insight to our understanding of this portion of scripture.[2]

A basic understanding of how the Old Testament came to be compiled is a good starting place for making sense of the relationship between Account A and Account B. For generations, oral tradition preserved and passed down Israel's origin stories, as well as its poems, plays, and proverbs. In the sixth century BC, a national crisis forced a change in that custom when King Nebuchadnezzar laid siege to Jerusalem, destroying the city and its temple. Though some Jews remained in conquered Jerusalem, many others were enslaved and taken from their homeland; that scattering, known as the Diaspora, caused both groups to begin to lose their national identity and beloved religion. Israel's dire circumstances called for the compilation and dispersion of written Hebrew scripture, accomplished by Jewish scribes gathering centuries of material, much of it oral, and adding their own reflections, colored by the current crisis, to their codification.[3]

Not surprisingly, some significant pieces of their past merited multiple retellings from multiple perspectives. Most biblical scholars believe this is the case with the consecutive Creation accounts in Genesis.[4] This historical background helps us examine each account separately and objectively, recognizing that what we are reading is the work of different storytellers using different methods and highlighting different elements to effectively address different audiences.[5]

GENESIS ACCOUNT A

This account, told in just six verses (Genesis 1:26–31), contains several enlightening pieces of information to help expand our understanding, both of Adam and Eve's physical introduction and of our own place in the physical world. It seems Account A has perpetually lived in the shadow of Account B, perhaps because it is so much shorter, but more likely because it is simple and relatively uncontroversial in its assertions. I find each part of this telling to be straightforward and beautiful.

Significant Pronouns

One of the first things we notice as we examine Account A is the use of plural pronouns, specifically *us* and *our:*

"And God said, Let us make man in our image, after our likeness" (Genesis 1:26).

The Moses version features a first-person narration, with God the Father as speaker, and specifies that His Only Begotten was included in the *us* He was directing:

"And I, God, said unto mine Only Begotten, which was with me from the beginning: Let us make man in our image, after our likeness; and it was so" (Moses 2:26).

The Abraham version highlights the Divine Council as the *us* that worked together in the creation of the first physical bodies:

"And the Gods took counsel among themselves and said: Let us go down and form man in our image, after our likeness" (Abraham 4:26).

The parallels across these versions support and bear witness to our belief that at least two and quite possibly more than two divine beings participated in this critical step of the plan of salvation. With this basic understanding in place, when we then read Genesis 1:27, "male and female created he them," we might deduce that the Divine Council included *both* male and female deity. A wide array of scholars—linguistic, Hebrew, and biblical—have long maintained that the *-im* suffix added to certain Hebrew words is generally meant to indicate a plurality.[6] This convention has even lingered in some adopted English words, such as *cherub* (singular) and *cherubim* (plural).[7] Indeed, the Prophet Joseph Smith taught, "The word *Eloiheam* ought to be in the plural all the way through—Gods."[8] Given what we understand regarding premortality and our Heavenly Parents, it makes beautiful sense that the most sacred name with which we address our Father in Heaven is *Elohim*. My faith is strengthened by considering that perhaps the name *Elohim* represents our Heavenly *Parents*.

The other significant pronoun that appears again and again throughout these verses is *them*. Everything is described as pertaining to *both* Eve and Adam (though their names are not mentioned in this account) in a completely equivalent, simultaneous way. There is no mention of who came first; they are introduced concurrently, with no concern for birth order. The use of *them* allows for no listing, no ranking whatsoever. *Them* says "side by side." Where the word *man* is used (verses 26 and 27), it is clearly meant to refer to *human* or *humanity*, rather than exclusively the male of this duo, a convention of the English language that has been employed for centuries. And when the wording shifts in the final verses from *them* to *you*, it is still clear that this is to be interpreted as *you* in the plural form, not the singular. This male and female are a united pair, a coupled twosome from the moment of their introduction and throughout this beautiful narrative.

Blessings

One of my favorite ideas in Account A is encapsulated in the word *bless*—reminiscent of the tender experience of receiving a father's blessing.

"And God *blessed* them" (Genesis 1:28; emphasis added).

This statement immediately precedes God's five-part directive: be fruitful, multiply, replenish the earth, subdue it, and have dominion over it. Based on our familiarity with Account B, we generally think of this as a list of *commandments*. Though we certainly recognize commandments as blessings in our lives,[9] there is empowering significance in the loving tone embraced in the idea that these directives are *blessings*.

The ability to use our agency as we work and create productively—as we are fruitful—both in specifically rearing children and in generally making our way through the world, is a powerful gift because it allows us to personally and individually take part in God's work and glory, as discussed in chapter 4. Likewise, our relationship with the earth and its resources is an amazing opportunity for learning and growth through responsible stewardship. In just a few brief sentences, we see how generously God prepared the earth with all we would need to get started, and then entrusted it to us for our education and progression.

Very Good

The final statement of Account A denotes God's satisfaction with this preparatory phase of His master plan:

"And God saw every thing that he had made, and, behold, it was very good" (Genesis 1:31).

This declaration employs a simple, refreshingly understated method of emphasis. On six different occasions throughout the account of Earth's creation (Genesis 1:1–25), God has repeatedly deemed the work "good." Now, at its culmination, with the introduction of the complementary and unified male and female and the bestowal of the great blessings earth would allow them, *good* is significantly elevated to *very good.*

This description implies that not only did our First Parents begin life in a state of "very good" but that each child born to earth likewise begins life *very good,* as opposed to entering mortality in a state of wickedness or depravity, or "original sin," as some mistakenly label this incorrect notion.[10] As the poet William Wordsworth so eloquently and famously put it, we come "trailing clouds of glory" from our former heavenly home. Rarely recited is the following line, in which he accurately describes the change that sadly and unavoidably overtakes us all, to some degree or another:

Shades of the prison-house begin to close
Upon the growing Boy.[11]

Unfortunately, some misunderstand and misapply the often-quoted doctrine that "the natural man is an enemy to God,"[12] believing it to mean we begin life in an unworthy, damaged state, far from "very good." Rather, President Spencer W. Kimball taught that the natural man is better thought of as "the 'earthy man' who has allowed rude animal passions to overshadow his spiritual inclinations."[13] In other words, the natural man is something we may gradually become if we allow mortality's inherent difficulties to tarnish our divine nature. Elder David A. Bednar explained this frustrating reality further, stating: "As sons and daughters of God, we have inherited divine capacities from Him. But we presently live in a fallen world. The very elements out of which our bodies were created are by nature fallen and ever subject to the pull of sin, corruption, and death."[14] It's that pull of sin and its inevitable corruption that damages and taints us. Modern revelation clarifies what Wordsworth intuitively understood: living in a fallen, mortal world can at times feel like imprisonment, particularly when we succumb to temptations and the effects of mortal weakness.

Human nature, and specifically the nature with which we are born, has been disputed through the ages, but that debate is put to rest with two simple words: *very good.* Account A's beautiful introduction of Eve and Adam makes clear, even in its brevity and simplicity, that the earth is not just good but *very good;* each child of God begins life not just good but *very good;* and the great plan of happiness is not just good but *very good.*

GENESIS ACCOUNT B

Let's now turn our attention to the second account, far lengthier and more symbolically descriptive than the first, and examine Genesis 2:4–25. The anonymous scribe of Genesis's Account B could not possibly have known at the time he recorded his poetic narrative what impact his choice of imagery and metaphor would have on men and women for centuries, even millennia, to come. Eve's secondary creation from Adam's rib, along with her apparent designation as his "help meet," would give unscrupulous men supposed cause to oppress and dominate women, and mistreated women plenty of reason to question their role and value, both to tragic effect. Sadly, what this author likely intended to be a lyrically poignant way of portraying our First Parents' perfectly balanced interdependence has been repeatedly mistranslated, misconstrued, and misapplied until its purpose seems to have been to reiterate woman's second-class position in man's unkind world. A closer look at each significant element of this account sheds much-needed light on the complementary beauty meant to be portrayed in our poet's figurative approach.

Dirt and Bone

Though Account B depicts Adam's physical body being formed from the ground and Eve's subsequent formation from Adam's rib, since the beginning of the Restoration, both unusual birth processes have been repeatedly explained as symbolic and figurative. President Kimball almost dismissively insisted, "The story of the rib, of course, is figurative."[15]

Such a metaphoric description of so common an event as birth denotes powerful symbolism rather than complete obstetric ignorance. In Adam's case, his name is the link to the dirt's meaning. Jewish scribes seemed to relish playing with words, like expert crossword creators. Accordingly, the Hebrew *'adamah* means "ground" or "earth,"[16] so some feel "earthling" is the most accurate translation of *'adam*. This draws a powerful connection between mortality and its earthly basis. Additionally, as a common noun, *'adam*[17] is generally translated as *humankind*, effectively creating a new category for our First Parents. Recall that, to this point in the origin story, we've been introduced to Deity and the animals They have created, but not yet to any mortal humans. So Adam's creation from "the dust of the ground" represents humanity's interconnected relationship with the earth as our mortal home and our unique role as stewards of it—a fine example of this story's grand theme of balance, mutuality, and complementarity.[18]

But another enlightening bit of clarity is gained by understanding the evolution of the proper name *Adam* as well. In its plural form, *Adam* represents *both* Adam and Eve, a subtle though significant nuance we hear in several biblical verses, including throughout Account A, in which the linkage of *man* to *them* sounds grammatically incorrect. Later, in Genesis 5:2, as prelude to the genealogy of Adam, we read that God "called *their* name Adam."[19] President Kimball addressed this important detail when he explained, "Man here is always in the plural. It was plural from the beginning," further noting that this referred to "not a separate man, but a complete man, which is husband and wife."[20] President Kimball suggested that the name *Adam* should be considered the First Couple's surname, as in "Mr. and Mrs. Adam" or "Brother and Sister Adam."[21] Elder Bruce R. McConkie concurred, teaching, "The name of Adam and Eve as a united partnership is Adam. They, the two of them together, are named Adam."[22]

Turning our attention now to Eve's creation from Adam's rib, we see a similar use of metaphor with the same goal of portraying interdependence. And, like *Adam*, her name has great significance as well. Again, a close look at translation increases our understanding.

The Hebrew word *tsela*, from which English translations derive the figurative *rib*, is used more than forty times in the Old Testament. Oddly, only in the case of Eve's creation is it translated as "rib." Otherwise, *tsela* is consistently interpreted as "side," most frequently found in descriptions of constructing an altar, tabernacle, or temple.[23] Also of interest is the Hebrew word *banah*, translated in verse 22 as "made"; this is translated elsewhere throughout the Bible as "build" or "construct."[24] With this in mind, perhaps an alternate rendering of Genesis 2:21–22 would paint a picture of the Master Builder taking one side of *'adam* (humanity) and constructing a separate, complementary human, with the two individuals now symbolizing the inherent, sacred interconnectedness between male and female, man and woman.[25]

BYU professor of ancient scripture Dr. Camille Fronk Olson states, "The imagery of the rib, or side, symbolizes that man and woman are made of the same substance and are to exist together, side by side, not beneath or above."[26] Even as far back as the Middle Ages, Dominican friar and renowned theologian Thomas Aquinas recognized the complementary significance in the rib, noting that "it was entirely appropriate for the woman to come from the side, or rib, since if she came from the head she might exert supremacy over the man, while if she came from the feet, she might be a slave."[27] And President Russell M. Nelson concurs, as well, stating that the rib denotes "partnership" and "signifies neither dominion nor subservience, but a lateral relationship as partners, to work and to live, side by side."[28]

I particularly appreciate the insight with which BYU adjunct professor of ancient scripture Dr. Sherrie Johnson analyzes the deep symbolism of Adam's figurative creation from dirt and Eve's figurative creation from bone. In her opinion, "They were made of different materials and for different purposes."[29] Had Eve been metaphorically made from muscle, Adam might have had power to move her; had she been made from his heart, she might have been obligated to feel as he felt; had she been made from his mind, she might have been compelled to think as he thought; but she was made from bone, "the part of the body that gives structure and stature and where the marrow which produces the life-giving element of mortality . . . is found."[30] Furthermore, with his rib removed, Adam was now incomplete.

What a beautiful depiction of their balance, interdependence, and equality, as they begin their lives together, side by side.

Genesis's Account B does not technically include mention of the First Woman's name; the name *Eve* is revealed to the reader at different points among the various versions, but we shall consider it here, as we did Adam's.

When we think of Eve, we often think of her glorious epithet, the Mother of All Living.[31] This title of honor and respect derives directly from her Hebrew name, *Chavvah*, meaning "Life"[32]—so fitting, since she and all women who follow her will be the bearers and nurturers of life. But Eve's role is unique, and her name represents her sacred calling. Hers is the solemn responsibility to choose to cross the threshold into mortality, with Adam at her side, to usher in life and progress to all Creation. Truly, she is *Life* and *Mother* to *all* that lives.

Restoration scripture and revelation add important insight to our understanding of Eve's name. If one were to read only Genesis, he or she might suppose that Adam simply chose a name to his liking for this newly created woman, akin to his methods for naming the animals that had previously been presented to him. We are blessed with added understanding that this was not the case. Eve's name, unlike Adam's, is an honorific title.[33] In this case, Joseph Smith's translation of Genesis 3:20 adds a crucial phrase, italicized below:

"And Adam called his wife's name Eve, because she was the mother of all living; *for thus have I, the Lord God, called the first of all women, which are many*" (Moses 4:26; emphasis added).

Eve's name is a beautiful symbol representing her unique qualities, roles, and gifts, separate and distinct from Adam's. She had a calling and mission of her own that, when combined with his, would unify and complete them both.

'Ezer Kenegdo

Acknowledging Adam's currently incomplete and lonely state, God announces to Adam in Genesis 2:18 that He will provide "an help meet for him." Oh, what sad misunderstanding the combination of two such harmless words has facilitated! Perhaps the interweaving of the animal parade[34] has led some to feel as if the woman is being offered as a pet, though a two-legged one that talks. Or maybe the term feels subservient to some because it evokes another feminine characterization Christians know quite well: a handmaid, historically a female servant or slave. Though young Mary uses this label in submissive reverence in response to the angel's wholly singular divine annunciation,[35] it would be grossly inaccurate to represent the ideal relationship between a husband and wife in such an inequitable way. These factors may influence why even the most objective reader can hardly help but sense that Eve enters the scene as a sidekick. Yet neither careful translation nor greater context supports such interpretations, though these attitudes have proven stubbornly persistent across cultures and through the ages.

Countless scholars, concerned with the negative connotation perceived in the term, have closely examined the Hebrew phrase *'ezer kenegdo*, so commonly perceived as "help meet." Their findings repeatedly affirm the balanced strength and interdependence of Eve and Adam. Contextually, *'ezer* is used throughout the Old Testament, and though it is regularly translated as "help," it is useful to look closely at *whose* help and *what kind* of help it typically describes.

A little research reveals that *'ezer* is used frequently in the praising poetry of the Psalms, as in the repetitive rhythm of Psalm 115:9–11:

> *O Israel, trust thou in the Lord: he is their* help *and their shield.*
> *O house of Aaron, trust in the Lord: he is their* help *and their shield.*
> *Ye that fear the Lord, trust in the Lord: he is their* help *and their shield.*

And in Psalm 121:1–2, it is used similarly:

I will lift up mine eyes unto the hills, from whence cometh my help.
My help *cometh from the Lord, which made heaven and earth.*

These verses demonstrate beautifully that *'ezer* refers to the kind of help the Lord gives—divine assistance that succors, delivers, and rescues. Some of our hymns, though not of Hebrew origin, similarly refer to the Lord as our Helper. For example, in the moving sixteenth-century hymn "A Mighty Fortress Is Our God," Martin Luther penned these beautiful words:

A mighty fortress is our God,
A tower of strength ne'er failing.
A helper *mighty is our God,*
O'er ills of life prevailing.[36]

One of the Church's most respected musicians and composers, Evan Stephens, also wrote of the Lord as our Helper in "Let Us All Press On." Verse 3 reads:

If we do what's right we have no need to fear,
For the Lord, our helper, *will ever be near;*
In the days of trial his Saints he will cheer,
And prosper the cause of truth.
Fear not, though the enemy deride;
Courage, for the Lord is on our side.[37]

Hebrew etymology shows that *'ezer* originated from two roots, "to save" and "to be strong," which, over time, merged into one, rendered "to help."[38] In fact, *'ezer* was so representative of these godly characteristics that it evolved into several theophoric names, names that evoked God's protection by either embedding His name within them or attesting to His virtues.[39] *Ebenezer* ("rock of help")[40] and *Ezra* ("a helper")[41] are two examples of the latter that have withstood the test of time and translation. So while "helper" would be a fair translation for this quality of Eve, a more accurate and complete term might be "rescuer" or "deliverer."

Lest we think Eve's unique strength now surpasses Adam's, the coupled Hebrew word that follows and qualifies *'ezer* restores their equilibrium. *'Ezer kenegdo* is the Hebrew pairing that we read as "an help meet for him." Though used only this once in the Old Testament, *kenegdo* is elsewhere translated as "equal to."[42] Modern English readers typically mentally divide this phrase, *'ezer kenegdo,* into two distinct parts: *an help meet* + *for him*. But considering the actual meanings of *'ezer* and *kenegdo,* those two distinct parts should more accurately be divided as follows: *an help* + *meet for him*. In King James's seventeenth-century English, *meet for* was a standard way of saying "worthy of" or "equal to." Unfortunately, the Old English understanding of *meet for* has become archaic, making way for a corrupted interpretation of this significant phrase in the King James Version of the Bible,[43] leading to the misguided adoption of the terms *helpmeet* and *helpmate*. Other biblical translations remedy this by translating the phrase in more accurate ways:

New King James Version	NKJV	**"a helper comparable to him"**
New Living Translation	NLT	**"a helper who is just right for him"**
New International Version New American Standard Version Hebrew Names Version	NIV NASV HNV	**"a helper suitable for him"**
English Standard Version Revised Standard Version	ESV RSV	**"a helper fit for him"**
Christian Standard Bible	CSB	**"a helper corresponding to him"**

Modern-day prophets understand the true implications of the broadly misused term. President Howard W. Hunter declared that the Lord intended for a man's wife to be "a companion equal and necessary in full partnership."

He went on to illuminate the importance of shared responsibility in marriage, noting that "for a man to operate independent of or without regard to the feelings and counsel of his wife in governing the family is to exercise unrighteous dominion."[44] Our Heavenly Parents' intentions for holy matrimony were set forth from the very beginning: husband and wife are and always have been intended to be equal partners, supporting each other in balanced unity.

"Bone of My Bones, and Flesh of My Flesh"

Account B, and more specifically Genesis 2:23–25, is generally believed to depict the marriage of Adam and Eve.[45]

> *And Adam said, This is now bone of my bones, and flesh of my flesh: she shall be called Woman, because she was taken out of Man.*
>
> *Therefore shall a man leave his father and his mother, and shall cleave unto his wife: and they shall be one flesh.*
>
> *And they were both naked, the man and his wife, and were not ashamed.*

In the earliest days of the Restoration, the Prophet Joseph Smith declared marriage "*an institution of heaven*, instituted in the Garden of Eden."[46] Since mortal life had not yet begun, this *institution of heaven* was an eternal covenant; as of yet, there was no alternative. And since our First Parents had not yet been separated from Deity, their eternal marriage would have been performed by Deity, "whose work endures forever."[47]

The phrase "bone of my bones, and flesh of my flesh" indicates just such a covenant relationship, both in these verses and in other places in the Bible. For example, in both accounts of David being anointed king of Israel,[48] his people rejoice in their new relationship with him, declaring, "We are thy bone and thy flesh." In the New Testament, Paul evokes this same imagery in his letter to the Ephesians, noting that, as covenant-making members of Christ's Church, we are "of his flesh, and of his bones."[49]

There is yet an additional way we might look at the phrase "bone of my bones, and flesh of my flesh." If we allow bone to represent physical strength and flesh to represent human weakness, this ancient oath might be akin to a pledge to be bound together "through thick and thin," in the best circumstances as well as the worst. Seen in this light, it appears to be antiquity's precursor to the standard modern wedding vows: "from this day forward, for better, for worse, for richer, for poorer, in sickness and in health."

Account B concludes with Adam being directed to "cleave" to Eve, symbolically becoming "one flesh" (Genesis 2:24). *Cleave* is a fascinating word. Like many English words, it has two meanings, but unlike most homonyms, its two definitions are diametrically opposed to each other, with one meaning "to part, divide, or separate," and the other meaning "to stick, adhere, or cling."[50] No word could be more fitting for this account, since what began as one (*'adam* or "humanity") became two (male and female), and those two are now directed to once again become one through the balanced unity of eternal marriage. As they are united both spiritually and physically as husband and wife, their unique qualities and roles perfect and complete each other.[51]

Each and every element of both Account A and Account B has been carefully crafted to highlight Adam and Eve's divinely designed interdependence. As they take their first steps away from their Father and their Mother, they reflect the divine image of their Heavenly Parents in their beautifully balanced duet. For "neither is the man without the woman, neither the woman without the man, in the Lord. For as the woman is of the man, even so is the man also by the woman; but all things of God."[52] So they begin their journey together, side by side.

NOTES

1. Pope Francis, "Pope Francis's Homily at the Family Synod's Opening Mass."
2. I strongly recommend a close personal study of the various accounts, in which you prayerfully consider their similarities and differences. Though it is impractical for

me to go into extensive detail here, and it has been done well by other authors, such study has significantly strengthened my testimony of the gospel of Jesus Christ and its ongoing Restoration.

3. See Wilson, *Christ's Emancipation of Women*, 6.
4. Researchers have so thoroughly examined the two parts that, based on the different tones and styles, they have assigned names to the two unidentified scribes: the Priestly source (Account A) and the Jahwist source (Account B). Other sections of the Old Testament have been attributed to each of them as well. Specifically, Genesis 5:1–2 (Moses 6:8–9), which reads like yet another account of the creation of Adam and Eve, has been attributed to the Priestly source (author of Account A). Interestingly, these verses are considered the prelude to the genealogy of Adam through Seth, rather than an additional Creation account. They are brief and poetic, echoing the tone and intent of Account A.
5. It is interesting to consider that, from a Restoration perspective, Account A and Account B's parallel structure in Moses and Abraham have had ample opportunity to be altered, added to, or completely disregarded by way of prophetic revelation. However, with relatively minor exceptions, the dual narratives have been preserved, perhaps because of their insightful and harmonious differences.
6. Brown, *Brown-Driver-Briggs Hebrew and English Lexicon*, 43. A simple way to study the meaning and occurrence of Hebrew words in the Bible is through the website blueletterbible.org. There is a tools function for each verse that shows the original Hebrew word with its English translation. It also conveniently allows for reading various translations for each verse.
7. A second interesting example of this plural suffix is seen in the term *Urim and Thummim*, which has been interpreted to mean "lights and perfections" (see Bible Dictionary).
8. Smith, *The Words of Joseph Smith*, 379.
9. See also D&C 59:3–4, which also likens commandments to blessings.
10. The doctrine of "original sin" traces back to Augustine and the Catholic Church's Council of Carthage (AD 418) and Council of Orange (AD 529). Officially, it teaches that "the sin of Adam made the whole human race a 'mass of sin' worthy of damnation," and declares that "the sin of Adam is passed on 'by propagation not by imitation'" (Collinge, *The A to Z of Catholicism*, 385). This Catholic doctrine provides their rationale for infant baptism. The critical error here is the assumption that *sin* is the result of Adam and Eve's decision to partake. The true doctrine is that *mortality* (and thereby *death*) are the result of their action, and the Atonement of Jesus Christ is the great remedy, clearly explained in 1 Corinthians 15:22: "As in Adam all die, even so in Christ shall all be made alive." *Sin* is a byproduct of the exercise of *agency* in a mortal world. It is also interesting to note Moses 5:13 when considering when sin first reared its ugly head. Taking place some time after Adam and Eve's mortal sojourn began, that verse reads, "And

men began from that time forth to be carnal, sensual, and devilish." For further insight, I strongly recommend the excellent research and writing of Terryl and Fiona Givens in their book *The Christ Who Heals.*

11. Wordsworth, "Ode: Intimations of Immortality from Recollections of Early Childhood."
12. This doctrine is taught by both the Apostle Paul and King Benjamin in 1 Corinthians 2:14 and Mosiah 3:19, respectively.
13. Kimball, "Ocean Currents and Family Influences."
14. Bednar, "We Believe in Being Chaste." The prophet Brigham Young made a similar statement: "The body is of the earth . . . and is under the mighty influence of that fallen nature that is of the earth" (Young, *Complete Discourses of Brigham Young,* 2:922). In a later discourse, he expanded on that doctrine, teaching: "[Mankind] naturally love and admire righteousness, justice and truth more than they do evil. . . . When we do an evil, we do it in opposition to the promptings of the Spirit of Truth that is within us. Man[kind], the noblest work of God, was . . . designed for an endless duration, for which the love of all good was incorporated in [our] nature. It was never designed that [we] should naturally do and love evil" (Young, *Complete Discourses of Brigham Young,* 4:2020).
15. Kimball, "The Blessings and Responsibilities of Womanhood." The prophet Brigham Young declared in characteristic fashion: "[God the Father] created man, as we create our children; for there is no other process of creation in heaven, on the earth, in the earth, or under the earth, or in all the eternities, that is, that were, or that ever will be. . . . There exist fixed laws and regulations by which the elements are fashioned . . . and this process of creation is from everlasting to everlasting" (in *Journal of Discourses,* 11:122). Though these concepts are currently beyond our full mortal comprehension, President Joseph F. Smith said Adam and Eve were "born of woman into this world, the same as Jesus and you and I" (*Deseret Evening News,* 27 December 1913, section 3, Church News, 7). President George Albert Smith simply described Account B's birth descriptions as "a symbolic representation" (see Lee, *Ye Are the Light of the World,* 284).
16. Brown, *Brown-Driver-Briggs Hebrew and English Lexicon,* 9.
17. Brown, *Brown-Driver-Briggs Hebrew and English Lexicon,* 9.
18. There are several excellent sources for an extended and fascinating study of Adam's name. Three of my favorites are Meyers's *Discovering Eve*; Rockwood's "The Redemption of Eve"; and Spackman's "'Adam, Where Art Thou?' Onomastics, Etymology, and Translation in Genesis 2–3."
19. See also Moses 6:9; emphasis added.
20. Kimball, "The Blessings and Responsibilities of Womanhood."
21. Kimball, "The Blessings and Responsibilities of Womanhood."
22. McConkie, "Eve and the Fall."
23. Brown, *Brown-Driver-Briggs Hebrew and English Lexicon,* 854.

24. Brown, *Brown-Driver-Briggs Hebrew and English Lexicon*, 124.
25. Rockwood's "The Redemption of Eve" makes a thorough and enlightening study of Eve's creation from Adam's rib. Sister Rockwood received her Master of Theological Studies from the Harvard Divinity School.
26. Olson, *Women of the Old Testament*, 9.
27. Moore, *Women in Christian Traditions*, 22.
28. Nelson, "Lessons from Eve."
29. Johnson, *Man, Woman, and Deity*, 12.
30. Johnson, *Man, Woman, and Deity*, 12.
31. Genesis 3:20.
32. Brown, *Brown-Driver-Briggs Hebrew and English Lexicon*, 295.
33. Sister Patricia T. Holland and Sister Sheri L. Dew have both spoken memorably regarding the significance of the fact that Eve's title as "the mother of all living" preceded her maternity. See Holland, "'One Thing Needful': Becoming Women of Greater Faith in Christ" and Dew, "Are We Not All Mothers?"
34. Genesis 2:19–20.
35. Luke 1:38.
36. *Hymns of The Church of Jesus Christ of Latter-day Saints*, no. 68; emphasis added.
37. *Hymns*, no. 243; emphasis added. Composer Evan Stephens served as the president of the Mormon Tabernacle Choir from 1890 to 1916. He composed eighty-four of the hymns in the 1927 *Latter-day Saint Hymns*, eighteen of which remain in the current edition of the hymnal.
38. Brown, *Brown-Driver-Briggs Hebrew and English Lexicon*, 470.
39. A few good examples of Hebrew names that embed the sacred name of Deity (*El*, as in *Elohim*) are Ariel ("lion of God"), Daniel ("God is my judge"), Elizabeth ("my God is a vow" or "my God is abundance"), and Gabriel ("God is my strength" or "a hero of God"). There are also Christian theophoric names, such as Timothy ("one who honors God") and Theodora ("gift of God"). See Youngberg, *Sacred Baby Names*.
40. Youngberg, *Sacred Baby Names*. This is the name the prophet Samuel gave to a monument erected in honor of the Lord's assistance in defeating the Philistines, the same monument referred to in lyrics of the beautiful hymn "Come, Thou Fount of Every Blessing": "Here I raise my Ebenezer; hither by thy help I come." See 1 Samuel 7:10–12.
41. Youngberg, *Sacred Baby Names*.
42. Brown, *Brown-Driver-Briggs Hebrew and English Lexicon*, 612, 1102.
43. See Rockwood, "The Redemption of Eve," for a more thorough look at this phrase.
44. Hunter, "Being a Righteous Husband and Father." Similarly, Elder G. Homer Durham stated, "Man and woman walk together before the Lord as companions, as loving helpmeets to each other, not as self-seeking competitors" (Durham, "Woman's Responsibility to Learn," 33).

45. President Harold B. Lee noted that Genesis 2:23–24 "were very likely the words spoken by Adam reciting the vows of the first marriage upon this earth" (Lee, *Decisions for Successful Living*, 125).
46. Smith, *Doctrines of Salvation*, 2:70–71; emphasis in original.
47. President Joseph Fielding Smith stated, "Marriage as established in the beginning was an eternal covenant. The first man and the first woman were not married until death should part them, for at that time death had not come into the world. The ceremony on that occasion was performed by the Eternal Father himself whose work endures forever" (Smith, *Doctrines of Salvation*, 2:71).
48. 2 Samuel 5:1 and 1 Chronicles 11:1.
49. Ephesians 5:28–31. These same verses also address the need for husband and wife to love each other as "one flesh."
50. *Oxford English Dictionary Online*, "cleave."
51. The beauty of such a relationship is further represented in the Hebrew word for "bride." *Kallah* is derived from the primary root *kalal*, meaning "to complete, to make perfect, or to finish" (Brown, *Brown-Driver-Briggs Hebrew and English Lexicon*, 480, 483).
52. 1 Corinthians 11:11–12.

CHAPTER 6

THE GARDEN OF GOD

Adam and Eve knew God personally.
They saw him and talked with him.
They were taught the gospel of Jesus Christ
even in that early time.

—Elder Mark E. Petersen[1]

I've heard it said that life is one grand adventure. A contrarian might contend that life, in fact, is a long series of overlapping adventures and *mis*-adventures, some planned, some unpredictable; some anticipated with nervous excitement, some accompanied by anxious dread; some delightfully exhilarating, some downright nauseating. Life is a wild ride: at any given moment, we're trying to catch our breath, recover, or brace for what's next. I imagine I'm not the only one who regularly wishes I could just press pause. If I could, I'd retreat to a tranquil sanctuary. It would be unabashedly beautiful, filled with the fragrance of gardenias and the soothing sound of a little stream. My most dedicated mentors would be calmly awaiting my arrival, ready to love, encourage, and motivate. Most important, there would be no clocks, no deadlines, and no rushing; time would simply stand still until I said, "Go." It would be just like paradise.

Newly embodied, Eve and Adam were introduced to just such a place, a peaceful precursor to their grand adventure. Eden's sacred garden[2] was a place like no other, where time literally stood still, "for as yet the Gods had not appointed unto Adam his reckoning."[3] Ezekiel dubbed it "the garden of God,"[4] a temple-garden where divine mentors could tutor and prepare our First Parents for all that lay ahead.

DUTIES AND QUALIFICATIONS

God's garden was so much more than flower beds. Elder James E. Talmage taught that "the Garden in Eden was the first sanctuary of earth, for therein did the Lord first speak unto man and make known the Divine law."[5] This supports earlier prophetic statements from Joseph Smith, explaining that Adam and Eve "received revelations, commandments and ordinances at the beginning."[6]

Recognizing the unique nature of this holy temple-garden brings meaningful clarity to the introductory charge given to "till," "dress," and "keep" this sacred place.[7] Serious students of scripture have likely been confused by this directive, having understood that the garden was self-sufficient, existing in a paradisiacal state of plenty.[8] It seems perfectly fitting that the Hebrew name *'Eden* translates to "delight" or "pleasure."[9] This pleasantly delightful place provided everything Eve and Adam required for their current, though temporary, state. Work was something that would come later and in a much different realm, requiring physical labor and "the sweat of [their] brow."[10] But a desire to better understand these specific duties to "dress and keep" Eden's garden guides us to once again examine the broader biblical context of those words—where and how they are used and understood elsewhere in scripture. Such research reveals that these terms, *'abad*[11] and *shamar*,[12] refer to priesthood responsibilities related to serving in the house of the Lord. Specifically, they are the same words used to describe the Levite priests' duties while serving in the Tabernacle, such as in Numbers 18:5–6:[13]

> *And ye shall keep the charge of the sanctuary, and the charge of the altar: that there be no wrath any more upon the children of Israel.*
>
> *And I, behold, I have taken your brethren the Levites from among the children of Israel: to you they are given as a gift for the Lord,* to do *the service of the tabernacle of the congregation.*

In modern English, "dress and keep" might be better understood as "serve and protect," particularly as such priesthood service and protection facilitate others' worship. In a sense, Adam and Eve were called as earth's first temple president and matron.

Just as today, such responsibility is reserved for the most dedicated and faithful, and in this regard our First Parents had previously proven themselves extremely well qualified, as outlined in chapter 3.

GARDEN LIVING

Though we each attained various levels of "stature, capacity, and intelligence"[14] as spirit children in the premortal realm, a veil of forgetfulness separates us from the memories of that place and time;[15] we enter mortality pure and innocent, quite literally with a world of learning ahead of us. Restored doctrine teaches that Adam and Eve likewise donned that same veil as they received their physical bodies, but their role as our First Parents necessitated a transition that included a period of divine tutelage in Eden's garden-temple. Though some depictions of the garden lead us to assume their sojourn there was brief, that is likely a combination of literary device and dramatic license meant to move the storytelling along. From the early days of the Restoration, inspired prophetic statements have repeatedly confirmed that life in the garden, though transitional, was a period of great learning, a special time of divinely led preparation for all that was to come.[16] The Prophet Joseph Smith explained that "God conversed with [Adam] face to face: in his presence he was permitted to stand, and from his own mouth he was permitted to receive instruction—he heard his voice, walked before him and gazed upon his glory—while intelligence burst upon his understanding."[17] President Brigham Young reiterated this truth and personalized it, adding, "Adam was as conversant with his Father who placed him upon this earth as we are conversant with our earthly parents."[18] And President Joseph Fielding Smith added a third powerful witness, stating, "When Adam was in the Garden of Eden he was in the presence of the Father and was taught by him. He learned his language. He was as familiar with our Eternal Father in that garden as we are with our fathers in mortal life."[19]

Clearly, *innocence* and *knowledge* are *not* mutually exclusive, as these prophetic statements make clear. Crucial learning was happening in the garden's holy intersection of cloistered virtue and divine tutelage. But *what* were Adam and Eve being taught during their sacred interactions with Deity?

Respected gospel scholar and author Beverly Campbell, in her seminal work *Eve and the Choice Made in Eden*, introduced this topic for thoughtful contemplation, urging dedicated students toward deeper reflection. She compellingly wrote: "Because they were the . . . only ones who could bring to pass mortal life so that His own promises to all His children can be fulfilled, we can feel confident that God did not visit them to speak of trifling matters. Each meeting was surely a time of important instruction."[20]

Indeed, no less weighty matters than the plan of salvation were being taught to them during this pivotal time of tutoring. It is *critical* to our overarching understanding of the gospel plan to comprehend this crucial truth: Adam and Eve were being taught the gospel by Deity while residing in the garden. Jumping slightly ahead in the account's chronology, let's carefully consider Elder Jeffrey R. Holland's thoughts related to this often-overlooked detail of Adam and Eve's story:

> *They—like us—were able and willing to venture [the terrible risks of sorrow and death] only with the knowledge that there would*

be safety at the end of the day for those who wanted it and lived for it. They were willing to transgress knowingly and consciously (the only way they could "fall" into the consequences of mortality, inasmuch as Elohim certainly could not force innocent parties out of the garden and still be a just God) only because they had a full knowledge of the plan of salvation, which would provide for them a way back from their struggle with death and hell.[21]

Elder Holland speaks to the extent of learning taking place in the garden, to the fact that Eve and Adam were innocent *but positively not ignorant.* Knowledge is a *prerequisite* of agency.[22] This is straightforward doctrine, reiterated each time an eight-year-old child is baptized: accountability is understanding based. That core tenet, so fundamental to our faith, has been true from the foundations of the world. It applied in the garden just as it applied in premortality and just as it applies to each of us now in mortality. We must have at least a rudimentary, if theoretical, understanding of our options in order to make a choice.

The perceived distance between innocence and knowledge has everything to do with *lack of experience,* and life in the garden epitomized this, as President Joseph Fielding Smith explained. Referring specifically to Adam, as was the custom at the time, though each of these points clearly applies to Eve as well, President Smith stated:

He was without knowledge of good and evil. He had knowledge, of course. He could speak. He could converse. There were many things he could be taught and was taught; but under the conditions in which he was living at that time it was impossible for him to visualize or understand the power of good and evil. He did not know what pain was. He did not know what sorrow was; and a thousand other things that have come to us in this life that Adam did not know in the Garden of Eden and could not understand and would not have known had he remained there.[23]

At this point of their story, the missing piece of the puzzle was *experience,* and it would require leaving the garden to find it.[24]

FAITHFUL COURAGE

Though their knowledge was more equivalent to book learning than to street smarts, Adam and Eve understood the plan, and they knew the players personally. Imagine the peace they felt in their garden sanctuary, being tutored by divine mentors intent on expressing Their love and assuring them of their ultimate safety. Much like our experience in premortality, where we built such a relationship with Jehovah as to enable us to trust in His role as our Savior, the faithful courage Eve and Adam were cultivating during this learning period was critical for the success of all that was to come. Though applied on a different scale and magnitude than we may typically face in day-to-day life, Adam and Eve were prepared to act because of their trust in the Savior. Elder David A. Bednar beautifully explained that powerful connection between trust, faith, and action, noting that "assurance and hope make it possible for us to walk to the edge of the light and take a few steps into the darkness—expecting and trusting the light to move and illuminate the way. The combination of assurance and hope initiates action in the present."[25]

Eve and Adam knew life's purpose and felt empowered through the combination of assurance and hope to exercise their agency to *choose* to usher in mortality for all of God's children, thereby opening the doorway to experience.[26] Even at this point of their story, they understood that life in the garden was not the ultimate goal, but that exaltation and celestial glory were.

NOTES

1. Petersen, "Adam, the Archangel."
2. It is worth noting that Eden and the Garden of Eden are not synonymous, though the terms are sometimes used interchangeably. The *Garden* of Eden is described as

a discrete area within the greater locale known as Eden. See Genesis 2:8; Moses 3:8; Abraham 5:8.

3. Abraham 5:13.
4. Ezekiel 28:13.
5. Talmage, *The House of the Lord*, 17.
6. https://www.josephsmithpapers.org/paper-summary/history-1838-1856-volume-c-1-2-november-1838-31-july-1842/551#historical-intro. For further insight on this topic, see Smith, *The Words of Joseph Smith*, 38–44. The editors include a first-hand account by Robert B. Thompson, 5 Oct 1840, explaining that Joseph had taught that God had revealed all the saving ordinances to Adam "'and set Adam to watch over them [and God intended] to reveal them from heaven to man or to send Angels to reveal them' in the event of their loss." It is worth reiterating that the name *Adam* refers to *both* Adam and Eve. President Spencer W. Kimball stated, "Man here is always in the plural. It was plural from the beginning," and Elder Bruce R. McConkie concurred, stating, "The name of Adam and Eve as a united partnership is Adam. They, the two of them together, are named Adam" (Kimball, "The Blessings and Responsibilities of Womanhood"; McConkie, "Eve and the Fall").
7. Genesis 2:5, 15; Moses 3:5, 15; Abraham 5:5, 11.
8. Joseph Fielding Smith taught that, before the Fall, Adam and Eve "could have remained in the Garden of Eden forever and all things that were created would have remained in that same condition forever" (Smith, *Doctrines of Salvation*, 1:92). Additionally, Bruce R. McConkie explained that the Fall's effects passed upon "all created things. They fall in that they too become mortal. Death enters the world; mortality reigns; procreation commences; and the Lord's great and eternal purposes roll onward" (McConkie, "Christ and the Creation"). Both statements corroborate Lehi's explanation to Jacob in 2 Nephi 2:22 that "all things which were created must have remained in the same state in which they were after they were created; and they must have remained forever, and had no end."
9. Strong, *The New Strong's Exhaustive Concordance of the Bible*, 103 (words #5730 and #5731).
10. Moses 5:1.
11. Brown, *Brown-Driver-Briggs Hebrew and English Lexicon*, 712.
12. Brown, *Brown-Driver-Briggs Hebrew and English Lexicon*, 1036.
13. Emphasis added. See also Numbers 3:7–8; 8:26; Deuteronomy 4:19; 1 Chronicles 23:32; and Ezekiel 44:14. For further study, I strongly recommend Faulconer's "Chaos and Order, Order and Chaos: The Creation Story as the Story of Human Community." Brown's *Gate of Heaven* also makes a close study of this point.
14. McConkie, "Eve and the Fall."
15. President Thomas S. Monson taught, "How grateful we should be that a wise Creator fashioned an earth and placed us here, with a veil of forgetfulness of our

previous existence so that we might experience a time of testing, an opportunity to prove ourselves in order to qualify for all that God has prepared for us to receive" (Monson, "The Race of Life").

16. Eve is unmentioned in many of these important prophetic statements, an unfortunate reality of the cultural context of the speakers' time. However, we can trust that Eve's inclusion was assumed in their comments, recalling the plural use of *Adam* as detailed in chapter 5.
17. *Lectures on Faith*, 13.
18. In *Journal of Discourses*, 9:148.
19. Smith, *Doctrines of Salvation*, 1:26. Again, recalling the plural use of *Adam* is important on this point. Gratefully, Elder Mark E. Petersen specifically described *both* Adam *and* Eve in his October 1980 general conference address, teaching: "Adam and Eve knew God personally. They saw him and talked with him. They were taught the gospel of Jesus Christ even in that early time." He further stated, still speaking of Adam *and* Eve, "They were well educated, having been taught by the Lord himself. What an education! What an instructor! Think of it, and remember that 'the glory of God is intelligence, or in other words, light and truth' (D&C 93:36). These gifts were imparted to Adam and Eve and their family. No one else could teach them, because they were the first human beings. That task was left to the Lord and his angels" (Petersen, "Adam, The Archangel").
20. Campbell, *Eve and the Choice Made in Eden*, 64–65. Besides writing her powerful book on Eve, Sister Campbell served for twelve years as the director of International Affairs for The Church of Jesus Christ of Latter-day Saints.
21. Holland, *Christ and the New Covenant*, 202–3.
22. Elder L. Lionel Kendrick taught, "Knowledge is essential for agency to exist" (Kendrick, "Our Moral Agency"); and Sister Elaine Cannon taught, "To use our agency wisely we need information to act upon. We need a knowledge of the laws of life, with their accompanying blessings and protective punishments" (Cannon, "Agency and Accountability"). This is basic doctrine taught in the Book of Mormon: "Men are instructed sufficiently that they know good from evil" so that they may "act for themselves and not . . . be acted upon" (2 Nephi 2:5, 26); "He that knoweth not good from evil is blameless" (Alma 29:5).
23. Smith, *Doctrines of Salvation*, 1:107–8.
24. Lehi's counsel to his son Jacob, found in 2 Nephi 2, is a beautiful extended discourse on this topic, deserving of extensive personal study.
25. Bednar, "Seek Learning by Faith."
26. Elder Jeffrey R. Holland declared that "sorrow and death were facts Adam and Eve were willing to face *in order that* 'men might be'" (*Christ and the New Covenant*, 202; emphasis added). This modern, prophetic witness further emphasizes and reiterates the degree of knowledge and understanding Eve and Adam possessed as they made their choice to leave the garden.

CHAPTER 7

THE CRUCIAL CONFLICT

If choice is to exist and agency is to have any meaning, alternatives must be presented.

—Elder Jeffrey R. Holland[1]

Like it or not, every one of our individual stories has conflict, lots of it. We regularly work through dilemmas and predicaments. We feel torn by competing demands or pressured by unrealistic expectations. Someone forces our hand, or we're forced to prioritize. Big or small, mutually exclusive alternatives are literally everywhere. The Prophet Joseph Smith referred to such challenging choices as "decision[s] of character."[2] Elder Jeffrey R. Holland called them "contending enticements,"[3] and President Dallin H. Oaks, "competing demands."[4]

In every realm, including the spiritual, we have a long list of things we *should* do, but time and energy are finite—we can't do everything, so we choose as best we can. Caring for small children might mean infrequent temple attendance for a time; a period of poor health or depression might preclude magnifying our calling as we'd otherwise like. Sometimes, things we *shouldn't do,* like shop on the Sabbath, come in direct conflict with things we *should,* like serve a sick neighbor who needs a prescription picked up from the pharmacy. And occasionally our only options seem to be equally undesirable alternatives, like bearing with immorality *or* alienating a family member.

The fact of the matter is that mortality has been designed to require tough decisions. "Opposition in all things"[5] doesn't always look like a boulder hedging up the way or feel like temptation leading us astray; it frequently manifests itself as a fork in the road, presenting us with puzzling alternatives.

As we begin to pick apart the details of Adam and Eve's crucial conflict, it's helpful to recall, as outlined in chapter 3, that agency, loving Heavenly Parents, and a perfect plan are the bedrock on which this true story is built. Every element has been carefully crafted by the Master Architect to create the ideal setting and circumstances to allow for maximum learning and growth. Remember, conflict is crucial: "*If choice is to exist and agency is to have any meaning, alternatives must be presented.*"[6] Faithfulness is cultivated by exercising agency, little by little, through a lifetime of choosing. With that stable groundwork in mind, let's now take a close look at the apparently conflicting alternatives Eve and Adam have laid out before them.

They have a beautiful list of "shoulds"—to "be fruitful, and multiply, and replenish the earth, and subdue it, and have dominion . . . over every living thing."[7] And those "shoulds" are offset by one very specific "should not," a warning given as they are introduced into their new garden home:

> *Of every tree of the garden thou mayest freely eat,*
>
> *But of the tree of the knowledge of good and evil, thou shalt not eat of it, nevertheless, thou mayest choose for thyself, for it is given unto thee; but, remember that I forbid it, for in the day thou eatest thereof thou shalt surely die.*[8]

This conflict is concerning: how can our noble First Parents be perfectly obedient if they are commanded to do two things that are mutually exclusive? They cannot multiply and replenish the earth—which they've been told to do—unless they eat the fruit of the tree of the knowledge of good and evil—which they've been told *not* to do. These two directives appear to be diametrically opposed to each other. Can God be kind and good if He is placing them in this predicament? But if we pause and ponder those three foundational components—agency, loving parentage, and a perfect plan—understanding emerges: Adam and Eve have been placed in the ideal circumstances for maximum learning and growth.

First, there's agency: *thou mayest choose for thyself, for it is given unto thee.* They've been given the privilege of choice, but they must have options to nudge them forward. As President Boyd K. Packer explained, "There was too much at issue to introduce man into mortality by force. That would contravene the very law essential to the plan."[9] Rather, opposing alternatives are the perfect impetus for action. If they eat, they keep the first directive but disobey the second; if they don't eat, they disobey the first but keep the second, so even inaction is action, in a sense. The conflict requires a choice, and agency allows for it to be their own.

Second, they have a personal relationship with their Heavenly Father, so they recognize and understand His defining characteristics: He is a God of love and a God of truth. Since He wants the very best for His beloved children, He must warn them of pain and suffering. Regardless of its many benefits, eating this fruit will, by divine design, lead to pain and suffering and eventually death. All the other fruits can be eaten without repercussions, *freely,* but not this one; this one comes with *consequences,* and He will not, *He cannot,* keep that truth from them.

The third key element is a perfect plan, which they have been taught in its entirety. They learned long before Nephi did that a loving God does not give His children commandments without preparing a way to accomplish them.[10] Jesus Christ is that Way.[11] The doorway to mortality does have a threshold to be crossed, but it opens to progress and a path homeward made possible by our loving Savior and His perfect Atonement.

TRANSGRESSION

Ultimately, as we know, Adam and Eve choose to step across that threshold into mortality. That choice has been labeled a "sin" by many, even the "original sin" by some,[12] but it's designated a "transgression" in the vocabulary of the restored gospel of Jesus Christ.

In the Prophet Joseph's extended translation of the Genesis account, found in Moses, *transgression* is the term used by both Adam and Eve, as well as the Lord, when referring to that pivotal decision,[13] and it is also the word choice for the second article of faith: "We believe that men will be punished for their own sins, and not for Adam's transgression."

Though the two terms, *sin* and *transgression*, are often used synonymously, there are important distinctions. Specifically, *to sin* means to act in a reprehensible way, contrary to God's plan, while *to transgress* means to pass or cross over, as in the case of a limit or a boundary, which is exactly what our First Parents chose to do by partaking of the fruit. On at least one occasion, the Prophet Joseph made clear that Adam and Eve "did not commit sin in eating the fruits for God had decreed that [they] should eat and fall."[14] In other words, it was a necessary part of the plan. Other prophets and apostles have likewise reaffirmed this, adding their explanations of the difference between *sin* and *transgression*, especially in terms of this imperative choice. President Dallin H. Oaks explained that "some acts, like murder, are crimes because they are inherently wrong. Other acts, like operating without a license, are crimes only because they are legally prohibited. Under these distinctions, the act that produced the Fall was not a sin—inherently wrong—but a transgression—wrong because it was formally prohibited."[15] He noted, "It was Eve who first transgressed the limits of Eden in order to initiate the conditions of mortality. Her act, whatever its nature, was formally a transgression but eternally a glorious necessity to open the doorway toward eternal life."[16]

Occasionally, order seems to highlight significance, as we read in "The Family: A Proclamation to the World," which emphasizes, "The first commandment that God gave to Adam and Eve pertained to their potential for parenthood." President Oaks designated that commandment, to multiply and replenish the earth (as specifically applied to our First Parents), to be "first in sequence and first in importance."[17] Other apostles and prophets have likewise expounded on the preeminence of that command given to Adam and Eve. Elder James E. Talmage called it "the first and greater commandment";[18] Elder John A. Widtsoe similarly considered the command to procreate the "greater" of the two because it concerns the good of others, noting that "lesser laws" chiefly benefit ourselves;[19] Elder Bruce R. McConkie concurred, stating that the commandment to not partake of the fruit was "a lesser law—an infinitely lesser law."[20]

Indeed, the choice to *transgress*, to cross that threshold into mortality, was beneficial and necessary. Gospel scholar Truman Madsen declared Eve "the heroine who led the way into this obstacle course of mortality. . . . She did not leave the garden for trivial, selfish gratification but to open the way for the birth and rebirth of the whole human family."[21] President James E. Faust supported that stance, explaining, "The choice was really between a continuation of their comfortable existence in Eden, where they would never progress, or a momentous exit into mortality with its opposites: pain, trials, and physical death in contrast to joy, growth, and the potential for eternal life."[22] He wisely concluded, "We all owe a great debt of gratitude to Eve."[23] Her courageous choice to step across mortality's threshold, Adam at her side, allowed for the activation of each premortal spirit's deliberate decision to brave mortality as well.

DECEPTION

Let's return to the story, backing up momentarily because in our examination of one conflict, we've conveniently set aside another. In the interim between the issuance of the two key commandments and Eve's decision to partake, a new character has entered the scene.[24] Here is Lucifer, figuratively portrayed as a serpent,[25] cunningly misrepresenting himself and lying to Eve in order to cause trouble, introduce uncertainty, and derail the plan. Saying his arrival introduces complications and further conflict would be an epic understatement.

Though he's known by many names, *Lucifer* appears to have been his name in premortality; it means *the shining one, light bringer,* or *light bearer.*[26] These glowing descriptions were appropriate prior to his rebellion—scripture teaches he was "an angel of God who was in authority in the presence of God" before his fall.[27] The name *Lucifer* now strikes us as ironic, since post-rebellion he has become the prince of darkness,[28] a master of disguise, an impostor who seeks to portray himself as an angel of light.[29]

The "father of all lies"[30] confronts Eve in her innocence—she is educated in certain ways but as yet inexperienced with deception and unpracticed in discernment, having interacted only with the perfectly trustworthy. Though it is true that eating the fruit of the tree will open her eyes, allowing for the recognition of good and evil, it is *not* true that it is harmless; mortality's unavoidable consequence is death, as God had truthfully and lovingly warned Adam and Eve. On realizing the error in her assumption regarding Lucifer's nature and intent, it's no wonder that she felt "beguiled,"[31] regardless of how heroic or courageous her subsequent choice to partake proved to be.

UNCERTAINTY

In spite of Satan's deception, we know his opposition was necessary. Though his primary objective is to tempt and try each member of the human family, his earliest encounters with Eve and Adam were singular because of their *innocence* and significant because of their *agency*. Since God *will not* exert any compulsory means and Satan *cannot*, sometimes the most the adversary can do in his attempts to cause trouble and derail plans is to introduce uncertainty.[32]

Uncertainty in such circumstances allows us to truly, freely, and fully choose for ourselves because, during these questioning moments, we are *unsure* of what the "right" choice is—we are *uncertain* of precisely what God would have us do. In my estimation, such was the case in the serpent's interaction with Eve. Without Satan's opposition—his introduction of uncertainty among alternatives—causing her to sincerely question and consider, her choice would not have been *completely* her own. I believe Eve needed to feel at least slightly unsure of what she was *supposed* to do because *certainty* would have diminished her agency.

Parenting with such impartiality requires restraint; some decisions are so pivotal that wisdom recommends a challenging degree of parental neutrality. Few parents want to be blamed for influencing a choice that leads to serious difficulty and discomfort. Elder John A. Widtsoe seemed to recognize this dilemma. Describing the pivotal decision, he explained that God "had *warned* Adam and Eve of the hard battle with earth conditions if they chose to eat of the tree of the knowledge of good and evil. He would not subject his son and daughter to hardship and the death of their bodies unless it be of their own choice. They must choose for themselves."[33]

The uncertainty introduced by the serpent appears to have caused some period of pondering and reflection. Genesis 3:6 follows Genesis 3:5[34] in rapid succession because that's the nature of written text, but proximity on the page has no correlation to chronological timeline—it merely denotes the order of events. We have no idea of the length of the nearly invisible interlude between verses 5 and 6, but one might deduce that there was *some* interval of time because of one word the Prophet Joseph altered in his Moses translation: *became.* "And when the woman saw that the tree was good for food, and that it was pleasant to the eyes, and a tree to be desired . . . ," he changed to, "And when the woman saw that the tree was good for food, and that it became pleasant to the eyes, and a tree to be desired . . . " This was a pivotal point, perhaps the first opportunity for Eve to powerfully demonstrate her ability to reason.

Various portrayals depict Eve's character at this moment falling somewhere between wise and wicked. As members of The Church of Jesus Christ of Latter-day Saints, we emphatically believe it was the former. Recall President Oaks's explanation: "Some Christians condemn Eve for her act, concluding that she and her daughters are somehow flawed by it. Not the Latter-day Saints! Informed by revelation, we celebrate Eve's act and honor her wisdom and courage in the great episode called the Fall."[35] Her decision, irrevocably illustrated by that first bite, places Eve and Adam on the lifelong path of *becoming* like our Heavenly Father and His Beloved Son, that eternal progression which had been the goal from the start.[36]

STEWARDSHIPS

It's natural to focus on Eve during this suspenseful period of deception and uncertainty, even to the extent that we temporarily lose sight of Adam. But one might pause to wonder if he was nearby, especially since the Middle English *ye* is slightly ambiguous—able to be interpreted as either a singular pronoun or a plural one. The Genesis account includes eight uses of such equivocal pronouns in just the six verses of Genesis 3:1–6.[37] Here is a prime example of an opportunity for language and cultural bias to influence our interpretation of the story, as described in chapter 1. Since modern Western culture tends to value individualism, our default is to imagine Eve alone when she chooses to eat the fruit. However, the Eastern world esteems collectivism, so a reader from that culture may well assume Adam is nearby. In fact, scholarly research bears that assumption out, noting plural Hebrew pronouns throughout these verses.[38]

Even while acknowledging ancient linguistics, perhaps the specific detail of whether or not they were both present matters little, since there is no discrepancy among the accounts regarding who partook of the fruit first.[39] Perhaps, as the Mother of All Living, this initial choice was Eve's to make. Eve, and each of her daughters who would follow, would embody "the living fountain from which flows the stream of humanity."[40] I feel at peace when I consider that her independent decision might be seen as a meaningful precursor to women's sacred stewardship—the responsibility to usher each child of our Heavenly Parents into mortality.

The complementary stewardships of women and men have been a timeless topic of study and debate, but one thing is fairly indisputable: though their responsibilities are diverse, often interchangeable, and undoubtedly interdependent, actually *giving birth* is a privilege reserved for women. As early Church leader Martha Horne Tingey declared in 1893, "Woman has been given the power, the honor to open the door through which all must pass ere they can enter that advanced stage of action and go forward in the work of progression which has been designed and marked out by our Heavenly Parents."[41]

More recently, in 2010, Dr. Valerie Hudson Cassler similarly addressed women's and men's unique stewardships. Closely examining the symbolism of the tree of the knowledge of good and evil and the tree of life, she went a step further than we did in chapter 2. You may recall that there I offered my opinion that the tree of the knowledge of good and evil might be thought of as "the mortality tree," while the tree of life might be considered "the eternity tree." Considering complementary stewardships, Dr. Cassler shared her understanding that the tree of knowledge of good and evil, or "the mortality tree," might symbolize "the role and power of women in the Great Plan of Happiness." If so, Dr. Cassler believes, the choice to first partake of that tree's fruit was rightly Eve's. As Dr. Cassler explained, "Those who would bear the responsibility of bringing all of the children through the doorway, and risk their life in this task, had the right to make that decision."[42]

Similarly, perhaps part of Adam's, and by extension all men's, specific stewardship focuses on the second tree—the tree of life, or "the eternity tree." By virtue of priesthood office and authority, he would have the responsibility of helping their posterity partake of the fruit of that tree, the gift of eternal life, made available through the sacred saving ordinances and covenants of the gospel.[43]

MOTIVATION

Just as Eve had exercised her agency, so Adam would now have the opportunity to exercise his. Our two written texts depict his decision most simply: Eve gave him the fruit "and he did eat."[44] Adam chose to join Eve, to follow her lead, and to accept her offer of the fruit that would enable them to cross the threshold into mortality *together,* as well as open that doorway for all of humanity to follow.

Elder Holland, noting that they *willingly* and *consciously* chose to leave the garden in order "that men might be," deems the privilege of mortality to be their principal gift to each of us.[45] Summarizing this divine doctrine, he writes:

> *Thus, and only with this knowledge, can a student of the gospel of Jesus Christ grasp the full import of the magnificent line already cited: "Adam fell that men might be." That doctrine, fully understood*

and thoroughly taught only in the restored gospel, is as important as any taught in the entire Book of Mormon. Without it the world would be ignorant of the true nature of the fall of Adam and Eve, ignorant of their life-giving decision, and ignorant of the unspeakable love they demonstrated for all of God's sons and daughters.[46]

The climactic peak of their story features Adam accepting the fruit from Eve in order that they might jointly progress, leaving the garden to embark on their divine mortal mission together. Unlike Catholicism's notion of *felix culpa*,[47] or "happy fault," Adam and Eve's decision to leave the garden was not a Curious George–like episode of innocent naughtiness that luckily worked out for the best.[48] That damaging worldview, so eloquently described by Terryl and Fiona Givens, "of life as the consequence of moral failure rather than triumph, of human nature as depraved and evil rather than good but encumbered, and of Christ himself primarily as repairman of a cosmic catastrophe and shield against God's wrath, rather than the co-architect of an original plan of induction into the society of heaven,"[49] is one of the serious repercussions of the world's misunderstanding and misinterpretation of Eve's decision to partake.

NOTES

1. Holland, *Christ and the New Covenant*, 202.
2. https://www.josephsmithpapers.org/paper-summary/history-1838-1856-volume-c-1-addenda/62#foot-notes.
3. Holland, *Christ and the New Covenant*, 202.
4. Oaks, "The Plan and the Proclamation."
5. 2 Nephi 2:11.
6. Holland, *Christ and the New Covenant*, 202; emphasis added.
7. Moses 2:28. Joseph Fielding Smith addressed the curious use of the word *replenish* in this verse, explaining, "The original Hebrew word appears many times in the Old Testament; only *once* is it translated 'replenish.' . . . This same Hebrew word is translated more than a score of times in other parts of the Bible and always as 'fill,' or 'make full,' never as 'replenish'" (Smith, *Doctrines of Salvation*, 1:93–94). Other Bible translations of Genesis 1:28 make this adjustment: "Be fruitful and multiply

so as to fill the earth and subdue it" (Catholic Bible); "Be fruitful, multiply, fill the earth, and subdue it" (Smith and Goodspeed translation).

8. Moses 3:16–17. See also the corresponding verses in the other versions, respectively: Genesis 1:28 and 2:16–17; Abraham 4:26, 28 and 5:12–13. Because each version is slightly different, I have chosen to quote only selectively, preferring to keep a broader perspective, though I strongly recommend further personal examination and reflection of the similarities and differences between the various versions and accounts. It is interesting to recognize that, though we typically group these together, the first directive (Moses 2:28, Genesis 1:28, and Abraham 4:26, 28) is from Account A, while the second directive (Moses 3:16–17, Genesis 2:16–17, and Abraham 5:12–13) is from Account B, as explained in chapter 5.
9. Packer, "Atonement, Agency, Accountability."
10. 1 Nephi 3:7.
11. John 14:6. Interestingly, the earliest disciples of Christ, following His death and Resurrection, referred to themselves as followers of The Way before becoming known as Christians, which originally was a derogatory term applied to them by others (see Acts 9:2; 19:9, 23; 24:14, 22).
12. For a basic summary of the Catholic Church's doctrine of "original sin," refer to chapter 5, note 10.
13. See Moses 5:10–11; 6:53 for Adam's, Eve's, and the Lord's designations, respectively. Biblical scholar and Duke University Mary Grace Wilson Professor Emerita of Religious Studies, Carol Meyers, who has extensively researched the Genesis 3 narrative, notes this fascinating insight: "Interpreters may label this act as disobedient; exegetes may consider it sinful. But *God* does not provide such a judgment within either the narration or the discourse of Genesis 3. Nor . . . does the Hebrew Bible ever associate any of the many sins later perpetrated individually or collectively by the children of Israel with the behavior of the woman and the man in Eden. Not until Cain and Abel . . . are involved in the act of murder does sin make its strange and fateful appearance. . . . Not even the horrendous deed of the offspring of Eve and Adam is linked with a parental model of sinful disobedience. Even the prophets, whose writings are filled with harangues against the sinful behavior of the Israelites and other nations, never mention Eve or Adam. In their concern for judgment, punishment, and banishment, the prophets could cogently cite the Eden story. Yet they do not" (Meyers, *Discovering Eve*, 87–94).
14. Smith, *The Words of Joseph Smith*, 63.
15. Oaks, "The Great Plan of Happiness." President Brigham Young questioned and then clarified, "How did Adam and Eve sin? Did they come out in direct opposition [sin] to God and to His government? No. But they transgressed a command of the Lord, and through that transgression sin came into the world. The Lord knew they would do this, and He had designed that they should" (in *Journal of Discourses*, 10:312). If we had the audacity to amend President Young's statement,

we might clarify that "through that transgression [mortal life began, and mortality allowed for sin to come] into the world." Similarly, President Joseph Fielding Smith explained, "I never speak of the part Eve took in this fall as a sin, nor do I accuse Adam of a sin. . . . This was a transgression of the law, but not a sin . . . for it was something that Adam and Eve had to do! . . . We can hardly look upon anything resulting in such benefits as being a sin" (Smith, *Doctrines of Salvation*, 1:114–15).

16. Oaks, "The Great Plan of Happiness."
17. Oaks, "The Great Plan of Happiness."
18. Talmage, *Articles of Faith*, 59.
19. Widtsoe, *Gospel Interpretations*, 78. Elder Widtsoe's comment echoes a powerful statement from President Thomas S. Monson: "Never let a problem to be solved become more important than a person to be loved" (Monson, "Finding Joy in the Journey"). Similarly, Elder John C. Pingree Jr. wisely suggested we "approach decision points in our lives . . . in the context of helping others" (Pingree, "I Have a Work for Thee").
20. McConkie, *The Promised Messiah*, 221.
21. Madsen, "House of Glory, House of Light, House of Love."
22. Faust, "What It Means to Be a Daughter of God."
23. Faust, "What It Means to Be a Daughter of God."
24. See Genesis 3:1–6; Moses 4:5–12.
25. I find it both informative and enlightening that Hebrew scribes chose to figuratively represent Lucifer as a serpent because, anciently, serpents were associated with healing. The Greek myth of Asclepius and his snake-entwined rod popularized this idea and led to the image still frequently used to represent the medical profession. The Hebrews also linked snakes with wellness in connection with Moses's use of a brazen serpent to represent Christ and His healing powers (Numbers 21:9); the Nephites and Lamanites were likewise familiar with this symbolism, as the Book of Mormon reiterates on several occasions (see 1 Nephi 17:41; 2 Nephi 25:20; Alma 33:19–22; 37:46). During His mortal ministry, the Lord Himself referred to the lifting up of the serpent as a type of His own lifting up on the cross, "that whosoever believeth in him should not perish, but have eternal life" (John 3:14–15). By portraying "the father of all lies" (Moses 4:4) with this saving, healing type, the Hebrew scribes were illustrating, as compellingly as they knew how, Satan's skillfulness in the art of deception.
26. See the Bible Dictionary. See also Lawrence, "The War Goes On."
27. D&C 76:25–28; see also Moses 4:1–4.
28. JST, John 14:30.
29. 2 Corinthians 11:14; 2 Nephi 9:9; D&C 128:20. Similarly, Korihor describes how the devil deceived him by appearing in the form of an angel (Alma 30:53). Additionally, author Matthew Brown writes: "The extracanonical [apocryphal]

First Book of Adam and Eve says that this most evil of spirits once appeared to Adam and Eve dressed in 'a garment of light' and a 'bright girdle' in an apparent attempt to imitate the vesture of the holy angels who minister in God's heavenly temple (see Daniel 10:5; Revelation 1:13; 15:5–6)" (Brown, *The Gate of Heaven*, 29). Likewise, the Qur'an includes a similar reference, in the seventh surah, verses 21–22, where it describes Lucifer deceitfully swearing an oath to Adam and Eve, saying, "Truly, I am a well-intentioned counselor to you" (see Peterson, "The Qur'anic Tree of Life," 197).

30. Moses 4:4.
31. Because of the unique connotations of the word *beguiled*, it may be helpful to consider that of the sixteen times the Hebrew word *nasha'* is used in the Old Testament, the King James Version renders it *only here* as *beguiled*; elsewhere, it is consistently translated as *deceived* (Brown, *Brown-Driver-Briggs Hebrew and English Lexicon*, 674). Compare 2 Kings 18:29; 19:10; 2 Chronicles 32:15; Isaiah 19:13; 36:14; 37:10; Jeremiah 4:10; 29:8; 37:9; 49:16; Obadiah 1:3, 7. Several alternative Bible translations translate Genesis 3:13 as "deceived," rather than "beguiled," including the New King James Version, the New Living Translation, the New International Version, the English Standard Version, the Christian Standard Bible, the New American Standard Bible, and the Darby Translation.
32. Regarding the doctrine of agency, Joseph Smith was reported to have taught the Saints in Nauvoo, on May 16, 1841, "that satan was generally blamed for the evils which we did, but if he was the cause of all our wickedness, men could not be condemned. The devil cannot compel mankind to evil, all was voluntary. . . . Those who resist the spirit of God, are liable to be led into temptation, and then the association of heaven is withdrawn from those who refuse to be made partakers of such great glory—God would not exert any compulsory means and the Devil could not; and such ideas as were entertained by many were absurd." https://www.josephsmithpapers.org/paper-summary/discourse-16may-1841-as-reported-by-times-and-seasons/1.
33. Widtsoe, *Gospel Interpretations*, 77–78; emphasis in original. I also find the following statement by President Dallin H. Oaks helpful to consider: "For reasons that have not been revealed, this transition, or 'fall,' could not happen without a transgression—an exercise of moral agency amounting to a willful breaking of a law (see Moses 6:59). This would be a planned offense, a formality to serve an eternal purpose" ("The Great Plan of Happiness").
34. Moses 4:12 and Moses 4:11, respectively.
35. Oaks, "The Great Plan of Happiness."
36. Significantly, Eve promptly displays her nascent powers of discernment, as portrayed in some depictions that show her, soon after her decision to partake, recognizing the serpent's deceit and labeling his true identity. As gospel scholars Terryl and Fiona Givens have insightfully written, "We are continuing . . . on the

trajectory inaugurated by Adam and Eve, becoming more like God, as we become ever more adept at discerning good and evil. . . . And in so doing, we grow more capable of discerning a kind and merciful God among His many counterfeits" (Givens and Givens, *The God Who Weeps*, 20).

37. Moses 4:5–12.
38. Rockwood, "The Redemption of Eve," 19–20.
39. I appreciate the way the Book of Mormon addresses the issue of them successively partaking of the fruit. Rather than calling out Eve as the one who first transgressed, on three separate occasions and by three different prophets (Jacob, Abinadi, and Moroni), Eve and Adam are referred to jointly, as a united duo, *"our first parents,"* when referring to the consequences of their individual decisions to partake, effectually confirming their unity in triplicate. See 2 Nephi 9:9; Mosiah 16:3; Ether 8:25.
40. McKay, *Gospel Ideals*, 449.
41. Tingey, "The School of Experience," 85. Sister Tingey was a delegate of the Young Ladies' Mutual Improvement Association sent by the Church to address the World's Congress of Representative Women, part of the 1893 Chicago World's Fair. She presented this memorable speech to a diverse audience from around the world and across religions.
42. Hudson, "The Two Trees." This speech was presented in 2010 at the twelfth annual FairMormon conference. It is worth noting that pondering this divine division of labor in light of the particular challenges women would face in mortality is quite personal to Dr. Cassler; much of her extensive and groundbreaking academic research focuses on the treatment of women throughout the various nations and cultures of the world. With that sobering expertise as backdrop to her feelings, she went on to surmise: "Surely when we considered all the elements of the Plan of Christ, and we considered what would befall us in the fallen world, surely the daughters of God were given at least an inkling of what would befall them—rape, forced marriage, sex trafficking, treated as chattel throughout much of human history. If no woman was willing to open the door to mortal life and all that it would mean for women, I don't think it would have been opened, and that would only be just."
43. Regarding the righteous stewardship of priesthood-holding men, and particularly how the practical application of their stewardship impacts women, Elder Richard G. Scott notably taught: "The purpose of priesthood authority is to give, to serve, to lift, to inspire—not to exercise unrighteous control or force. In some cultures, tradition places a man in a role to dominate, control, and regulate all family affairs. That is not the way of the Lord. In some places the wife is almost owned by her husband, as if she were another of his personal possessions. That is a cruel, unproductive, mistaken vision of marriage encouraged by Lucifer that every priesthood holder must reject. It is founded on the false premise that a man

is somehow superior to a woman. Nothing could be farther from the truth" (Scott, "Honor the Priesthood and Use It Well").

44. Genesis 3:6; Moses 4:12.
45. You may recall from the previous chapter Elder Holland's words: "They [Adam and Eve] were willing to transgress knowingly and consciously (the only way they could 'fall' into the consequences of mortality, inasmuch as Elohim certainly could not force innocent parties out of the garden and still be a just God) only because they had a full knowledge of the plan of salvation, which would provide for them a way back from their struggle with death and hell." He goes on to write, "But Adam and Eve made their choice for an even more generous reason than those of godly knowledge and personal progress. They did it for the one overriding and commanding reason basic to the entire plan of salvation and all the discussions ever held in all the councils of heaven. They did it 'that men might be.'" He then states, "The privilege of mortality granted to the rest of us is the principal gift given by the fall of Adam and Eve" (Holland, *Christ and the New Covenant*, 202–5; see also 2 Nephi 2:25).
46. Holland, *Christ and the New Covenant*, 205.
47. In Catholicism's Easter Vigil *Exultet*, also called the Paschal Proclamation, the choir sings, "*O felix culpa quae talem et tantum meruit habere redemptorem*," translated as "O happy fault that merited such and so great a Redeemer!" http://catholicism.org/o-happy-fault.html.
48. Curious George, a beloved children's book character, is a well-intentioned yet naughty monkey who consistently causes trouble, but his escapades somehow always work out for the best. See Rey, *Curious George*.
49. Givens and Givens, *The Christ Who Heals*, 32.

CHAPTER 8

NAKEDNESS

Paradise is lost,
but divinity appears on the distant horizon.

—Terryl and Fiona Givens[1]

Eve's and Adam's decisions to partake of the fruit are immediately followed by consequences. Recall that the Father's perfect plan required that they transgress a law in order to initiate mortality; regardless that it was "a glorious necessity,"[2] the breaking of a law comes with consequences. And in this completely singular event, the consequences were mortal life and all its accompanying challenges. But first, they were blessed with a period of calm, careful, *loving* preparation recorded in Genesis 3:7–24 and Moses 4:13–31, to which we now turn our attention, one piece at a time.

The first verse of this section (Genesis 3:7; Moses 4:13) highlights an immediate and impactful change: "And the eyes of them both were opened." What their new sight instantly reveals—"and they knew that they were naked"—is momentous: not only were they naked but they *had been* naked all along. Due to their newfound power of comparison, the peaceful safety they hadn't even known to appreciate has been supplanted by precarious vulnerability. Where every need had been divinely met, with improved vision they now see not only that they *have needs* but that it's time for them to get to work to meet those needs.

The second half of the verse shows their creative and industrious problem solving: "And they sewed fig leaves together and made themselves aprons." Not bad for beginners, but fig-leaf aprons will hardly be sufficient for the climate and conditions of the lone and dreary world that awaits them.

The choice of fig leaves seems meaningful, though they may have simply been what was closest at hand or best suited for coverage. As a symbol, figs are unusual among fruits because of their plethora of tiny seeds, anciently thought to represent fertility and posterity, much like the pomegranate.[3] The deep green color of the leaves not only brings to mind life and growth (two concepts that are about to become very real), but their verdant quality also reflects another meaning: they are green in the metaphorical sense of lacking experience and sophistication—a fair description of Adam and Eve in their current state.

And where is Lucifer while they are busy sewing? One can imagine him nearby, celebrating his supposed victory—after all, he believed their eating the deadly fruit would ruin everything, but "he knew not the mind of God."[4] What he *thought* would destroy the plan was, in fact, precisely what was *divinely designed* to facilitate our eternal progression, as paradoxical as that might seem. We are comfortably familiar with Father Lehi's explanation that Eve and "Adam fell that men might be."[5] Less often quoted, but certainly just as meaningful, is his declaration that precedes it: "But behold, all things have been done in the wisdom of him who knoweth all things."[6]

As the serpent eagerly (though mistakenly) awaits the trouble ahead, he selfishly seeks to enhance his revelry by adding some shame to the complicated mix of new feelings and emotions Eve and Adam are suddenly experiencing. After all, they likely felt some regret that eternal progression had required the transgression of a law; there simply was no other way. Still, whether in Eden's garden or in our own mortal circumstances, the whispered suggestion to hurry and hide usually comes from that same adversarial source intent on our further harm.

In the fallen world, it is helpful to recognize shame as guilt's evil impostor. Where guilt prompts penitent action, shame fuels fear. Guilt nudges us closer to the Lord as we accept accountability; shame forces us out of the light as we search for dark places to hide. Guilt is guided by humility, but shame is governed by humiliation. We *choose* humility with the help of the Spirit and the increased understanding that comes from experience; humiliation is often heaped upon us in the form of judgment and criticism, systematically disabling our ability to separate any misguided action from our divine identity. When shame says, "hide," guilt says, "repair."

In Eve and Adam's unique case, there is no inherent shame in their nakedness. On the contrary, their recognizing their vulnerable state is an enlightened and humble realization that they need help and protection. As we'll see shortly, this section of the story is set off and held together as if by two symbolic bookends—their initial, inadequate attempt to fend for themselves with fig-leaf aprons and the far better, grace-lined coats of skin the Lord will provide to cover and protect them. The space between is filled with a fascinating dialogue between our full cast of characters.

QUESTIONS AND ANSWERS

The discussion begins with the arrival of Divinity and a series of direct questions for Adam and Eve (Genesis 3:9–13; Moses 4:15–19). The opening question noticeably varies between accounts, but both versions draw attention to their attempt to hide. Genesis's "Where art thou?" seems almost playful, since an all-seeing God certainly knows their exact location; Moses's "Where goest thou?" seems more directed at their turned backs as they attempt to hide. Each has clear metaphorical application to us during the mortal moments following our inevitable errors. Will humble feelings of guilt help us step forward and take responsibility for our choices, or will a humiliating sense of shame keep us in the shadows, denying our need for assistance? Either way, we frequently find ourselves figuratively naked before an omniscient God. This is the moment when our willingness to truthfully admit our weakness requires soul-baring vulnerability. At least in Adam and Eve's case, Satan's influence quickly fades as they step out of the darkness to plainly state, "[We] heard thy voice, . . . [we were] afraid, . . . and [we] hid."[7]

The second question, "Who told thee thou wast naked?"[8] suggests God's acknowledgment of an unfortunate correlation between Satan's influence and humankind's susceptibility to shame. Getting right to the heart of the matter, the next question, direct and dignifying, makes room for them to step up and take responsibility for their actions: "Hast thou eaten of the tree?"[9] Before they can answer, God restates the rule and repercussion for that specific tree, reminding them of His previous warning: "Thou shouldst not eat [of it], if so thou shouldst surely die,"[10] a reminder that they knew they could eat "freely" from any other tree, but this one would have unavoidable and life-altering results.

Adam answers first, accepting responsibility for his actions by truthfully explaining that Eve gave him the fruit, and he ate it. He adds the additional information, almost by way of a reminder, that they had been commanded to stay together. "The woman thou gavest me, and [added in Moses] commandest that she should remain with me, she gave me of the fruit of the tree and I did eat."[11]

Eve is equitably given a chance to explain her actions as well, with God's final question, "What is this thing which thou hast done?"[12] Eve also answers truthfully: she "did eat." She too adds a detail, prefacing her truth by noting the serpent's deception.[13] Given the far-reaching misunderstandings related to her decision to eat, I find it meaningful that though she acknowledges Satan's involvement with her reply, she does not specifically *blame* her decision on him—she does not say, "I was deceived *so* I ate." Rather, she maintains her autonomy and her agency, accepting full responsibility as did Adam, by confidently and forthrightly answering, "The serpent beguiled me, *and* I did eat."[14]

CURSES AND CONSEQUENCES

Eve's straightforward admission is followed by an intensifying shift in the dialogue (Genesis 3:14–24; Moses 4:20–31). It's now time for God the Father to powerfully and personally outline the changes that lie ahead as a direct result of recent choices. He curses Satan for his blasphemous deception, and He informs Eve and Adam of the new realities they will face in the fallen world. I interpret these new realities as *consequences,* not *punishments,* and the difference is worth noting. Whereas a punishment is generally a harsh treatment imposed to cause suffering, a consequence is often simply the natural result of a given action. As promised, eating the fruit had *consequences,* specifically mortality and all that accompanies that fallen state.

In the course of relating this information, God guards the tree of life, protecting Adam and Eve from the truly dire result that would accompany eating of its fruit while in their newly mortal, and therefore imperfect, physical condition. The interim between the partaking of the fruit of the tree of knowledge of good and evil and the departure from the garden is a blessing: it allows our First Parents a final empowering interaction directly with Deity before their mortal adventure begins.

SATAN

In the second century AD, just before the Great Apostasy really took root, the Greek bishop and Christian theologist Irenaeus openly taught,

"The curse *in all its fulness* fell upon the serpent."[15] He rightly recognized that Satan was the only player deserving and receiving punishment. Moses 4:20 reads: "Because thou hast done this thou shalt be cursed above all cattle, and above every beast of the field; upon thy belly shalt thou go, and dust shalt thou eat all the days of thy life."[16]

And what precisely was *this* that merited such punishment? His deception perpetrated on Eve both usurped the role of Deity and spurned the words of God. Such malicious dishonesty was deliberate and deadly, meriting his relegation to the lowest symbolic position of the animal kingdom.[17]

The second portion of God's declaration to Satan (Moses 4:21) is a grave condemnation for Lucifer but simultaneously describes a profound blessing for all humankind: "And I will put enmity between thee and the woman, between thy seed and her seed; and he shall bruise thy head, and thou shalt bruise his heel."[18]

These poetic phrases weave together multiple layers of meaning. In a very personal sense, I like to think of the "enmity" placed between Satan's followers and Eve's descendants as our innate aversion to evil—what we sometimes call the Light of Christ, or our conscience. As Lehi taught Jacob, every child of God enters mortality "instructed sufficiently that they know good from evil."[19] This inherent ability to discern between right and wrong—at least at the most elementary level—is a divine endowment of aid, almost like armor.[20] The Light of Christ can serve as a protective barrier or at least a preliminary impediment to the dangerous lures of the adversary.

Furthermore, and on a much grander scale, God specifically assures that though Satan's power will be injurious to many (able to bruise the heel), the Savior's power will prove victorious for all (able to crush Satan's head).[21] Good *will* conquer evil; indeed, "the way is prepared from the fall of man, and salvation is free."[22]

THE TREE OF LIFE

The second frequent misunderstanding during this interim period of preparation concerns the guarding of the tree of life. Certain accounts rearrange this portion of the tale slightly, though significantly, so we shall follow that lead and examine it now. Moses 4:28, 31 reads:

> *And now lest he put forth his hand and partake also of the tree of life, and eat and live forever, . . . I placed at the east of the Garden of Eden, cherubim and a flaming sword, which turned every way to keep the way of the tree of life.*[23]

When approached in this order, we see Deity's foremost concern following Satan's banishment as protecting Eve and Adam from the damningly irreversible results of prematurely eating the fruit of the tree of life. The urgency for such a precaution highlights the respect our Father in Heaven has for eternal laws; as the Moses account adds in verse 30, His "words cannot return void, for as they go forth out of [His] mouth they must be fulfilled."[24] If Adam and Eve were to partake of the fruit of the tree of life in their current condition, they would be tragically doomed to "live forever" in their fallen state, completely nullifying the Savior's redeeming Atonement and God's great plan of happiness and progress for His children.

This protective precaution allowed them a probationary period: a time to learn from mortal experiences and mistakes while being blessed with the opportunity to repent. They would temporarily be denied access to the tree's immortalizing effects in order that the Savior's life, Atonement, and Resurrection could provide a well-lit path back to their heavenly home. The account is ambiguously brief on this point; it isn't until the New Testament's book of Revelation that the Bible provides any guidance regarding *how* to eventually return to the tree of life. There John writes, "To him that overcometh will I give to eat of the tree of life, which is in the midst of the paradise of God."[25]

Thankfully, the Book of Mormon goes into great detail expounding on this merciful gift; it practically leads off with a description of its great significance, vividly depicted in Lehi's dream and further explained in Nephi's vision.[26] With that imagery fixed in our minds, nearly every subsequent prophet identifies mortality as a preparatory state, "a space granted unto man in which he might repent" and "prepare to meet God," and highlights the necessity of the Savior's Atonement in helping us gain exaltation and eternal life.[27]

It is through obedience to God's commandments, as well as participation in sacred ordinances and covenants available through the priesthood, that we can be properly equipped to eventually make that return journey and partake of the fruit of the tree of life. As Brigham Young taught:

> *Your endowment is, to receive all those ordinances in the House of the Lord, which are necessary for you, after you have departed this life, to enable you to walk back to the presence of the Father, passing the angels who stand as sentinels, being enabled to give them the key words, the signs and tokens, pertaining to the Holy Priesthood, and gain your eternal exaltation in spite of earth and hell.*[28]

EVE

God the Father next directs His attention to Eve, delivering a four-part message—brief enough to be recorded in just one verse but controversial enough to fill volumes. Making sense of the two couplets of Genesis 3:16 calls for objective examination as well as careful interpretation.

> *I will greatly multiply thy sorrow and thy conception; in sorrow thou shalt bring forth children; and thy desire shall be to thy husband, and he shall rule over thee.*[29]

To discern the true meaning and intention of this message, two words in the first couplet require thoughtful study: the twice-used *sorrow* and its magnifier, *multiply. Sorrow* is emotionally packed, evoking deep sadness infused with a sense of loss, so its use here seems to allude to forthcoming tragedy. But, in fact, the Hebrew word from which *sorrow* is drawn, *'itstsabown*, is generally translated as *pain, labor, toil,* or *struggle,* all very fair descriptors of the realities of childbirth.[30] Various Bible translations use different combinations of these words to different effect. For example, the New International Version translates the phrases of the first couplet, "I will make your pains in childbearing very severe; with painful labor you will give birth to children," and the Christian Standard Bible settles on, "I will intensify your labor pains; you will bear children with painful effort." In this light, these statements seem to be an accurate though simplistic account of childbirth, mentally preparing Eve for the pain, work, and struggle becoming a mother will require.

But what of *multiply?* Some have mistakenly pointed to this word as evidence that Eve is being *punished* for her choice to partake. But *multiply* is a descriptor that can be used in various ways. Specifically, as Dr. Camille Fronk Olson has noted, the Hebrew original implies *repetition,* rather than intensification; Dr. Olson describes the difference as "something happening over and over again, not something being added to or increased."[31] So rather than recoiling from a spiteful God intent on escalating Eve's torturous punishment, we can instead feel drawn toward a loving God who is promising her a vast posterity, even while mentally preparing her for the unavoidable discomforts of the birthing experience.

The second couplet, "and thy desire shall be to thy husband, and he shall rule over thee," appears, on its surface, to institute a subservient relationship between husband and wife, plain and simple. But our story, to this point, supports the ideal relationship between husband and wife as being one of beautifully balanced interdependence. The uncomfortable contradiction in this verse suggests a lingering misunderstanding, most likely influenced by some combination of language limitations and cultural biases.[32]

Dr. Alma D. Sorensen, professor emeritus of political science at BYU, and his former colleague and coauthor, Dr. Valerie Hudson Cassler, have extensively researched this apparent inconsistency of women's status found in Eve and Adam's story. In their book *Women in Eternity, Women of Zion,* Dr. Sorenson examines the contradiction with faith and a critical eye, explaining that it's easy "to see how these texts could be interpreted to justify, on the basis of divine authority, a society that favors men and upholds the exercise of dominion by men over women. But all such interpretations are mistaken."[33]

He supports that opinion with a two-point summary of their findings regarding the concerning phrase, "and he shall rule over thee."

"First," he explains, "the Hebrew term rendered here as 'rule over' can also mean 'rule with.' In fact, we understand that when the Hebrew word '*msh'l*' (usually translated as 'rule') is used in conjunction with '*bet*' (in most cases translated as 'with,' 'in,' 'by,' or 'at'), the better translation is 'rule with' rather than 'rule over.'"[34]

Second, he notes that "the 'rule' referred to here is that authorized by the Holy Priesthood (see D&C 84:17; 107:5, 40–44)."[35] And it is important to remember that "'rule' by means of the priesthood is rule according to the celestial order, the order of the gods, and that order is one of equal power (D&C 76:54–58, 94–95). In particular, it is an order in which couples who are married for eternity by the Holy Priesthood rule with one another as . . . equal partners on earth as well as in heaven."[36]

Regarding the celestial order of marriage, and specifically the equal power shared by husband and wife, we have been taught repeatedly that man and woman have divinely designed complementary stewardships. President M. Russell Ballard reiterated this beautiful doctrine, stating:

"Men and women have different but equally valued roles. Just as a woman cannot conceive a child without a man, so a man cannot fully exercise the power of the priesthood to establish an eternal family without a woman. In other words, in the eternal perspective, both the procreative power and the priesthood power are shared by husband and wife."[37]

Elder Bruce C. and Sister Marie K. Hafen have also written extensively about the beautiful balance God ordains between husband and wife. Concurring that "rule *with*" is a more accurate translation than "rule *over*," Elder and Sister Hafen affirm that "the concept of interdependent, equal partners is well-grounded in the doctrine of the restored gospel."[38]

In D&C 132:19–20, we read of the new and everlasting covenant, and what a sealed couple might expect as they progress toward exaltation:

> *Ye shall . . . inherit thrones, kingdoms, principalities, and powers, dominions, all heights and depths . . . and they shall pass by the angels, and the gods, which are set there, to their exaltation and glory in all things, as hath been sealed upon their heads, which glory shall be a fulness and a continuation of the seeds forever and ever. Then shall they be gods, because they have no end; therefore shall they be from everlasting to everlasting, because they continue; then shall they be above all, because all things are subject unto them.*

With each additional use of the pronouns *they, their,* and *them,* those glorious phrases of the Doctrine and Covenants support our understanding of eternal marriage as a joint partnership between man and woman. The restored gospel of Jesus Christ, as detailed in scripture, the sacred liturgy of the temple, and the words of modern-day prophets and apostles, powerfully and repeatedly reinforces that divine doctrine.

With our understanding of the second half of the couplet reconciled, the first half, "and thy desire shall be to thy husband," can now be recognized as loving assurance that Eve will have a yearning, or a longing, to work closely and cooperatively with Adam; together their faithful and complementary efforts will lead them successfully home to their Heavenly Parents, where they will jointly govern their vast posterity. Eve's verse of instruction is no punishment; rather, it is a description of what to expect in mortality, as well as a God-given endowment of purpose, posterity, and potential.

ADAM

God the Father now turns His attention to Adam, bestowing upon him a similarly realistic description of the changes that will accompany mortality, encapsulated in three verses. Moses 4:23–25 reads:

> *Cursed shall be the ground for thy sake; in sorrow shalt thou eat of it all the days of thy life.*
>
> *Thorns also, and thistles shall it bring forth to thee, and thou shalt eat the herb of the field.*
>
> *By the sweat of thy face shalt thou eat bread, until thou shalt return unto the ground—for thou shalt surely die—for out of it wast thou taken: for dust thou wast, and unto dust shalt thou return.*[39]

Unlike Eve's message, Adam's does, in fact, contain a blatant curse, but not on *him*, and it includes a crucial mitigating caveat: "Cursed shall be the ground *for thy sake.*" *For thy sake* is an idiom of Middle English origin and has come to mean *for one's benefit, welfare, or advantage*[40]—in this case, Adam's. The impending change of environment and lifestyle, from dependent ease to independent effort, will be *for his benefit.* God knows, as most wise parents eventually learn, that thorns and thistles and the work required to tame them and cultivate goodness in spite of them will ultimately bless His children.[41]

Once we've reconciled the "curse," we can next examine its accompanying "sorrow," this time with added insight: "In *sorrow* shalt thou eat of [the ground] all the days of thy life."[42] Here is that same *'itstsabown—pain, labor, toil,* or *struggle*—that Eve was guaranteed. As with childbirth, farming is certainly challenging, laborious work, rife with toil, pain, and struggle, but not necessarily with regret and loss, as *sorrow* implies. In fact, few other vocations better teach that work comes before play and that "hard" heralds the harvest. As we determined in Eve's blessing, *sorrow* may not be the *best* word choice for Adam's upcoming learning opportunities, but it is interesting that it is the *same* word choice, highlighting the balance in their individual messages.

Elder George Q. Morris summarized their similarly prescribed *pain, labor, toil,* and *struggle* with wise insight. Rather than characterizing the consequences of their choices to partake as "punishments," he instead identified them as "real blessings."[43] Likening their challenges to our own, he offered this explanation for that somewhat surprising label: "We come to the earth with all these conditions arranged as they are so that we have to struggle constantly against evil, struggle to preserve our lives, struggle for everything of true value—that is the thing for us to understand—this is the course of life that is most desirable, and for our good. We have no need to find fault with these conditions. The Lord has ordained them all for our welfare and happiness."[44] Of course, hindsight is often required to recognize the truth in this statement. But as many of us have had the opportunity to learn over and over again, Christ's Atonement enables the Lord to consecrate our afflictions for our gain.[45]

Even so, as the final portion of Adam's message promises, mortality will prove fatal. Elder Morris spoke to this point as well, once again drawing important parallels to the realities of our timeless, human condition. He explained, "Though the Lord condemns us to death—mortal death—it is one of the greatest blessings that comes to us here because it is the doorway to immortality, and we can never attain immortality without dying."[46]

Death fulfils "the merciful plan of the great Creator"[47] by bringing closure to mortality's preparatory state and allowing for a glorious resurrection made possible by a loving Savior. President Joseph Fielding Smith reiterated that hopeful perspective, declaring death to be "just as important in the plan of salvation as birth is."[48]

In the course of this singular dialogue with Deity, Eve and Adam have each had the consequences of their choices realistically described to them; each has been similarly instructed and similarly endowed regarding the challenges that await them. As Elder Morris described, these distinct blessings, so often disguised as difficulties, are for our sake and for our good, providing us with the very struggles that will ultimately refine and transform us.

COATS OF SKINS

Like a counterbalanced bookend for this portion of the story, God finally provides a far superior covering for Adam and Eve's nakedness than that which they had initially managed on their own. Moses 4:27 reads: "Unto Adam, and also unto his wife, did I, the Lord God, make coats of skins, and clothed them."[49]

The protective "coats of skins" stand in stark contrast to their man-made counterpart—the woefully insufficient fig-leaf aprons. As with the aprons, the coats are described in just one, all-too-brief verse of scripture, but close examination coupled with inspired commentary aids our understanding of this grace-lined gift. Representing the perfect, protective covering of the Atonement of Jesus Christ, these divinely made coats are both tangible and emblematic, meant not only to literally defend them from the harsh elements of earth but also to figuratively shield them from the damaging effects of mortality. As Elder and Sister Hafen have beautifully penned: "The Savior's Atonement makes [mortality's] learning process possible by protecting us while we discover through practice what love really is or why wickedness cannot produce happiness. . . . Because of the Atonement, we can learn from our experience without being condemned by it."[50]

Unlike Adam and Eve's meager aprons, which left them exposed, vulnerable, and defenseless, this clothing would be warm, protective, and durable, symbolically strengthening them to resist temptation and combat evil while upholding truth.[51]

The actual act of clothing, performed here by Deity, is described by the Hebrew word *labash*.[52] This word is used frequently throughout ancient scripture and is translated in various thought-provoking ways, several of which further enrich our understanding of these coats of skins. For example, in Isaiah's exultations in Isaiah 61:10, it is translated as *clothed*, but with a connotation of noble investiture:

> *I will greatly rejoice in the Lord, my soul shall be joyful in my God; for he hath* clothed *me with the garments of salvation, he hath* covered *me with the robe of righteousness.*

Exodus 40:13 uses a similar translation, rendered *put*, this time adding a sense of sacred responsibility:

> *And thou shalt* put upon *Aaron the holy garments, and anoint him, and sanctify him; that he may minister unto me in the priest's office.*

Yet another insightful interpretation is found in 1 Samuel 17:38, where we read of the courageous young David preparing for battle, and hear in *labash* a strong sense of protection:

> *And Saul* armed *David with his armour, and he put an helmet of brass upon his head; also he* armed *him with a coat of mail.*[53]

Each endowed member of The Church of Jesus Christ of Latter-day Saints is similarly blessed with the opportunity to be clothed in and wear the garment of the holy priesthood, which President Russell M. Nelson has referred to as "part of the enduring armor of God."[54] Representative of

Adam and Eve's divinely made coats of skins, the garments are noble and protective, providing safe coverage for our mortal vulnerabilities thanks to our Savior and His atoning sacrifice.

Following these loving preparations, this part of the story concludes with a simple yet poignant phrase: "So I drove out the man."[55] A subtle scriptural detail, frequently overlooked—"I placed at the east of the Garden of Eden"[56]—informs us that they make their departure from the eastern side of Eden, implying that they set off in an eastward direction. This small clue yet again affirms the positive nature of their brave choice for mortality. Since antiquity, east has been the representative direction of God and godliness.[57] Indeed, Adam and Eve's eastward departure was a "positive and divinely foreordained event" and "a movement toward God in the truest sense."[58]

Though this parting scene has been portrayed throughout history as an angry act of expulsion, I picture it as a tender parental farewell, illuminated by this period of great care and compassion shown to Eve and Adam following their courageous decisions to partake. The Savior's redeeming and empowering Atonement, covering them like a protective cloak, will provide them safe passage and sure footing until their joyful reunion with Him.

NOTES

1. Givens and Givens, *The God Who Weeps*, 62.
2. Oaks, "The Great Plan of Happiness."
3. To provide further food for thought, this same species of tree notably makes an appearance in the final days of Christ's earthly ministry, when He displays His power over life and death by cursing the barren fig tree, likely a tangible reminder of the importance of the commandment to be fruitful, not just in terms of multiplying one's posterity but also in terms of productivity (see Matthew 21:19–21; Mark 11:12–14).
4. Moses 4:6. This verse is a hugely significant addition we are blessed with in Joseph Smith's Bible translation.
5. Adding Eve's name to this great declaration of doctrine, just as I have done here,

was noticeably and graciously done by President Dallin H. Oaks in his October 1993 conference address, "The Great Plan of Happiness."

6. 2 Nephi 2:24–25.
7. Genesis 3:10; Moses 4:16.
8. Genesis 3:11; Moses 4:17.
9. Genesis 3:11; Moses 4:17.
10. Genesis 3:11; Moses 4:17. The concluding phrase, "if so thou shouldst surely die," is a significant addition found in Moses 4:17.
11. See Genesis 3:12; Moses 4:18. Theirs is a beautifully balanced eternal marriage, as outlined in chapter 5; they have given themselves to each other in holy matrimony. The direct references we have of the command that they stay together are in Genesis 2:24, Moses 3:24, and Abraham 5:18, all of which state, "Therefore shall a man leave his father and his mother, and shall cleave unto his wife; and they shall be one flesh."
12. Moses 4:19; see also Genesis 3:13. The Prophet Joseph's addition of the word *thing* in verse 19 is meaningful, in that it further removes shame from the act of partaking of the fruit by acknowledging that it is Eve's *action* which is in question, not her character.
13. Genesis 3:13; Moses 4:19. Refer to chapter 7 for a detailed examination of Satan's "beguilement," or deception, of Eve.
14. Genesis 3:13; Moses 4:19; emphasis added.
15. Saint Irenaeus of Lyon, *Against Heresies*, 351; emphasis added.
16. Compare Genesis 3:14. The difference between these two accounts (*shalt be* in the Moses account, *art* in the Genesis) highlights yet again the value of this brief interim between the partaking of the fruit and the departure from the garden; this divine interchange is an important opportunity for instruction and preparation.
17. For further commentary on Satan's curse, see Rockwood, "The Redemption of Eve."
18. Compare Genesis 3:15.
19. 2 Nephi 2:5.
20. As previously mentioned, a basic awareness of the difference between right and wrong is also a prerequisite of agency.
21. As the LDS edition of the KJV footnote for Genesis 3:15 points out, the Hebrew word translated here as "bruise" (*shuwph*), is also broadly interpreted as "crush" or "grind" (see Brown, *Brown-Driver-Briggs Hebrew and English Lexicon*, 1003). Strong's *Concordance* further defines it as "figuratively, to overwhelm—break, bruise, cover." See also "Genesis 3: The Fall," *Old Testament Student Manual Genesis–2 Samuel* (1980), 38–43, which reads, "The seed of the woman (Christ) shall crush the head of the serpent (Satan and his kingdom) with the very heel that was bruised (the atoning sacrifice)."
22. 2 Nephi 2:4.

23. See Genesis 3:22–24; Moses 4:28–31.
24. Moses 4:30; note that there is no equivalent verse in the Genesis version of the story. This addition draws attention to the importance of eternal laws and consequences in the gospel plan.
25. Revelation 2:7.
26. See 1 Nephi 8 and 1 Nephi 11–14, respectively.
27. See Alma 12:20–34. Here, Alma is directly challenged on this very point of misunderstanding by the contentious chief ruler of Ammonihah. Trying to ensnare the prophet, Antionah points to Alma's declaration that "man should rise from the dead and be changed from this mortal to an immortal state," believing it contradictory to the scriptures' mention of guarding the tree of life, assuming that the presence of cherubim and a flaming sword precluded any possibility that man "should live forever." Alma responds that mortality is "a space granted unto man in which he might repent" and "prepare to meet God." The sword-wielding cherubim were placed there only temporarily; when the appropriate time arrives, those who are prepared will be given access to that special tree by virtue of priesthood ordinances and covenants.
28. Young, *Complete Discourses of Brigham Young*, 2:646. As we conclude our examination of God's actions to guard the tree of life, it is thought-provoking to consider that, had He wanted to, He certainly could have similarly guarded the tree of the knowledge of good and evil, if it had been His intent that they *not* partake of that tree's fruit.
29. See also Moses 4:22. It is worth noting that while these two accounts are identical, the temple account differs significantly, warranting careful comparison and thoughtful contemplation.
30. Brown, *Brown-Driver-Briggs Hebrew and English Lexicon*, 781.
31. Olson, *Women of the Old Testament*, 16.
32. See chapter 1 for a discussion of language limitations and cultural biases.
33. Sorensen and Cassler, *Women in Eternity, Women of Zion*, 69.
34. Sorensen and Cassler, *Women in Eternity, Women of Zion*, 91–92. Dr. Sorensen and Dr. Cassler note that they are indebted to BYU professor Dr. Donald W. Parry for his assistance in explaining this mistranslation. Additionally, theology scholar and Stanford University institute teacher Dr. Lynne Hilton Wilson addresses the same translation issue in her excellent book, *Christ's Emancipation of Women*. Referring to the Hebrew letters '*bet*,' she writes, "Hebrew dictionaries include its meaning as: in, at, to, on, among, with, towards, according to, by, because of, on top of, beside, and about 20 other such meanings. All are valid, depending on the interpretation of the passage," leading her to conclude that the common biblical translation [of *rule over*] "speaks more of the translators' belief, than of the text" (Wilson, *Christ's Emancipation of Women*, 109 n. 299).
35. Sorensen and Cassler, *Women in Eternity, Women of Zion*, 91–92.

36. Sorensen and Cassler, *Women in Eternity, Women of Zion*, 91–92. See also Brown, *Brown-Driver-Briggs Hebrew and English Lexicon*, 606.
37. Ballard, "This Is My Work and Glory." See also "The Family: A Proclamation to the World."
38. Hafen and Hafen, "Crossing Thresholds and Becoming Equal Partners." In this article, Elder and Sister Hafen definitively state that "*over* in 'rule over' uses the Hebrew *bet*, which means ruling *with*, not ruling *over*." See also Hafen and Hafen, *The Contrite Spirit*, for their extensive thoughts regarding the balanced stewardships of husband and wife.
39. Compare Genesis 3:17–19.
40. *Oxford English Dictionary Online*, "sake."
41. It is noteworthy that the Book of Mormon records several occasions when the land was cursed due to the breaking of a commandment (see, for example, 2 Nephi 1:7; Jacob 2:29; 3:3; Mormon 1:17). In Helaman 11:1–18, we read about the prophet Nephi petitioning the Lord to temporarily curse the land for the sake of the contentious Nephites who are destroying each other "by the sword." Nephi steps in to plead with the Lord for a famine, hoping their ensuing struggles will "stir them up in remembrance of the Lord their God." His tactic works—their hunger and thirst distract them from battle while leading them to humility and repentance. With the goal of the famine achieved, Nephi returns in prayer to supplicate the Lord for relieving rain, which He graciously provides, and "the people did rejoice and glorify God, and the whole face of the land was filled with rejoicing." Comparing this account to the message Adam receives from the Lord in Moses 4:23–25, we see that in both cases the breaking of a law, whether designated a necessary transgression or a grievous sin (see chapter 7 of this book), has a consequence. In both cases, the consequence (the "cursing" of the ground, or the change in conditions) results in important learning and growth.
42. Moses 4:23; emphasis added. See also Genesis 3:17.
43. Morris, in Conference Report, April 1958, 39. Elder George Q. Morris served as an Apostle from 1954 until his death in 1962.
44. Morris, in Conference Report, April 1958, 39.
45. See 2 Nephi 2:2.
46. Morris, in Conference Report, April 1958, 39.
47. 2 Nephi 9:6.
48. Smith, *Doctrines of Salvation*, 1:116.
49. Compare Genesis 3:21.
50. Hafen and Hafen, *The Contrite Spirit*, 28.
51. Elder Carlos E. Asay explained that Adam and Eve "received this clothing in a context of instruction on the Atonement" (Asay, "The Temple Garment: 'An Outward Expression of an Inward Commitment'"). Interestingly, one of the Hebrew words translated as *atonement* is *kafar*, which means "to provide protection or security

by covering" (Brown, *Brown-Driver-Briggs Hebrew and English Lexicon*, 496, 498). The other Hebrew word used for *atonement* is *kippur*, as in *Yom Kippur*, or Day of Atonement, Judaism's most sacred holiday. Closely related are the Arabic *kafara*, which connotes a tight squeeze, as in drawing a thing close to oneself, and the Arabic *kafata*, which represents a protective embrace. Dr. Hugh Nibley described the Arabic custom of *kafata* as a practice wherein one who is fleeing for his life may seek protection in the tent of a respected sheik. The victim cries out, "I am thy suppliant," whereupon the sheik places the hem of his robe over the victim's shoulder and declares that he is now under his protection. The prophet Nephi alludes to this custom in 2 Nephi 4:33: "O Lord, wilt thou encircle me around in the robe of thy righteousness! O Lord, wilt thou make a way for mine escape before mine enemies!" (Nibley, "The Atonement of Jesus Christ, Part I").

52. Brown, *Brown-Driver-Briggs Hebrew and English Lexicon*, 527, 1098.
53. In each of these three scriptural examples, emphasis has been added to clarify the various translations of the Hebrew *labash*.
54. Nelson, "Personal Preparation for Temple Blessings."
55. Moses 4:31; compare Genesis 3:24.
56. Moses 4:31; compare Genesis 3:24.
57. The original meaning of the English *east* is "light resplendent," and several other languages similarly connect this compass direction with the sunrise, strengthening its symbolic significance (see Gaskill, *The Lost Language of Symbolism*, 151–52).
58. Gaskill, *The Lost Language of Symbolism*, 152. Dr. Gaskill's research on biblical symbolism is enormously helpful for understanding subtle clues within the scriptures.

CHAPTER 9

THORNS AND THISTLES

I hope to do it better in time.
I myself am very far from satisfied with this
but, well, getting better must come
through doing *it and through trying.*

—Vincent van Gogh[1]

Let's now take a brief interlude to examine mortality's ideal setting for growth and its purpose in the great plan of happiness. Though we may not know much about our First Parents' initial transition to their new earthly home, we do know they experienced an abrupt change in learning methods. A close look at their new style of education increases our appreciation for their faithful courage while motivating our own.

In 1984, social psychologist David Kolb published what colleagues in the field of educational theory considered groundbreaking work. Describing this model in his book *Experiential Learning: Experience as the Source of Learning and Development*, he summed up his thesis in one sentence: "Learning is the process whereby knowledge is created through the transformation of experience."[2]

His research proved that the ideal "spiral of learning" begins with a concrete, real-world experience and continues in a fairly predictable pattern. This cyclical pattern tends to move through the following three steps:

1. Intellectual growth is initiated by an experience that leads to self-reflection.
2. That self-reflection involves the analysis and synthesis of the experience with its attendant feelings, effects, and consequences.
3. Such reflection then creates new or revised knowledge, which better equips the student for the next experience, thereby creating an upward cycle of learning.

As Kolb summarized, "Throughout the experiential learning process, the learner is actively engaged in posing questions, investigating, experimenting, being curious, solving problems, assuming responsibility, being creative, and constructing meaning, and is challenged to take initiative, make decisions, and be accountable for results."[3] Sounds like a perfect plan, even a divinely designed one—an ingenious laboratory for agency and accountability, learning and growth. This is exactly the laboratory Eve and Adam were placed in on entering the lone and dreary world.

HARDER THAN IT LOOKS

My teenage daughter wasn't familiar with Dr. Kolb's research, definitions, or model when she came home from school extremely agitated one day. "Let me tell you, Mom," she said with angry authority, "making stuff on a pottery wheel is harder than it looks!" She was a few weeks into a new semester, and her ceramics elective was turning out to be quite a challenge. She just couldn't make that clay do what she wanted! Granted, all she knew of ceramic making came from preconceived notions of what fun it would be to sit at the wheel with gooey hands and create works of art with ease, but she was quickly realizing that there was a learning curve to be climbed, and she wasn't too happy about the discomfort it was causing.

Ah, mortality. President Spencer W. Kimball paraphrased Elder Orson F. Whitney's eloquent summation of the spiritual benefits of experiential learning, given long before Dr. Kolb gained notoriety among educators for naming and modeling it:

> *No pain that we suffer, no trial that we experience is wasted. It ministers to our education, to the development of such qualities as patience, faith, fortitude and humility. All that we suffer and all that we endure, especially when we endure it patiently, builds up our characters, purifies our hearts, expands our souls, and makes us more tender and charitable, more worthy to be called the children of God, . . . more like our Father and Mother in heaven.*[4]

My daughter's struggle that semester opened the door for several philosophical conversations about the nature of life and learning. For a girl who had always enjoyed and excelled in school, that ceramics class proved to be a surprising source of humility and an ideal place to practice persistence, two timeless trademarks of experiential learning. Life is intended to be a laboratory for godly growth, one in which we gradually become like Him by choosing to live His way. In fact, that neatly sums up the everlasting covenant we made premortally—if we follow God's plan, we can become as He is.[5] We can develop Christlike attributes by struggling through experiences that teach us patience and persistence, hard work and humility. That's not to say that we will always succeed in our struggles—or that we will always be patient or persistent, hardworking or humble—but the beauty of mortality's plan is that, thanks to our Savior and His Atonement, mistakes, missteps, and errors can all be highly effective teachers. The secret of success seems to lie in the struggle—more precisely, in the way in which we *approach* and *respond* to the struggle.

DESIRABLE DIFFICULTIES

Teddy Roosevelt is one of American history's heroes who notoriously sought out and embraced hardship because of the unmatched opportunity it afforded for growth. While serving as United States president, he looked forward to spending weekends leading his young children, along with any friends, cabinet members, or dignitaries who might be visiting, on what he affectionately termed "scrambles." This hiking game was usually played in Rock Creek Park, a large wilderness area near the White House, but he could make it work most anywhere. President Roosevelt would choose an identifiable landmark on a distant ridge and then challenge everyone to join him in a "point-to-point" walk, not "turning aside for anything." The only rule was simple: proceed in a straight line until you reach the designated endpoint. Of course, that was easier said than done. When they met an obstacle in their path, players could go over, under, or through, but never around. Avoidance was against the rules, which meant the route might require scaling a boulder, digging under a felled tree, or swimming across a stream. The children loved the adventure, returning home quite muddy and tattered but proud of themselves for not giving up, and eager for the next family scramble.[6]

Their persistence and fortitude would likely have thrilled Dr. Kolb. Social scientists would term the obstructions the children faced during the scrambles "desirable difficulties." They've found that learning that emerges through meaningful challenging experiences is more durable than learning that comes easily.[7] But efficiency is so satisfying, and this method feels so *inefficient.* Isn't it easier to simply avoid the hard stuff? To transfer out of the hard class or pass on participating in the tough game?

Imagine how Nephi and his brothers must have felt when it took them three tries to get the brass plates from Laban, a task they were given by way of direct commandment. If the Lord planned to pave the way with drunkenness, why not do it in the first place and save the time and energy of everyone involved? Obviously, Heavenly Father is more concerned with *effectiveness* than *efficiency.* That's uncomfortably contrary to our modern "the-sooner-the-better" attitude. The brothers' struggle for the plates taught them patience, faith, and fortitude. The process of trying and failing and trying again requires advanced agency, demonstrated by persistence, resilience, and determination. God is after durable learning—deep understanding, gained through experience, that is powerful enough to effect lasting change.

PATIENT PRACTICE

Durable learning is strengthened by practice. Though children often roll their eyes at the thought of yet another hour sitting on the piano bench, it's hardly the waste of time they think it is. Parents and music teachers understand the lifelong benefits that accompany patient practice, such as increased willpower and improved problem-solving abilities. It's helpful to recognize that God also believes in practice, and He frequently allows, even *provides,* such practical opportunities. The story of the Jaredites' journey to the Promised Land is an excellent example of this. We're quite familiar with and fond of the second half of the story, especially their eight ingenious, ocean-worthy barges, but we often overlook some meaningful details in the first half of the story. In Ether 2:6, we read:

> *And it came to pass that they did travel in the wilderness,* and did build barges, *in which they did cross many waters,* being directed continually *by the hand of the Lord.*

Ten verses later, in 2:16, these preliminary barges are mentioned once again:

> *And the Lord said: Go to work and build,* after the manner of barges which ye have hitherto built.

Jared and his family were given training—effectively, practice—in barge building before their skills had to hold up to the mountain waves of the great deep. Once they realized what they had been being prepared for, they were likely quite grateful for those early trial runs.

Nobel Prize winner and renowned physicist Dr. Carl Wieman praised the virtues of this kind of training and hands-on research, noting that lectures and book learning are "just not how the brain learns. It does not learn to do [complex] things by watching someone write on a chalkboard or by listening to them talk."[8] By confronting problems personally, students become more invested and better prepared to listen to and learn from what a wise teacher can offer.

Imagine each subsequent time the Jaredites built barges; they probably asked more astute questions, which likely resulted in the gradual fine-tuning of their skills. In this way, a little extra time spent on practice, training, or research is anything but inefficient. Since the long-term results are far superior, practice is actually effective *and* efficient, resulting in durable, applicable, useful understanding. Rather than trying to "save time," we might see patient practice and the learning it facilitates as actually why we *have* time.

PURPOSEFUL PERSISTENCE

In addition to a misguided desire for efficiency at the sake of effectiveness, there's another common, modern mindset that interferes with our growth: a confused pursuit of perfection over progress. Part of the problem lies in the word English scriptures typically translate as *perfection,* as in, "Be ye therefore perfect . . ."[9] Ironically, this is a less-than-perfect word choice. In Martin Luther's German translation of the Bible, a version the Prophet Joseph Smith particularly appreciated, Luther selected the German word *vollkommen,* interpreted as *complete* or *whole,* suggesting that it is ultimately the Savior who completes us as we strive toward a godlike state.[10] As much as we might like to reach *completion, wholeness,* or *perfection* today, tomorrow, or next week, as if it were an endpoint on a map, such a condition is more like an algebraic asymptote—an evasive line that can be approached but never crossed, at least mortally remaining out of reach. If recognized as such, its very elusiveness leaves space for continued striving, but without such recognition, that gap can feel like a gulf of never-ending frustration. As Sister Sheri L. Dew explains: "Though perfection is our ultimate objective and destination, it is not something that will occur here and not something we earn. Ultimately, perfection will be a gift from our Father. So fixating on perfection during mortality can become an immobilizing distraction. Progress, however, is another thing entirely. We can make progress in countless ways, large and small, every day of our lives if we choose to."[11]

It is precisely by *choosing* to engage in the struggle for progress with its many attendant ups and downs, successes and failures, that growth occurs. Such purposeful persistence is not for the fainthearted. It takes "courage to be imperfect while striving for perfection."[12] Avoidance of life's obstacles just isn't an option; we can be creative and go under them or over them, but we must pass through challenges and adversity—we simply can't go around them.

Interestingly, researchers have found that those who recognize errors, mistakes, and even failures as part of learning exhibit greater resiliency and an increased willingness to tackle tough problems because they see *the struggle itself* as the path to mastery.[13] Journalist Kathryn Schulz's research supports this, as she shares in her book, *Being Wrong.* She explains that the ability to make mistakes is crucial to human cognition. Far from being a liability, fallibility is an asset, contributing to the development of some of our most honorable qualities, such as empathy, optimism, conviction, creativity, and courage.[14]

Elder Neal A. Maxwell testified that "to deprive ourselves of those experiences, much as we might momentarily like to, would be to deprive ourselves of the outcomes over which we shouted with anticipated joy when this life's experiences were explained to us so long ago, in the world before we came here."[15] Though currently uncomfortable, imperfection and weakness are all part of the plan.

GODLY PROGRESS

That common idiom, *harder than it looks,* became our family's catchphrase to remind us of the purpose of mortality. When we started to listen for it and other colloquialisms like it, we realized that the notion of experiential learning is everywhere: "live and learn"; "nothing ventured, nothing gained"; "if at first you don't succeed, try, try again"; "trial and error"; "practice makes perfect"; "easier said than done"; and, my personal favorite, "good grief!" But even though we throw around these phrases, as if it's obvious that life's learning experiences are good for us, we sometimes feel cheated when we go through something tough, as if we'd procured a guarantee of ease and comfort before agreeing to this mortal adventure. On the contrary, the only guarantee we were given was that life would be hard but worth it, that all these things would give us experience and would be for our good.[16] So perhaps the most critical thing for us to keep in mind is that *we chose this,* as Elder Jeffrey R. Holland explained. "We (through Adam and Eve) made the conscious choice to live in and endure this mortal sphere of opposition in all things, for only through such an experience was godly progress possible."[17] Thanks to the great gift of agency, "Adam and Eve—and we—knowingly and lovingly absolved God of the responsibility for the 'thorns and thistles' of a fallen world [because it] was personally chosen by us, not capriciously imposed by him."[18]

Now let's turn our focus back to our First Parents, whom we left at the end of chapter 8 being escorted out of the garden. Eve and Adam now discover what their brave choice for progress looks and feels like as they cross the threshold into the lone and dreary world—mortality's perfectly designed, experiential-learning-based laboratory. "They traded their innocence," explained Brother Tad R. Callister, "for the prospect of perfection—that was the deal."[19] And to that end, mortality would provide them "unlimited opportunities to progress toward [their] destiny of godhood."[20] But those unlimited opportunities would be in a place removed from God's presence, to which they had certainly grown accustomed. Elder Holland reflected on how this change might have felt:

> *When Adam and Eve willingly stepped into mortality, they knew this telestial world would contain thorns and thistles and troubles of every kind. Perhaps their most challenging realization, however, was not the hardship and danger they would endure but the fact that they would now be distanced from God, separated from Him with whom they had walked and talked, who had given them face-to-face counsel. After this conscious choice, as the record of creation says, "they saw him not; for they were shut out from his presence" (Moses 5:4). Amidst all else that must have troubled them, surely this must have troubled them the most.*[21]

It's easy to imagine that, as the reality of that separation set in, they experienced the same sinking sensation we occasionally do when we're reminded that life is sometimes "harder than it looks." But Eve and Adam had been equipped with three amazing gifts, as are we, to help acquire the attributes of godliness as they progressed toward their heavenly home: they had bodies, they had each other, and they had a Savior. Their intelligent use of these blessings would see them through life's prickly patches, perhaps with a few scrapes and scratches but better for having learned from their experiences. It is to these three gifts that we now turn our attention.

NOTES

1. From a letter written by Vincent van Gogh to his brother Theo, The Hague, 26–27 November 1882; emphasis in the original. Available at *Vincent van Gogh: The Letters*, vangoghletters.org, Letter 288.
2. Kolb, *Experiential Learning*, 38.
3. See the Association for Experiential Education's website, www.aee.org, for more information.
4. Quoted in Kimball, *Faith Precedes the Miracle*, 98.
5. Dr. Terry Ball, former dean of Religious Education at BYU, wrote: "Expressed simply, the covenant promises that if we follow Heavenly Father's plan, we can become like Him. The everlasting covenant includes many principles and ordinances, such as the new and everlasting covenant of marriage and the new and everlasting covenant of baptism. In some periods of history some aspects of the covenant have varied. For example, in Abraham's day the covenant included ordinances of circumcision and blood sacrifice. In our dispensation it includes the ordinance of the sacrament. Despite these slight differences, the promise of the covenant has been consistent in all ages. If we follow God's plan, we can become as He is" (Ball and Winn, *Making Sense of Isaiah*, 70).
6. Roosevelt, *All in the Family*, 88–89.
7. Psychologists Elizabeth and Robert Bjork coined the term "desirable difficulties" to refer to short-term impediments that make for stronger learning. For fascinating insights and applications of their research, I highly recommend Brown, Roediger, and McDaniel, *Make It Stick*; and Lahey, *The Gift of Failure*.
8. Scott, "Should We Lose the Lecture?"
9. Matthew 5:48.
10. Givens and Givens, *The Crucible of Doubt*, 5.
11. Dew, *Worth the Wrestle*, 61–62.
12. Holland, "'One Thing Needful': Becoming Women of Greater Faith in Christ."
13. Brown, Roediger, and McDaniel, *Make It Stick*, 91.
14. Schulz, *Being Wrong*, 5–6.
15. Maxwell, *All These Things Shall Give Thee Experience*, 28.
16. See D&C 122:7.
17. Holland, *Christ and the New Covenant*, 203–4.
18. Holland, *Christ and the New Covenant*, 203–4.
19. Callister, "Our Identity and Our Destiny."
20. Callister, "Our Identity and Our Destiny."
21. Holland, "The Ministry of Angels."

CHAPTER 10

ACCORDING TO THE FLESH

The spirit and the body are the soul of man.

—Doctrine and Covenants 88:15

As Eve and Adam begin mortality, physical changes in their bodies certainly added to their brave adventure. Though we're given few details, we've been taught that blood began to course through their veins, and aging, with all its attendant processes, followed suit.[1] Imagine their surprise at some of the odd sensations that accompanied these changes but also their delight at their expanded abilities to express their feelings. Physical pain and pleasure suddenly presented them with a wide spectrum of sensations and experiences in their new environment. They must have felt a heightened sense of vitality, realizing their previous physical-yet-immortal state had now been "added upon"[2] in order to provide expanded opportunities for learning and growth.

The doctrine of Jesus Christ establishes that *the soul* is comprised of the spirit *and* the body.[3] And the interplay of spirit *and* body is a fundamental part of mortality.[4] The Prophet Joseph Smith taught, "The great principle of happiness consists in having a body."[5] And scripture confirms that "spirit and element, inseparably connected, receive a fulness of joy."[6] Though our bodies, with all their current natural-world weaknesses,[7] can occasionally feel more like a liability than an asset, happiness, joy, and even exaltation depend on them working cooperatively with our spirits.

Anciently, the ideal relationship between the two was thought to be friendly—that of "consort and ally."[8] However, today's prevailing attitude might be summed up by the word *embattled*. Many throw around the maxim, "The spirit is willing, but the flesh is weak,"[9] as if that's just how it is and always will be. Sadly, we sometimes feel like innocent bystanders watching a street fight between the two, with hunger and lust inevitably beating out the noble desires of our hearts.

There are several common attitudes regarding the relationship between the body and the spirit, which could be graphically represented by the following diagram:

Common Perspectives of the Relationship Between Body and Spirit

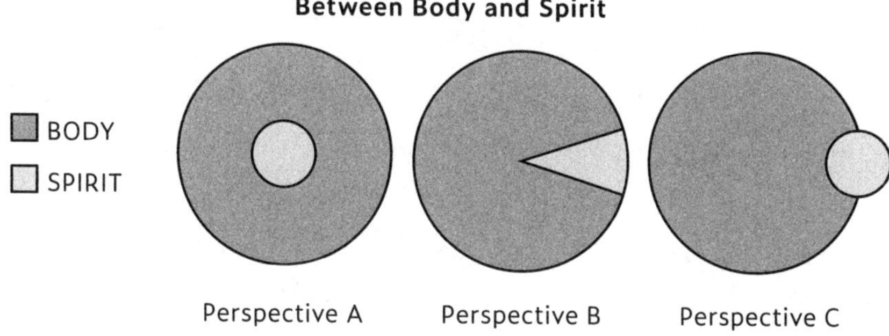

On various occasions, we might feel that our spirit is buried somewhere deep inside our body, hard to locate and even harder to access (Perspective A); or that our body is virtually devouring our spirit, gobbling it up with ravenous physical appetites (Perspective B); or that there is barely even a connection between the two, the spirit taking lead at church on Sundays but the body calling the shots the rest of the time (Perspective C). But what if we could embrace the divinity of both our spirit *and* our body, regularly remembering that it is when spirit and element inseparably connect that godliness becomes possible? Though physical sensations were new to Adam and Eve, they surely recognized the divine potential the union of spirit and body afforded them. Personally acquainted with resurrected Deity as they were, they had likely longed for such mortal embodiment, since their sincerest desire was to become like their Heavenly Parents. If that were our working attitude, as well, we too might see the relationship between body and spirit as something balanced and beautiful, like this:

Perspective D

After all, working in harmony with our spirits, our bodies are intended to be "instruments of power" and "of order and creation."[10] They allow us to be agents unto ourselves, to *do* what we *choose* to *do*, to assist us in *becoming* like our Heavenly Parents little by little and *right now*, not just in the eternities.

GIFTS OF THE BODY

The fulness of the earth, its intoxicating aromas and tastes, its enchanting sights and sounds, nourish both the physical and the spiritual in order to "strengthen the body and to enliven the soul."[11] These gifts of the body can be as beneficial and transformative as the various gifts of the Spirit. Indeed, our bodies are spectacular, information-gathering "filters for sifting the world," passing "light through our eyes, sounds through our ears, smells through our noses, tastes through our tongues . . . and symbols through our brains."[12] In addition to physical sensations, emotions provide compelling evidence of the dual nature of the soul—a racing heartbeat, nervous stomach, broad smile, or tear-stained cheeks—making feelings, hopes, and fears tangible.[13]

Few feelings are more valuable in our learning and growth than physical manifestations of the Spirit. Consider how you experience your most powerful spiritual impressions. Perhaps you feel your heart swelling, or you sense the warmth of a blanket being wrapped around you, or you see things more clearly. For me, the Spirit often leaks from my eyes. What wonderful ways our bodies and spirits work in concert with each other to testify of truth! Perhaps this is why the Lord discounts the earthly distinction of temporal versus spiritual; He recognizes the power inherent in body and spirit working together, allowing for "all things" to impact our spirituality.[14]

Elder David A. Bednar summarized the inestimable benefits of life's embodied experience. "Our physical bodies make possible a breadth, a depth, and an intensity of experience that simply could not be obtained in our premortal existence. Thus, our relationships with other people, our capacity to recognize and act in accordance with truth, and our ability to obey the principles and ordinances of the gospel of Jesus Christ are amplified through our physical bodies." He concluded, "Simply stated, there are lessons we must learn and experiences we must have, as the scriptures describe, 'according to the flesh.'"[15]

Physicality is practically a required condition for experiential learning; gospel guidelines seem to be designed to facilitate full body-spirit cooperation. For example, fasting is an effective way to add extra power to prayer; it helps us access "a fulness of joy" and strengthens our bulwarks against the adversary—proof that mighty power often results from the synergy between body and spirit.[16] And the blessings promised to those willing to live by the Word of Wisdom are spectacular: physical moderation and restraint empower us to "find wisdom and great treasures of knowledge, even hidden treasures," ultimately protecting us from "the destroying angel."[17] Even our participation in sacred ordinances employs the beautiful balance between body and spirit for our benefit. Ordinances are divinely prescribed physical representations of spiritual commitments; they provide opportunities for us to exercise agency as we actively demonstrate our discipleship, thereby compounding their meaningful impact.

THE GIFT OF SELF-COMPASSION

Though our bodies are meant to be a divine gift, too often the adversary manipulates them into a heavy burden. For many, especially women and girls, when it comes to our physical selves, the fun of effortful learning has been pushed aside by the facade of effortless perfection,[18] viciously fueled by Photoshop, social media, and the entertainment industry. The futile pursuit of society's unattainable physical ideals fosters unhealthy comparison and unnecessary competition, leading to both reckless pride and debilitating discouragement.

Sadly, so many of us accept Satan's lies that appearance is everything and that the easier we make it look, the better. Intellectually, we understand that self-discipline is necessary for self-mastery, but we fall for the adversary's twisted implication that self-criticism is required for self-control. Research consistently shows just the opposite: self-criticism drains motivation and undermines self-control.[19] Perhaps most significantly, negative self-talk, so prevalent in our relationships with our bodies, effectively disables healthy risk taking—that special type of courage that welcomes uncertainty and enables transformative growth. As Elder Jeffrey R. Holland wisely advised, "As children of God, we should not demean or vilify ourselves, as if beating up on ourselves is somehow going to make us the person God wants us to become."[20] Our mortal bodies sometimes fail, and even our immortal spirits sometimes falter. This is the time when self-compassion is most crucial.

Elder Paul E. Koelliker taught that distractions, like the hopeless hunt for effortless physical perfection, pull us toward the world, while focusing our agency on seeking the Lord and His love "[opens] our hearts to a celestial force which draws us toward Him."[21] Self-compassion directs our focus toward our divine identity and toward our loving Savior—the ultimate Source for confidence, support, and self-discipline.

THE GIFT OF A COMPASSIONATE SAVIOR

Christ's approach is always kind, never critical. Even He required an earthly body, not only as a fundamental component to allow for His Resurrection but to provide us a flawless example while simultaneously becoming perfectly equipped with infinite compassion. He can coach us through all of life's challenges—even the physical ones—because He has experienced them all. Throughout His life and ministry, and specifically as He wrought His Atonement, He took upon Himself our "infirmities, that his bowels [would] be filled with mercy, *according to the flesh*, that he [would] know *according to the flesh* how to succor his people."[22] The process of mastering our physical bodies, as well as learning to properly respect them, is a crucial part of becoming like Him and is graciously facilitated by His help—help only He can give because He was willing to become like us. As we gain that mastery, the unification of body and spirit enables our physical countenances to literally shine with His divine image.[23]

What a steep learning curve our First Parents had to climb as, with great faith and trust, they figured out the balance between body and spirit in the progress of the soul. Like us, they must have been repeatedly bruised, wounded, and scarred as they learned by experience to safely navigate the physical challenges of mortality. Such was the case even for the Prince of Peace, who has chosen "to retain for [our] benefit . . . the wounds in His hands and in His feet and in His side" as "signs . . . that painful things happen" but "problems pass and happiness can be ours."[24] Patient courage, in spite of such problems and pain, allowed Eve and Adam to keep their focus on the Savior and His promise of ultimate success for those who strive to follow Him.

NOTES

1. Regarding the introduction of blood to their mortal bodies, President Joseph Fielding Smith taught that "the immortal body is quickened by spirit, but the mortal body is quickened by blood" (Smith, *Doctrines of Salvation*, 1:76–77); see also Brown, *Gate of Heaven*, 30.
2. Abraham 3:26.
3. D&C 88:15–16; 2 Nephi 9:13.
4. President Joseph Fielding Smith taught that the two main purposes of mortality are "to gain experience that could not be obtained in any other way" and "to obtain these tabernacles of flesh and bones." Both, he noted, "are vital to the existence of man" (Smith, *Doctrines of Salvation*, 1:66).
5. https://www.josephsmithpapers.org/paper-summary/discourse-5-january-1841-as-reported-by-unknown-scribe-a/1.
6. D&C 93:33.
7. Brigham Young taught that " . . . the body is of the earth, . . . and is under the mighty influence of that fallen nature that is of the earth" (Young, *The Complete Discourses of Brigham Young*, 2:922).
8. Clement of Alexandria called the body the soul's "consort and ally" (Givens and Givens, *The Christ Who Heals*, 29).
9. See Matthew 26:41.
10. Eubank, "Eyes to See, Discipline to Create, Glue to Bind—Converted unto the Lord."
11. D&C 59:16–20.
12. Miller, "Theoscatology: On Dirt, Dung, and Digestion in God's Garden," 82–83.
13. Whether emotion is primarily physical or mental in source or experience has been a prime subject of debate for psychologists for over a century. Some researchers theorize that emotion is merely a mental state of awareness of a physiological response to stimuli, while others have postulated that bodily and mental responses to stimuli occur separately but simultaneously, that they work in tandem, or that there is no thinking involved at all (see Myer, *Psychology*, 460–63).
14. D&C 29:34.
15. Bednar, "We Believe in Being Chaste."
16. See Matthew 17:21; Mark 9:29; 1 Corinthians 7:5; Helaman 3:35; 3 Nephi 27:1;

and D&C 59:13–14 for these insights into the power available when the physicality of fasting is coupled with the spirituality of prayer.

17. D&C 89:19, 21.
18. Dr. Donna Lisker of Duke University coined this phrase as part of research she did to support Duke's Women's Initiative in the early 2000s. See Farrelly, "Freshman Women at Duke University Battle 'Effortless Perfection.'"
19. Simmons, *Enough As She Is*, 127–35. Rachel Simmons is the leadership development specialist at Smith College and cofounder of the national nonprofit Girls Leadership. She is a researcher, educator, and author focused on helping girls and young women find courage and confidence. She wisely notes, "If you don't beat yourself up when you fail, failure becomes a lot less scary" (135).
20. Holland, "Be Ye Therefore Perfect—Eventually."
21. Koelliker, "He Truly Loves Us."
22. Alma 7:12; emphasis added.
23. Alma 5:14 makes this point by poignantly asking if we have received His image in our countenance.
24. Holland, *Trusting Jesus*, 43–44.

CHAPTER 11

COMPLEMENTARY NATURE

Thee lift me and I'll lift thee,
and we'll ascend together.

—Quaker proverb[1]

The second valuable asset Adam and Eve entered mortality equipped with was teamwork, though this element is tragically missing from the Bible's telling of the tale and, subsequently, generally overlooked. Moses 5:1–16 comprises one of the longest continuous additions the Prophet Joseph Smith made to the Genesis account of the story, and its details are priceless.

Here we discover that everything Adam and Eve did, they did *together.* Adam worked the land, "and Eve . . . did labor with him" (v. 1). With Adam by her side, Eve labored in childbirth, and "they began to multiply and replenish the earth" (v. 2). Together, they "called upon the name of the Lord, and they heard the voice of the Lord" (v. 4). Jointly, "they made all things known unto their sons and their daughters" (v. 12) and "ceased not to call upon God" (v. 16) for guidance and direction.

Whether providing the necessities of life, worshipping the Lord, or parenting and protecting their posterity, they worked interdependently—not just side by side, but hand in hand, cooperative in their efforts and united in their goals, each using his or her unique gifts and stewardships to strengthen the other. Relying only on the Genesis account tragically discounts Eve's place in their partnership because these crucial details are completely absent. As Dr. Camille Fronk Olson has observed, "An acceptance and appreciation for the mutual dependence that God designed to exist between man and woman is one of the most important purposes of the scriptural record."[2] The significance of this restored section is apparent from the very first verse: "and Eve . . . did labor *with* him." President Marion G. Romney expounded specifically on the powerful implications of this phrase, explaining, "The word *with* as used here is very significant. It means more than physical labor. It connotes a common purpose, understanding, cooperation, and love."[3] It means they were *united.*

THE IDEAL PATTERN

As President Ezra Taft Benson explained, "From this inspired record we see that Adam and Eve provide us with an ideal example of a covenant marriage relationship."[4] Elder Bruce R. McConkie elaborated, extending that idea to their posterity, testifying that Adam and Eve's cooperative and united approach presents "the perfect pattern" for parenting. He went on to declare, "God be praised for the infinitely wondrous and glorious system of family unity which he has provided—the system that enables a man and a woman to unite together, provide bodies for the children of our Eternal Father, bring them up in light and truth and righteousness, and prepare and qualify them to return to the Father's presence and be inheritors of eternal life."[5]

"Ideal," "perfect," "wondrous and glorious"—such a stellar union presupposes equality between its participants, but not equality limited by *sameness,* rather equality enhanced by *balance.* The Apostle Paul seemed to be describing the caring cooperation that accompanies this brand of parity when he wrote to the Corinthians, recommending "that . . . your abundance may be a supply for their want, that their abundance also may be a supply for your want."[6]

This sort of balanced husband-wife relationship is built on "giving, serving, sharing, sacrificing, and selflessness."[7] Clearly, each member of the marriage must give himself or herself completely to the other, and fully receive the other as well. As President Russell M. Nelson has taught, "The complete contribution of one partner to the other is essential to exaltation."[8] Equal parts generosity and humility are required for such committed giving and receiving, and the combination of these two Christlike attributes unleashes the powerful synergy of wholeness as united partners recognize that neither is complete without the other.

HARMONIZED VOICES

If such an interdependent partnership is to succeed, both voices *must* be heard and respected, never silenced or suppressed. As President Spencer W. Kimball boldly declared, in The Church of Jesus Christ of Latter-day Saints, women are not intended "to be *silent* partners or *limited* partners" *to* their husbands but should absolutely and unequivocally be "*contributing* and *full*" partners *with* their husbands.[9] President Nelson recently reiterated this crucial message, urging women to speak up and speak out, declaring: "We, your brethren, need your strength, your conversion, your conviction, your ability to lead, your wisdom, *and your voices*. The kingdom of God is not and cannot be complete without women . . . who can *speak* with the power and authority of God!"[10]

This portion of our story, the "bonus" section of Moses 5, peaks with the scriptures' quintessential display of husband-and-wife complementarity, balance, and unity, as recorded in Adam and Eve's side-by-side testimonials. Their individual voices ring out even while harmonizing beautifully:

And in that day Adam blessed God and was filled, and began to prophesy concerning all the families of the earth, saying: Blessed be the name of God, for because of my transgression my eyes are opened, and in this life I shall have joy, and again in the flesh I shall see God.

And Eve, his wife, heard all these things and was glad, saying: Were it not for our transgression we never should have had seed, and never should have known good and evil, and the joy of our redemption, and the eternal life which God giveth unto all the obedient.[11]

While their dual declarations mutually express faith-filled understanding, they are both noteworthy *and* powerful because of their differences. What is most striking is their individual choice of pronouns. Adam speaks independently, using *my* and *I*, while Eve speaks relationally, using *our*, *we*, and *all*. That juxtaposition hints at a meaningful lesson, kindly acknowledged by President Nelson at the women's general session of general conference in October 2018: "Women see things differently than men do, and oh, how we need your perspective! Your nature leads you to think of others *first*, to consider the effect that any course of action will have on others."[12]

Research strongly supports the pervasiveness of this female perspective. Dr. Deborah Tannen, professor of linguistics at Georgetown University, has extensively documented that women tend to approach life as a network of connections through which they seek to preserve intimacy and avoid isolation. Men, on the other hand, tend to look at life as a series of oppositions through which they struggle to preserve their independence and avoid failure.[13] Given women's and men's unique, divinely appointed stewardships, each approach has its benefits. Used concurrently and in concert with each other, the combination of the two viewpoints strengthens and blesses families. Still, men and women can learn much from each other by humbly acknowledging the gaps in each approach, while generously guiding each other toward healthy improvements.

In addition to the gentle recognition of the different communication styles of men and women, Adam and Eve's tandem testimonials contain a second, more subtle, doctrinal message as well. Thoughtful examination reveals that our First Parents are each focused on slightly different, though interrelated, aspects of the next stage of the plan of redemption. In Adam's praises, he highlights the blessings of salvation—"again in the flesh I shall see God"; in Eve's, she specifies the blessings of exaltation—"the eternal life which God giveth unto all the obedient." Both declarations praise the Savior, the source of these priceless gifts, while recognizing that salvation and exaltation are not synonymous. Salvation, or immortality, is unconditional, given to every child of God thanks to Christ's Resurrection. Exaltation, sometimes referred to as eternal life or celestial glory, is conditional, referring to "the highest state of happiness and glory in the celestial realm."[14] Exaltation is contingent on obedience to the laws and ordinances of the gospel and the sacred covenants and sealing authority available in holy temples, all made possible by virtue of the power of the priesthood.

Though we may not typically articulate the difference between the two, we often read of salvation and exaltation in similar, coupled-yet-distinct ways, as in Moses 1:39, when God explains His work and His glory: "to bring to pass the immortality [salvation] and eternal life [exaltation] of man." In "The Family: A Proclamation to the World," we read of the opportunity "for individuals to return to the presence of God [salvation] and for families to be united eternally [exaltation]." Adam and Eve's pronoun selections powerfully reinforce the important truth taught by President Nelson: "In God's eternal plan, salvation is an individual matter; exaltation is a family matter." The loving connections of family make possible "the highest state of happiness and glory."[15] How thrilling and fitting to hear Eve, by her own voice and in her own words, teach and testify of the ultimate purpose of life! Her beautiful witness has fittingly been reverenced and honored as "one of the most profound doctrinal declarations ever made."[16]

UNIFIED PARTNERSHIPS

As Eve and Adam exemplify so beautifully, working interdependently to lead a family toward exaltation is the purpose of marriage. It was never intended to be a solo effort; it wasn't done alone in the premortal realm, it isn't meant to be done alone here on earth (though sometimes, of necessity, it is), and it won't be done alone in the eternities. Former General Relief Society President Julie B. Beck designated the family "a great and eternal organization" and taught that wise women lead such a family "in equal partnership with their husbands."[17] Elder L. Tom Perry elaborated on the balanced unity required to lead effectively, declaring: "There is not a president or a vice president in a family. The couple works together eternally for the good of the family. They are united together in word, in deed, and in action as they lead, guide, and direct their family unit. They are on equal footing. They plan and organize the affairs of the family jointly and unanimously as they move forward."[18]

United leadership requires focus and dedication, something I learned from my husband a few years ago in an unexpected way. Since he began medical school, I've worked to stabilize his stressful hospital career by striving to maintain peaceful order at home with our children. At times, our balancing act has resembled a comically unnerving two-person tightrope routine—not particularly calm or graceful. Truth be told, I've experienced some dark days of resentment, feeling like I was privately carrying the full load at home while wishing I was publicly earning recognition and respect somewhere else. Of course, he was making sacrifices and experiencing frustrations as well, watching from a distance as our little circus troupe learned new tricks while he missed out on all the fun. But eventually, thanks to patience and practice, humility and generosity, we both got better at our jobs and at supporting each other. As the children grew up and became more independent, I started to find some discretionary time in my schedule, freedom I hadn't had for many years. I happily filled it with community activities, humanitarian work, continuing education classes, and ladies' tennis groups. It was at this stage that he came home one evening and shared an interesting experience with me.

Some of the doctors had been discussing the pros and cons of allowing partners to moonlight in their free time. Moonlighting (working for another doctor, on a per-hour basis, as available) has traditionally been frowned upon by medical partnerships, though it's quite appealing to a young doctor drowning in student loans. I commented that I didn't really see the harm in a side job if it was done on vacation days and could help pay down loans. My husband stopped to think for a moment, then replied with an unusual hint of gravity: "If doctors are part of a partnership and have signed a contract, they've linked together their livelihood and well-being, so they've committed to give their very best to the group. If they spend their free time working elsewhere, and then come back worn out, they've cheated their partners." As I listened to his response, new understanding emerged in my mind, shining a light on a little corner of my conscience. That moment of enlightenment gently transformed how I looked at my responsibilities to our balanced marriage, our cooperative efforts, and our united goals. I realized that I could do better at preserving my best for my eternal partner, rather than rationalizing that as long as the home and family were running smoothly, any extra time and energy I had were free to be used for my own interests and pursuits. I realized that sort of self-centered attitude had resulted in the sense that we were sometimes living parallel lives—cooperative, successful parallel lives but not exactly the united, interdependent life we had set out to share.

Over the next few days, I thought long and hard about that moonlighting discussion, and I did a little experimenting to see if rededicating my focus to our marriage could increase our unity. I certainly didn't give up my other interests and pursuits, but I did use extra care in preserving the best part of myself—my energy and my intellect—for my relationship with my husband, rather than using it all up in my volunteer work, at my art class, or on the tennis court. Surprisingly, that slight shift helped me feel *more* capable and *more* accomplished, not less, because I was making room for his support and involvement. By saving some time and energy to discuss my feelings and ideas with him, even about hobbies he had no personal interest in, I was allowing him the opportunity to demonstrate he cared about what I was doing. Giving him the chance to express interest in my side pursuits provided him similar license to share more with me, and that virtuous cycle brought us closer together. I discovered that President Henry B. Eyring was exactly right when he testified to a group of international leaders in Rome "that a man and a woman, united in marriage, have a transcendent power to create happiness for themselves, for their family, and for the people around them."[19] As the Prophet Joseph taught, "By union of feeling we obtain power with God."[20]

Since that moonlighting discussion several years ago, I've paid special attention to quality partnerships, specifically watching for common traits that facilitate success. I've observed that the best teams communicate effectively *and* deliberately. They avoid surprises and keep each other apprised of what is coming. Even more, they counsel with each other, not just on joint ventures but on individual efforts and pursuits as well. And they keep each other's well-being in the forefront; they promote and encourage one another, never undermine or take unfair advantage.

President Eyring pointed to one particular factor as the key to unity in marriage: unselfishness. "Where there is unselfishness, differences become complementary and provide opportunities to help and build each other. Spouses and family members can lift each other and ascend together if they care more about the interests of the other than their own interests."[21]

Humility and generosity are the complementary keys that unlock the door to balanced interdependence in marriage. To lift each other as we ascend together is what the process of exaltation is all about. These days, our togetherness might not see us laboring in the field side by side, as our First Parents did, as much as touching base throughout the day with a text and emoji, then a quick handoff of the baby between a work meeting and Church assignment. What matters is that we work together, cooperatively united in striving jointly to provide the necessities of life, to worship the Lord, and to parent and protect our posterity, just as Eve and Adam did. Their faithful courage, founded on complete trust in their loving Savior, establishes their premier example as the "hallmark of marital partnership."[22]

NOTES

1. This traditional Quaker proverb is generally attributed to American Quaker poet John Greenleaf Whittier.
2. Olson, *Women of the Old Testament*, 19.
3. Romney, in Conference Report, Mexico City Area Conference 1977, 16.
4. Benson, "To the Elect Women of the Kingdom of God," 70.
5. McConkie, "Our Sisters from the Beginning."
6. 2 Corinthians 8:14.
7. Kimball, "Marriage and Divorce."
8. Nelson, "Lessons from Eve."
9. Kimball, "Privileges and Responsibilities of Sisters"; emphasis in original.
10. Nelson, "A Plea to My Sisters"; emphasis added.
11. Moses 5:10–11.
12. Nelson, "Sisters' Participation in the Gathering of Israel"; emphasis in original.
13. Tannen, *You Just Don't Understand!* 23–25.
14. Nelson, "Salvation and Exaltation."
15. Nelson, "Salvation and Exaltation."
16. McConkie, "Christ and the Creation."
17. Beck, "Mothers Who Know."
18. Perry, "Fatherhood, an Eternal Calling."

19. Eyring, "Renaissance of Marriage: To Become as One."
20. Nauvoo Relief Society Minute Book, 9 June 1842, 61. See Derr, Madsen, Holbrook, and Grow, *The First Fifty Years of Relief Society*, 78.
21. Eyring, "Renaissance of Marriage: To Become as One."
22. Olson, *Women of the Old Testament*, 19.

CHAPTER 12

DIVINE COLLABORATION

God will not act to make us something
we do not choose by our actions to become.

—Elder D. Todd Christofferson[1]

As we begin to examine the third, unparalleled gift Eve and Adam are blessed with as they undertake their mortal journey—the gift of a Savior—let's pause for a moment to review the facets of their mortal adventure that we've already examined. In chapter 9, we established that learning by experience is hard but effective. Mortality's path will be strewn with errors and mistakes, but it is precisely our inevitable imperfection that supplies ample opportunity for learning and growth. In chapter 10, we paid homage to the powerful relationship between body and spirit, honoring the body as the sacred, individualized gift that allows the soul to fully embrace life. And in chapter 11, we examined the complementary nature God so lovingly designed for women and men in order to allow them to faithfully partner and lead their families toward exaltation. At times, those first two gifts—physical bodies and loving companionship—might feel like some of the very obstacles we're tripping over along the challenge-strewn path to our heavenly home. Mustering our best long-suffering, we may even occasionally resort to the rote prayer of exasperation, "Lord, grant me the patience to endure my blessings!"

But rounding out this three-part divine endowment is the ultimate gift of a loving Savior: the perfect answer to our heartfelt pleading, the best solution for every problem, and the key component of true success. Adam and Eve are privileged to begin their earthly adventure with the benefits of a trusting, personal relationship with Him, and we are blessed with the opportunity to faithfully follow their fine example.

Christ's help is crucial since the uncomfortable reality is that life wends its way through some treacherous territory. Recall how Teddy Roosevelt taught his children about life's obstacles: avoidance is not an option. President Joseph Fielding Smith offered one explanation by way of comfort: "We are in the mortal life to get an experience, a training, that we couldn't get any other way. And in order to become gods, it is necessary for us to know something about pain, about sickness, and about the other things that we partake of in this school of mortality."[2]

"IN EVERY OTHER WAY"

As we navigate the inescapable dangers of life, we are occasionally privileged to meet fellow travelers who inspire and encourage us because of how they've learned from their challenges. Dr. Elisabeth Kübler-Ross, a psychiatrist who did groundbreaking work in the field of death, dying, and grieving, interacted regularly with such heroic individuals. Her research led her to strongly believe that "beautiful people do not just happen."[3] In an essay written by funeral directors Roy and Jane Nichols, which Dr. Kübler-Ross included in one of her research compilations, we are led to understand that "the most beautiful people we have known are those who have known defeat, known suffering, known struggle, known loss, and have found their way out of the depths. These persons have an appreciation, a sensitivity, and an understanding of life that fills them with compassion, gentleness, and a deep loving concern."[4]

My friend Christina is one of those "beautiful people." Her faithful commitment to the Lord softly illuminates her countenance and the road around her, drawing others toward her. Hearing a portion of her family's story has impacted my journey by clarifying how Christ can help us through our struggles.

In January 2005, Christina's daughter Catherine and her husband and young children were traveling home on the freeway one evening when the large wheel assembly of a semitrailer on the opposite side of the interstate broke loose, bounced across the divider, and struck their minivan, tragically taking the life of her husband.

Writing about the anguish she felt watching her precious daughter struggle with the pain of such a loss and the many new challenges it presented, Christina recalls, "She was 28 years old and had four children, ages 7 years to 8 months, to raise by herself. It was hard to do this alone. . . . As her mother, I wanted to take this from her. So, I pleaded with the Lord to help her in some way to lift the burden she carried."

The response to her prayerful pleading came with great clarity and compassion: "I cannot take away this experience from her, but I can bless her *in every other way*."[5]

Truly, Christ is our Guide, and He covenanted premortally with us that, although He would not shield us from mortality's painful experiences, He could be with us and bless us *in every other way*. And we trusted His promise. As He comforted the Prophet Joseph Smith through one of his greatest periods of struggle, He assures each of us: "All these things shall give thee experience, and shall be for thy good."[6] We will each pass through difficulties and problems, but He has set protective boundaries and will support our learning, provide resources, and ensure our safety. He is there to encourage and assist us in turning hard experience into durable, transformative learning, resulting in our gradually becoming like Him.

COMMITMENT AND EFFORT

As with all covenants, receiving His promised blessings is contingent on our commitment—we must put our agency to work and *try*. That willing, self-directed effort, however insignificant it may seem, is the key to divine collaboration because it unlocks the power of His Atonement to work in our lives. With conviction born of personal, faithful pioneering, Sister Eliza R. Snow taught this truth in 1869 to a group of Relief Society sisters and general leaders of the Church: "When you see one step before you, take it, and do not wait to see where is the next—if we see one step, it is not for us to stand still until we can see the way clear in the distance, but move forward and the way will be opened before us, step by step. This is a principle. God requires us to make the effort and thus prove our faith and trust in him, and then he is sure to extend his aid."[7]

One of the precious details we have of Eve and Adam's mortal experience describes this kind of trying—taking that next step, even while not knowing exactly why or precisely where it will lead. Their faithful sacrifices, both literally and figuratively, were a critical part of proving their trust in the Lord, a physical *and* symbolic demonstration of their reaching up to clasp His offered hand, allowing Him to guide them along. We read the beautiful account of what followed their faithful offerings in Moses 5:6–9:

> *And after many days an angel of the Lord appeared unto Adam [and Eve], saying: Why dost thou offer sacrifices unto the Lord? And Adam said unto him: I know not, save the Lord commanded me.*
>
> *And then the angel spake, saying: This thing is a similitude of the sacrifice of the Only Begotten of the Father, which is full of grace and truth.*
>
> *Wherefore, thou shalt do all that thou doest in the name of the Son,*

> *and thou shalt repent and call upon God in the name of the Son forevermore.*
>
> *And in that day the Holy Ghost fell upon [them], which beareth record of the Father and the Son, saying: I am the Only Begotten of the Father from the beginning, henceforth and forever, that as thou hast fallen thou mayest be redeemed, and all mankind, even as many as will.*[8]

These verses provide an excellent example of what we each frequently and personally experience: faithful, trusting actions are eventually rewarded with further enlightenment, in the form of either explanation or direction or a little of each. Those impressions motivate, encourage, and gradually transform us, thanks to the powerful witness of the Holy Ghost. As we repeatedly discover, the first step of this perfecting process always involves agency—*trying*.

Elder D. Todd Christofferson provides his additional witness to this fundamental gospel principle, stating, "Through the Atonement of Jesus Christ and His grace . . . we are enabled to develop a Christlike character. Justice demands, however, that none of this happen without our willing agreement and participation."[9]

Our willing agreement and participation, our *trying*, is Christ's only stipulation; as Elder Jeffrey R. Holland has emphatically confirmed, "The great thing about the gospel is we get credit for *trying*, even if we don't always succeed."[10] Once the Lord has concrete evidence of our desire to collaborate, of our reaching up to take His offered hand, He joyfully blesses us *in every way* short of removing our learning experiences. As Christina and her family and countless others, including our First Parents, have learned, it is the combination of bitter and sweet, our struggles plus His strength, that best allows for divine progress and exalting growth.

Elder Neal A. Maxwell, himself no stranger to life's painful sorrow and suffering due to his extended battle with leukemia, gained firsthand wisdom about life's bittersweet experiential learning. He shared: "The more we come to understand the plan of happiness, the more we come to understand how incomplete and unfinished we were in our first estate and how much we needed this difficult mortal experience. We finally realize that there is no other way." Then, with tender vulnerability, he acknowledged that the perfecting process can be quite painful. "Remembering this reality helps, especially when the only way is so difficult and discouraging at times and when we experience sadness as participants in the great plan of happiness."[11]

Sadness in spite of a perfect plan can be perplexing, even to the faithful. Christina helped her family battle discouragement and despair by leading them in watching for and recording all the many ways the Savior was blessing them. Three days after the death of her son-in-law, she asked her daughters to join her in writing down the many small gifts they were receiving from the Lord during that terrible time. A few months later, Elder David A. Bednar would label these "in-every-other-way" blessings *tender mercies*, popularizing that gentle scriptural term that so beautifully describes one aspect of the Atonement of Jesus Christ.[12] "After a few months," Christina shares, "we had 13 pages of tender mercies. We learned that those mercies came to remind us the Lord is mindful of us and what we are experiencing though He will not always take away the experience. These mercies build our faith and help us have courage to keep moving forward even when life is difficult."[13] That faithful courage—exhibited by Eve when she acknowledged the blessings of mortality's pains as precursor to eternity's joys—is just the impetus we need to keep us collaborating with the Lord as we bravely take one step at a time through life's challenging journey.

SACRED ASSISTANCE

Each of those moments when we recognize and acknowledge the Lord's mindfulness of our mortal difficulties gives the Spirit opportunity to witness of God's great love for us. Just as the angel taught Adam and Eve, the Spirit reminds us: "As thou hast fallen thou mayest be redeemed."[14] In order for us to more fully understand the infinite scope of Christ's Atonement, it's helpful to break down the Lord's sacred assistance into three subsets—redeeming blessings, empowering blessings, and compensatory blessings—each of which requires our active participation.

Redeeming Blessings

Because of His Atonement, Christ is able to redeem us from mortality's inevitable mistakes, oversights, errors, and sins. Agency, the very essence of the plan of salvation, is of necessity a two-part gift: its crucial counterpart is repentance. Christ's Atonement *preserves* agency by *allowing* for repentance. As Elder Christofferson phrased it, "Repentance respects and sustains our moral agency." He then clarified the collaborative piece of this doctrine beautifully, explaining, "Christ died not to save indiscriminately but to offer repentance. We rely 'wholly upon the merits of him who is mighty to save' (2 Nephi 31:19) in the process of repentance, but acting to repent is a self-willed change. So by making repentance a condition for receiving the gift of grace, God enables us to retain responsibility for ourselves."[15]

Used in tandem, agency and repentance allow for learning, change, and growth with the help of our Savior's redeeming power. President Thomas S. Monson testified, "One of God's greatest gifts to us is the joy of trying again, for no failure ever need be final."[16] If we think of repentance as the "desire to improve,"[17] it need not be frightening or overwhelming; it simply requires that we *try*. Elder Dale G. Renlund promised that "no matter how long we have been off the path or how far away we have wandered, the moment we decide to change, God helps us return."[18] It doesn't require some cruel and unusual punishment or any extended length of time. Noting that there's a difference between *faith* and *infallibility*, Elder Holland encouraged, "You can change anything you want to change, and you can do it very fast. . . . It takes exactly as long to repent as it takes you to say, 'I'll change'—and mean it."[19] Imperfection is such "a clever place for God to hide holiness."[20] The blessings are there for us if we are just willing to "repent and call upon God in the name of the Son forevermore."[21]

Empowering Blessings

In addition to His redemptive power, the infinite love of Christ, demonstrated and sanctified by His Atonement, allows Him to empower, enable, and strengthen us. This can occur frequently, even constantly, when we ally ourselves with the Holy Ghost. Sister Sheri L. Dew articulated the far-reaching blessings of seeking out such divine companionship, noting that "the cumulative effect of repeated witnesses of the Spirit becomes something of an inoculation against the ups and downs, the confusion and bewilderment, and the plain old agonies of life."[22] Learning to recognize and decipher spiritual promptings and impressions is like putting on the armor of God, preparing ourselves to be able to safely and effectively "counteract deception, distortion, and untruths."[23]

Once Adam and Eve had left God's presence in the garden, though clothed in their protective coats of skins, it might have taken them a bit of practice to perceive and apply that spiritual guidance that "fell upon [them]."[24] We can imagine them honing those new skills to the degree that they could wisely recognize the difference between heavenly messages and worldly ones, and the different intentions of those delivering them.

Compensatory Blessings

At times, in spite of all our effort and all our trying, the realities of life in this fallen world, complicated by the choices others make in exercising their agency, seem almost too much to bear. At those times, the compensatory powers of Christ's Atonement can prove a veritable lifeline. Even this is collaborative, since it is a particular gift for the obedient. While it is true that all of God's children are worthy of His blessings, for those who choose to keep God's commandments and acknowledge and express gratitude for His hand in their lives, there are additional, compensating blessings. Elder Andersen has spoken powerfully and repeatedly about this aspect of divine help. In a BYU devotional address given as part of the 2015 Campus Education Week, he shared profound prophetic insight, testifying: "As evil increases in the world, there is a compensatory spiritual power for the righteous. As the world slides from its spiritual moorings, the Lord prepares the way for those who seek Him, offering them greater assurance, greater confirmation, and greater confidence in the spiritual direction they are traveling. The gift of the Holy Ghost becomes a brighter light in the emerging twilight."[25]

We all experience days that feel frightening and unfair, when through no choice of our own we are under attack from all sides. In those formidable moments, our faithful obedience can be just that: full of faith. Though uncertainty may temporarily overwhelm us, our faith need not be blind or unfounded if it is built on trust.

When asked why we continue to obey, we can answer as our First Parents did, "I know not, save the Lord commanded me."[26] Though we may not understand everything, and we may not "know the meaning of all things," we can hold firmly and confidently to the Lord's hand, knowing "that he loveth his children."[27] And because of His divine love and our trusting obedience, He will bless us beyond our capacity to measure, thereby compensating for life's difficult injustices.

THE PROCESS OF EXALTATION

As Eve and Adam advanced through their mortal journey, though their fallen, human condition precluded face-to-face interaction with the Lord, they still "heard the voice of the Lord from the way toward the Garden of Eden, speaking unto them,"[28] guiding them along their way. Together, they diligently and faithfully obeyed, even when their understanding lagged behind their actions.

Little by little, they received additional insight and sacred assistance, sometimes by way of angelic messengers but also through personal revelation facilitated by the Holy Ghost. All that they learned pointed toward the Savior and His atoning sacrifice, "which is full of grace and truth."[29] All that they did, they did in His name. In exchange for their trust, faith, and obedience, they were assured redemption, "*and* all mankind, even as many as will,"[30] thanks to the Great Redeemer.

Ultimately, their story teaches that life is a process, quite literally "a progressive work,"[31] and exaltation is the two-part goal: both grand endpoint *and* gradual ascent. We look forward to "the glorious reward of receiving [our] full inheritance"[32] as children of Heavenly Parents, but in the meantime, we benefit from a Savior who "binds Himself to sustain, sanctify, and exalt us in return for our commitment to serve Him and keep His commandments."[33] The miracle of His Atonement is its power to lift us *each step of the way*. Brother Tad R. Callister has called this divine assistance "the crowning aim of the Atonement."[34] As he has explained, "Knowledge brings power; purity brings power; love brings power. The acquisition of each divine trait brings power. Power and godhood are directly related."[35] As we avail ourselves of that power, we gradually become more like God.

The Prophet Joseph acknowledged this gradual process, describing it while defining its goal: "Here, then, is eternal life—to know the only wise and true God; and you have got to learn how to be Gods yourselves . . . by going from one small degree to another, and from a small capacity to a great one; from grace to grace, from exaltation to exaltation until you attain to the resurrection of the dead, and are able to . . . sit enthroned in everlasting power."[36]

This ascent to our heavenly home is challenging, but no one has been asked to climb solo. Since mortality's thorns and thistles are for our sakes and for our growth, we've been lovingly offered spectacular help. Without taking away our strengthening experiences, Christ willingly and eagerly blesses us *in every other way,* if only we will turn toward Him and *try.*

With charming imagery, the revered theologian C. S. Lewis described the real-life process of exaltation: "*No amount* of falls will really undo us if we keep on picking ourselves up each time. We shall of course be very muddy and tattered children by the time we reach home. But the bathrooms are all ready, the towels put out, and the clean clothes in the airing cupboard. The only fatal thing is to lose one's temper and give it up." And then he added this final insight: "It is when we notice the dirt that God is most present in us: it is the very sign of His presence."[37]

As we learn from the true story of Eve and Adam, life demands courage. Watching their heroic efforts reminds us that mortality is sweaty, messy, uncomfortable work; there is simply no avoiding getting dirty. We've been both warned and assured that this is necessarily the case. Our journey's path will be strewn with obstacles, challenges, and seemingly impossible dilemmas, but Christ is the Way. With His help to supplement our humility, patience, and persistence, we too can heroically reach our final destination.

NOTES

1. Christofferson, "Free Forever, to Act for Themselves."
2. Smith, in Conference Report, October 1967, 122. Along these same lines, the prophet Brigham Young declared with conviction: "There is not a single condition of life [or] one hour's experience but what is beneficial to all those who make it their study, and aim to improve upon the experience they gain" (*Teachings of Presidents of the Church: Brigham Young,* 179, from a *Deseret News* article dated 9 July 1862).
3. Kübler-Ross, *Death: The Final Stage of Growth,* 96.

4. Nichols and Nichols, "Funerals: A Time for Grief and Growth," 96.
5. Shared with permission from a personal letter in possession of the author.
6. D&C 122:7.
7. Snow, "Let Us Cultivate Ourselves," 43.
8. Recall that Elder Bruce R. McConkie specified that "the name of Adam and Eve as a united partnership is Adam. They, the two of them together, are named Adam." See the discussion on the plural use of the name *Adam* in chapter 5.
9. Christofferson, "Free Forever, to Act for Themselves."
10. Holland, "Tomorrow the Lord Will Do Wonders among You"; emphasis in original.
11. Maxwell, *Lord, Increase Our Faith*, 49.
12. Bednar, "The Tender Mercies of the Lord."
13. Shared with permission from a personal letter in possession of the author.
14. Moses 5:9.
15. Christofferson, "Free Forever, to Act for Themselves."
16. Monson, "The Will Within."
17. Groberg, "The Beauty and Importance of the Sacrament."
18. Renlund, "Choose You This Day."
19. Holland, "For Times of Trouble."
20. In the optimistic words of Franciscan priest Father Richard Rohr, "What a clever place for God to hide holiness, so that only the humble and earnest will find it!" (Rohr, *Falling Upward*, xxii).
21. Moses 5:8.
22. Dew, *Worth the Wrestle*, 35.
23. Dew, *Worth the Wrestle*, 35.
24. Moses 5:9.
25. Andersen, "A Compensatory Spiritual Power for the Righteous."
26. Moses 5:6.
27. 1 Nephi 11:17.
28. Moses 5:4.
29. Moses 5:7.
30. Moses 5:9; emphasis added.
31. In *Journal of Discourses*, 16:165.
32. "Becoming Like God," Gospel Topics Essays, churchofjesuschrist.org.
33. Christofferson, "The Power of Covenants."
34. Callister, *The Infinite Atonement*, 52.
35. Callister, *The Infinite Atonement*, 68.
36. https://www.josephsmithpapers.org/paper-summary/history-1838-1856-volume-e-1-1-july-1843-30-april-1844/343#source-note.
37. Lewis, *The Letters of C. S. Lewis*, 470; emphasis in original.

EPILOGUE

EMBRACING LIFE WITH COURAGE

Life is so full of meaning and of purpose,
so full of beauty beneath its covering,
that you will find that earth but cloaks your heaven.
Courage, then, to claim it: that is all!

—Fra Giovanni Giocondo[1]

Courage is a complex concept. Part fleeting attitude, part acquired skill, it's the strength to persevere through danger, fear, and difficulty.[2] Its application looks different from person to person and from problem to problem, but what complicates courage even more is the cognitive dissonance that usually accompanies it. The human mind experiences uncomfortable tension when two conflicting or competing feelings coexist. That's usually the case when our courage is being called on—we *desire* a certain outcome but *fear* the path that leads there.

Part of the confusion of these mixed emotions is based on a simple misunderstanding of the nature of emotions. We think of opposites, like happy and sad, on a single spectrum, so a lot of one means a little of the other. But it's helpful, and probably more accurate, to imagine multiple, layered spectrums allowing for positive emotions to exist concurrently with negative ones. That paradoxical incongruity is hard to describe, but we've all felt it, like when we're grateful for a fun experience but sorry it's over, or when we've endured an excruciating ordeal but appreciate what we've learned. There's not really a perfect word for that feeling, but in English, we often use the term *bittersweet.*

Eve's choice in the garden may well be the origin of *bittersweet,* and her subsequent attitude in mortality is certainly the epitome of *courage.* She understood that the only way she and Adam could be "agents unto themselves,"[3] able to progress toward godly perfection, was through knowing *both* the bitter *and* the sweet, often simultaneously; life requires such a balance. Her faithful desire emboldened her to first partake of the fruit—to welcome hardship while holding firm to hope. That pivotal, representative action would set the standard for the attitude with which she and Adam would choose to embrace life. What bravery to willingly venture into such vast unknown, such frightening uncertainty!

Let's give Eve the last word. Listen closely and hear her wise encouragement. I believe she would counsel each of us to cherish agency, to seek the Lord and His love, and to embrace life. There is joy to be found and progress to be made, today and every day.

> *Were it not for our transgression we never should have had seed, and never should have known good and evil, and the joy of our redemption, and the eternal life which God giveth unto all the obedient.*[4]

NOTES

1. Giocondo, "A Letter to the Most Illustrious the Contessina Allagia degli Aldobrandeschi, Written Christmas Eve Anno Domini 1513."
2. *Merriam-Webster Online Dictionary,* "courage."
3. Moses 6:56; see also 2 Nephi 2:11.
4. Moses 5:11.

ACKNOWLEDGMENTS

One way to sum up my first foray into the complex world of publishing is with a favorite phrase of mine: harder than it looks. But in fact, a more accurate and more concise summation is this: collaboration. I have so many to thank for helping this work come to fruition; it was certainly the combined insights of a multitude that hopefully resulted in a book worth reading.

First, my thanks to those I know personally—my loving family and loyal friends, who tirelessly offered encouragement and support and sometimes, as needed, comic relief and cookies; my readers and confidants, whose kind and candid feedback helped me navigate the best path to my desired destination; the oh-so-talented Lisa DeLong, who created the perfect cover art to visually convey my heartfelt message; and the outstanding team at Deseret Book, who graciously shared their understanding, expertise, and impeccable standards. I am forever indebted to each of you for helping me make this dream a reality.

Second, my thanks to those I know only from a distance—the many enlightened thinkers, researchers, and writers who preceded me on this quest. Often, when my searching and digging yielded valuable insights and sparked new ideas, I was reminded that, thanks to these dedicated scholars, many of the answers I sought were hidden in plain sight. I sincerely hope I have built on your work in a way that pleases you.

And third, my thanks to those whose names I may not know but whose faith I have certainly felt—the countless, searching souls who have pled and wrestled with Divinity for explanations to the challenges of mortality, especially those related to the relationship between men and women. I bear witness to the cumulative effect of the prayers of so many. Thanks to each of our separate but similar efforts, I have repeatedly been overcome with the sense that "the veil o'er the earth is beginning to burst" ("The Spirit of God," *Hymns*, no. 2). I am so thankful for the continuing restoration of the fulness of the gospel of Jesus Christ.

And finally, I thank my dear husband, Doug—my personal Adam. He has generously and patiently supported me through this endeavor to an extent I never could have imagined. He has been at my side, providing those balancing elements I've needed to keep me upright and moving forward in so many ways these past four years. With the Lord as our Guide, there is no one with whom I would rather collaborate through the wild adventures of mortality. He is my best friend as well as my eternal partner—truly, my beloved *'ezer kenegdo.*

APPENDIX A

GENESIS 1:1–3:24

CHAPTER 1

1 In the beginning God created the heaven and the earth.

2 And the earth was without form, and void; and darkness was upon the face of the deep. And the Spirit of God moved upon the face of the waters.

3 And God said, Let there be light: and there was light.

4 And God saw the light, that it was good: and God divided the light from the darkness.

5 And God called the light Day, and the darkness he called Night. And the evening and the morning were the first day.

6 And God said, Let there be a firmament in the midst of the waters, and let it divide the waters from the waters.

7 And God made the firmament, and divided the waters which were under the firmament from the waters which were above the firmament: and it was so.

8 And God called the firmament Heaven. And the evening and the morning were the second day.

9 And God said, Let the waters under the heaven be gathered together unto one place, and let the dry land appear: and it was so.

10 And God called the dry land Earth; and the gathering together of the waters called he Seas: and God saw that it was good.

11 And God said, Let the earth bring forth grass, the herb yielding seed, and the fruit tree yielding fruit after his kind, whose seed is in itself, upon the earth: and it was so.

12 And the earth brought forth grass, and herb yielding seed after his kind, and the tree yielding fruit, whose seed was in itself, after his kind: and God saw that it was good.

13 And the evening and the morning were the third day.

14 And God said, Let there be lights in the firmament of the heaven to divide the day from the night; and let them be for signs, and for seasons, and for days, and years:

15 And let them be for lights in the firmament of the heaven to give light upon the earth: and it was so.

16 And God made two great lights; the greater light to rule the day, and the lesser light to rule the night: he made the stars also.

17 And God set them in the firmament of the heaven to give light upon the earth,

18 And to rule over the day and over the night, and to divide the light from the darkness: and God saw that it was good.

19 And the evening and the morning were the fourth day.

20 And God said, Let the waters bring forth abundantly the moving creature that hath life, and fowl that may fly above the earth in the open firmament of heaven.

21 And God created great whales, and every living creature that moveth, which the waters brought forth abundantly, after their kind, and every winged fowl after his kind: and God saw that it was good.

22 And God blessed them, saying, Be fruitful, and multiply, and fill the waters in the seas, and let fowl multiply in the earth.

23 And the evening and the morning were the fifth day.

24 And God said, Let the earth bring forth the living creature after his kind, cattle, and creeping thing, and beast of the earth after his kind: and it was so.

25 And God made the beast of the earth after his kind, and cattle after their kind, and every thing that creepeth upon the earth after his kind: and God saw that it was good.

26 And God said, Let us make man in our image, after our likeness: and let them have dominion over the fish of the sea, and over the fowl of the air, and over the cattle, and over all the earth, and over every creeping thing that creepeth upon the earth.

27 So God created man in his own image, in the image of God created he him; male and female created he them.

28 And God blessed them, and God said unto them, Be fruitful, and multiply, and replenish the earth, and subdue it: and have dominion over the fish of the sea, and over the fowl of the air, and over every living thing that moveth upon the earth.

29 And God said, Behold, I have given you every herb bearing seed, which is

upon the face of all the earth, and every tree, in the which is the fruit of a tree yielding seed; to you it shall be for meat.

30 And to every beast of the earth, and to every fowl of the air, and to every thing that creepeth upon the earth, wherein there is life, I have given every green herb for meat: and it was so.

31 And God saw every thing that he had made, and, behold, it was very good. And the evening and the morning were the sixth day.

CHAPTER 2

1 Thus the heavens and the earth were finished, and all the host of them.

2 And on the seventh day God ended his work which he had made; and he rested on the seventh day from all his work which he had made.

3 And God blessed the seventh day, and sanctified it: because that in it he had rested from all his work which God created and made.

4 These are the generations of the heavens and of the earth when they were created, in the day that the Lord God made the earth and the heavens,

5 And every plant of the field before it was in the earth, and every herb of the field before it grew: for the Lord God had not caused it to rain upon the earth, and there was not a man to till the ground.

6 But there went up a mist from the earth, and watered the whole face of the ground.

7 And the Lord God formed man of the dust of the ground, and breathed into his nostrils the breath of life; and man became a living soul.

8 And the Lord God planted a garden eastward in Eden; and there he put the man whom he had formed.

9 And out of the ground made the Lord God to grow every tree that is pleasant to the sight, and good for food; the tree of life also in the midst of the garden, and the tree of knowledge of good and evil.

10 And a river went out of Eden to water the garden; and from thence it was parted, and became into four heads.

11 The name of the first is Pison: that is it which compasseth the whole land of Havilah, where there is gold;

12 And the gold of that land is good: there is bdellium and the onyx stone.

13 And the name of the second river is Gihon: the same is it that compasseth the whole land of Ethiopia.

14 And the name of the third river is Hiddekel: that is it which goeth toward the east of Assyria. And the fourth river is Euphrates.

15 And the Lord God took the man, and put him into the garden of Eden to dress it and to keep it.

16 And the Lord God commanded the man, saying, Of every tree of the garden thou mayest freely eat:

17 But of the tree of the knowledge of good and evil, thou shalt not eat of it: for in the day that thou eatest thereof thou shalt surely die.

18 And the Lord God said, It is not good that the man should be alone; I will make him an help meet for him.

19 And out of the ground the Lord God formed every beast of the field, and every fowl of the air; and brought them unto Adam to see what he would call them: and whatsoever Adam called every living creature, that was the name thereof.

20 And Adam gave names to all cattle, and to the fowl of the air, and to every beast of the field; but for Adam there was not found an help meet for him.

21 And the Lord God caused a deep sleep to fall upon Adam, and he slept: and he took one of his ribs, and closed up the flesh instead thereof;

22 And the rib, which the Lord God had taken from man, made he a woman, and brought her unto the man.

23 And Adam said, This is now bone of my bones, and flesh of my flesh: she shall be called Woman, because she was taken out of Man.

24 Therefore shall a man leave his father and his mother, and shall cleave unto his wife: and they shall be one flesh.

25 And they were both naked, the man and his wife, and were not ashamed.

CHAPTER 3

1 Now the serpent was more subtil than any beast of the field which the Lord God had made. And he said unto the woman, Yea, hath God said, Ye shall not eat of every tree of the garden?

2 And the woman said unto the serpent, We may eat of the fruit of the trees of the garden:

3 But of the fruit of the tree which is in the midst of the garden, God hath said, Ye shall not eat of it, neither shall ye touch it, lest ye die.

4 And the serpent said unto the woman, Ye shall not surely die:

5 For God doth know that in the day ye eat thereof, then your eyes shall be opened, and ye shall be as gods, knowing good and evil.

6 And when the woman saw that the tree was good for food, and that it was pleasant to the eyes, and a tree to be desired to make one wise, she took of the fruit thereof, and did eat, and gave also unto her husband with her; and he did eat.

7 And the eyes of them both were opened, and they knew that they were naked; and they sewed fig leaves together, and made themselves aprons.

8 And they heard the voice of the Lord God walking in the garden in the cool of the day: and Adam and his wife hid themselves from the presence of the Lord God amongst the trees of the garden.

9 And the Lord God called unto Adam, and said unto him, Where art thou?

10 And he said, I heard thy voice in the garden, and I was afraid, because I was naked; and I hid myself.

11 And he said, Who told thee that thou wast naked? Hast thou eaten of the tree, whereof I commanded thee that thou shouldest not eat?

12 And the man said, The woman whom thou gavest to be with me, she gave me of the tree, and I did eat.

13 And the Lord God said unto the woman, What is this that thou hast done? And the woman said, The serpent beguiled me, and I did eat.

14 And the Lord God said unto the serpent, Because thou hast done this, thou art cursed above all cattle, and above every beast of the field; upon thy belly shalt thou go, and dust shalt thou eat all the days of thy life:

15 And I will put enmity between thee and the woman, and between thy seed and her seed; it shall bruise thy head, and thou shalt bruise his heel.

16 Unto the woman he said, I will greatly multiply thy sorrow and thy conception; in sorrow thou shalt bring forth children; and thy desire shall be to thy husband, and he shall rule over thee.

17 And unto Adam he said, Because thou hast hearkened unto the voice of thy wife, and hast eaten of the tree, of which I commanded thee, saying, Thou shalt not eat of it: cursed is the ground for thy sake; in sorrow shalt thou eat of it all the days of thy life;

18 Thorns also and thistles shall it bring forth to thee; and thou shalt eat the herb of the field;

19 In the sweat of thy face shalt thou eat bread, till thou return unto the ground; for out of it wast thou taken: for dust thou art, and unto dust shalt thou return.

20 And Adam called his wife's name Eve; because she was the mother of all living.

21 Unto Adam also and to his wife did the Lord God make coats of skins, and clothed them.

22 And the Lord God said, Behold, the man is become as one of us, to know good and evil: and now, lest he put forth his hand, and take also of the tree of life, and eat, and live for ever:

23 Therefore the Lord God sent him forth from the garden of Eden, to till the ground from whence he was taken.

24 So he drove out the man; and he placed at the east of the garden of Eden Cherubims, and a flaming sword which turned every way, to keep the way of the tree of life.

APPENDIX B

MOSES 2:1–5:16

CHAPTER 2

1 And it came to pass that the Lord spake unto Moses, saying: Behold, I reveal unto you concerning this heaven, and this earth; write the words which I speak. I am the Beginning and the End, the Almighty God; by mine Only Begotten I created these things; yea, in the beginning I created the heaven, and the earth upon which thou standest.

2 And the earth was without form, and void; and I caused darkness to come up upon the face of the deep; and my Spirit moved upon the face of the water; for I am God.

3 And I, God, said: Let there be light; and there was light.

4 And I, God, saw the light; and that light was good. And I, God, divided the light from the darkness.

5 And I, God, called the light Day; and the darkness, I called Night; and this I did by the word of my power, and it was done as I spake; and the evening and the morning were the first day.

6 And again, I, God, said: Let there be a firmament in the midst of the water, and it was so, even as I spake; and I said: Let it divide the waters from the waters; and it was done;

7 And I, God, made the firmament and divided the waters, yea, the great waters under the firmament from the waters which were above the firmament, and it was so even as I spake.

8 And I, God, called the firmament Heaven; and the evening and the morning were the second day.

9 And I, God, said: Let the waters under the heaven be gathered together unto one place, and it was so; and I, God, said: Let there be dry land; and it was so.

10 And I, God, called the dry land Earth; and the gathering together of the

waters, called I the Sea; and I, God, saw that all things which I had made were good.

11 And I, God, said: Let the earth bring forth grass, the herb yielding seed, the fruit tree yielding fruit, after his kind, and the tree yielding fruit, whose seed should be in itself upon the earth, and it was so even as I spake.

12 And the earth brought forth grass, every herb yielding seed after his kind, and the tree yielding fruit, whose seed should be in itself, after his kind; and I, God, saw that all things which I had made were good;

13 And the evening and the morning were the third day.

14 And I, God, said: Let there be lights in the firmament of the heaven, to divide the day from the night, and let them be for signs, and for seasons, and for days, and for years;

15 And let them be for lights in the firmament of the heaven to give light upon the earth; and it was so.

16 And I, God, made two great lights; the greater light to rule the day, and the lesser light to rule the night, and the greater light was the sun, and the lesser light was the moon; and the stars also were made even according to my word.

17 And I, God, set them in the firmament of the heaven to give light upon the earth,

18 And the sun to rule over the day, and the moon to rule over the night, and to divide the light from the darkness; and I, God, saw that all things which I had made were good;

19 And the evening and the morning were the fourth day.

20 And I, God, said: Let the waters bring forth abundantly the moving creature that hath life, and fowl which may fly above the earth in the open firmament of heaven.

21 And I, God, created great whales, and every living creature that moveth, which the waters brought forth abundantly, after their kind, and every winged fowl after his kind; and I, God, saw that all things which I had created were good.

22 And I, God, blessed them, saying: Be fruitful, and multiply, and fill the waters in the sea; and let fowl multiply in the earth;

23 And the evening and the morning were the fifth day.

24 And I, God, said: Let the earth bring forth the living creature after his kind, cattle, and creeping things, and beasts of the earth after their kind, and it was so;

25 And I, God, made the beasts of the earth after their kind, and cattle after their kind, and everything which creepeth upon the earth after his kind; and I, God, saw that all these things were good.

26 And I, God, said unto mine Only Begotten, which was with me from the beginning: Let us make man in our image, after our likeness; and it was so. And I, God, said: Let them have dominion over the fishes of the sea, and over the fowl of the air, and over the cattle, and over all the earth, and over every creeping thing that creepeth upon the earth.

27 And I, God, created man in mine own image, in the image of mine Only Begotten created I him; male and female created I them.

28 And I, God, blessed them, and said unto them: Be fruitful, and multiply, and replenish the earth, and subdue it, and have dominion over the fish of the sea, and over the fowl of the air, and over every living thing that moveth upon the earth.

29 And I, God, said unto man: Behold, I have given you every herb bearing seed, which is upon the face of all the earth, and every tree in the which shall be the fruit of a tree yielding seed; to you it shall be for meat.

30 And to every beast of the earth, and to every fowl of the air, and to everything that creepeth upon the earth, wherein I grant life, there shall be given every clean herb for meat; and it was so, even as I spake.

31 And I, God, saw everything that I had made, and, behold, all things which I had made were very good; and the evening and the morning were the sixth day.

CHAPTER 3

1 Thus the heaven and the earth were finished, and all the host of them.

2 And on the seventh day I, God, ended my work, and all things which I had made; and I rested on the seventh day from all my work, and all things which I had made were finished, and I, God, saw that they were good;

3 And I, God, blessed the seventh day, and sanctified it; because that in it I had rested from all my work which I, God, had created and made.

4 And now, behold, I say unto you, that these are the generations of the heaven and of the earth, when they were created, in the day that I, the Lord God, made the heaven and the earth,

5 And every plant of the field before it was in the earth, and every herb of the field before it grew. For I, the Lord God, created all things, of which I have spoken, spiritually, before they were naturally upon the face of the earth. For I, the Lord God, had not caused it to rain upon the face of the earth. And I, the Lord God, had created all the children of men; and not yet a man to till the ground; for in heaven created I them; and there was not yet flesh upon the earth, neither in the water, neither in the air;

6 But I, the Lord God, spake, and there went up a mist from the earth, and watered the whole face of the ground.

7 And I, the Lord God, formed man from the dust of the ground, and breathed into his nostrils the breath of life; and man became a living soul, the first flesh upon the earth, the first man also; nevertheless, all things were before created; but spiritually were they created and made according to my word.

8 And I, the Lord God, planted a garden eastward in Eden, and there I put the man whom I had formed.

9 And out of the ground made I, the Lord God, to grow every tree, naturally, that is pleasant to the sight of man; and man could behold it. And it became also a living soul. For it was spiritual in the day that I created it; for it remaineth in the sphere in which I, God, created it, yea, even all things which I prepared for the use of man; and man saw that it was good for food. And I, the Lord God, planted the tree of life also in the midst of the garden, and also the tree of knowledge of good and evil.

10 And I, the Lord God, caused a river to go out of Eden to water the garden; and from thence it was parted, and became into four heads.

11 And I, the Lord God, called the name of the first Pison, and it compasseth the whole land of Havilah, where I, the Lord God, created much gold;

12 And the gold of that land was good, and there was bdellium and the onyx stone.

13 And the name of the second river was called Gihon; the same that compasseth the whole land of Ethiopia.

14 And the name of the third river was Hiddekel; that which goeth toward the east of Assyria. And the fourth river was the Euphrates.

15 And I, the Lord God, took the man, and put him into the Garden of Eden, to dress it, and to keep it.

16 And I, the Lord God, commanded the man, saying: Of every tree of the garden thou mayest freely eat,

17 But of the tree of the knowledge of good and evil, thou shalt not eat of it, nevertheless, thou mayest choose for thyself, for it is given unto thee; but, remember that I forbid it, for in the day thou eatest thereof thou shalt surely die.

18 And I, the Lord God, said unto mine Only Begotten, that it was not good that the man should be alone; wherefore, I will make an help meet for him.

19 And out of the ground I, the Lord God, formed every beast of the field, and every fowl of the air; and commanded that they should come unto Adam, to see what he would call them; and they were also living souls; for I, God, breathed into

them the breath of life, and commanded that whatsoever Adam called every living creature, that should be the name thereof.

20 And Adam gave names to all cattle, and to the fowl of the air, and to every beast of the field; but as for Adam, there was not found an help meet for him.

21 And I, the Lord God, caused a deep sleep to fall upon Adam; and he slept, and I took one of his ribs and closed up the flesh in the stead thereof;

22 And the rib which I, the Lord God, had taken from man, made I a woman, and brought her unto the man.

23 And Adam said: This I know now is bone of my bones, and flesh of my flesh; she shall be called Woman, because she was taken out of man.

24 Therefore shall a man leave his father and his mother, and shall cleave unto his wife; and they shall be one flesh.

25 And they were both naked, the man and his wife, and were not ashamed.

CHAPTER 4

1 And I, the Lord God, spake unto Moses, saying: That Satan, whom thou hast commanded in the name of mine Only Begotten, is the same which was from the beginning, and he came before me, saying—Behold, here am I, send me, I will be thy son, and I will redeem all mankind, that one soul shall not be lost, and surely I will do it; wherefore give me thine honor.

2 But, behold, my Beloved Son, which was my Beloved and Chosen from the beginning, said unto me—Father, thy will be done, and the glory be thine forever.

3 Wherefore, because that Satan rebelled against me, and sought to destroy the agency of man, which I, the Lord God, had given him, and also, that I should give unto him mine own power; by the power of mine Only Begotten, I caused that he should be cast down;

4 And he became Satan, yea, even the devil, the father of all lies, to deceive and to blind men, and to lead them captive at his will, even as many as would not hearken unto my voice.

5 And now the serpent was more subtle than any beast of the field which I, the Lord God, had made.

6 And Satan put it into the heart of the serpent, (for he had drawn away many after him,) and he sought also to beguile Eve, for he knew not the mind of God, wherefore he sought to destroy the world.

7 And he said unto the woman: Yea, hath God said—Ye shall not eat of every tree of the garden? (And he spake by the mouth of the serpent.)

8 And the woman said unto the serpent: We may eat of the fruit of the trees of the garden;

9 But of the fruit of the tree which thou beholdest in the midst of the garden, God hath said—Ye shall not eat of it, neither shall ye touch it, lest ye die.

10 And the serpent said unto the woman: Ye shall not surely die;

11 For God doth know that in the day ye eat thereof, then your eyes shall be opened, and ye shall be as gods, knowing good and evil.

12 And when the woman saw that the tree was good for food, and that it became pleasant to the eyes, and a tree to be desired to make her wise, she took of the fruit thereof, and did eat, and also gave unto her husband with her, and he did eat.

13 And the eyes of them both were opened, and they knew that they had been naked. And they sewed fig leaves together and made themselves aprons.

14 And they heard the voice of the Lord God, as they were walking in the garden, in the cool of the day; and Adam and his wife went to hide themselves from the presence of the Lord God amongst the trees of the garden.

15 And I, the Lord God, called unto Adam, and said unto him: Where goest thou?

16 And he said: I heard thy voice in the garden, and I was afraid, because I beheld that I was naked, and I hid myself.

17 And I, the Lord God, said unto Adam: Who told thee thou wast naked? Hast thou eaten of the tree whereof I commanded thee that thou shouldst not eat, if so thou shouldst surely die?

18 And the man said: The woman thou gavest me, and commandest that she should remain with me, she gave me of the fruit of the tree and I did eat.

19 And I, the Lord God, said unto the woman: What is this thing which thou hast done? And the woman said: The serpent beguiled me, and I did eat.

20 And I, the Lord God, said unto the serpent: Because thou hast done this thou shalt be cursed above all cattle, and above every beast of the field; upon thy belly shalt thou go, and dust shalt thou eat all the days of thy life;

21 And I will put enmity between thee and the woman, between thy seed and her seed; and he shall bruise thy head, and thou shalt bruise his heel.

22 Unto the woman, I, the Lord God, said: I will greatly multiply thy sorrow and thy conception. In sorrow thou shalt bring forth children, and thy desire shall be to thy husband, and he shall rule over thee.

23 And unto Adam, I, the Lord God, said: Because thou hast hearkened unto the voice of thy wife, and hast eaten of the fruit of the tree of which I commanded

thee, saying—Thou shalt not eat of it, cursed shall be the ground for thy sake; in sorrow shalt thou eat of it all the days of thy life.

24 Thorns also, and thistles shall it bring forth to thee, and thou shalt eat the herb of the field.

25 By the sweat of thy face shalt thou eat bread, until thou shalt return unto the ground—for thou shalt surely die—for out of it wast thou taken: for dust thou wast, and unto dust shalt thou return.

26 And Adam called his wife's name Eve, because she was the mother of all living; for thus have I, the Lord God, called the first of all women, which are many.

27 Unto Adam, and also unto his wife, did I, the Lord God, make coats of skins, and clothed them.

28 And I, the Lord God, said unto mine Only Begotten: Behold, the man is become as one of us to know good and evil; and now lest he put forth his hand and partake also of the tree of life, and eat and live forever,

29 Therefore I, the Lord God, will send him forth from the Garden of Eden, to till the ground from whence he was taken;

30 For as I, the Lord God, liveth, even so my words cannot return void, for as they go forth out of my mouth they must be fulfilled.

31 So I drove out the man, and I placed at the east of the Garden of Eden, cherubim and a flaming sword, which turned every way to keep the way of the tree of life.

32 (And these are the words which I spake unto my servant Moses, and they are true even as I will; and I have spoken them unto you. See thou show them unto no man, until I command you, except to them that believe. Amen.)

CHAPTER 5

1 And it came to pass that after I, the Lord God, had driven them out, that Adam began to till the earth, and to have dominion over all the beasts of the field, and to eat his bread by the sweat of his brow, as I the Lord had commanded him. And Eve, also, his wife, did labor with him.

2 And Adam knew his wife, and she bare unto him sons and daughters, and they began to multiply and to replenish the earth.

3 And from that time forth, the sons and daughters of Adam began to divide two and two in the land, and to till the land, and to tend flocks, and they also begat sons and daughters.

4 And Adam and Eve, his wife, called upon the name of the Lord, and they

heard the voice of the Lord from the way toward the Garden of Eden, speaking unto them, and they saw him not; for they were shut out from his presence.

5 And he gave unto them commandments, that they should worship the Lord their God, and should offer the firstlings of their flocks, for an offering unto the Lord. And Adam was obedient unto the commandments of the Lord.

6 And after many days an angel of the Lord appeared unto Adam, saying: Why dost thou offer sacrifices unto the Lord? And Adam said unto him: I know not, save the Lord commanded me.

7 And then the angel spake, saying: This thing is a similitude of the sacrifice of the Only Begotten of the Father, which is full of grace and truth.

8 Wherefore, thou shalt do all that thou doest in the name of the Son, and thou shalt repent and call upon God in the name of the Son forevermore.

9 And in that day the Holy Ghost fell upon Adam, which beareth record of the Father and the Son, saying: I am the Only Begotten of the Father from the beginning, henceforth and forever, that as thou hast fallen thou mayest be redeemed, and all mankind, even as many as will.

10 And in that day Adam blessed God and was filled, and began to prophesy concerning all the families of the earth, saying: Blessed be the name of God, for because of my transgression my eyes are opened, and in this life I shall have joy, and again in the flesh I shall see God.

11 And Eve, his wife, heard all these things and was glad, saying: Were it not for our transgression we never should have had seed, and never should have known good and evil, and the joy of our redemption, and the eternal life which God giveth unto all the obedient.

12 And Adam and Eve blessed the name of God, and they made all things known unto their sons and their daughters.

13 And Satan came among them, saying: I am also a son of God; and he commanded them, saying: Believe it not; and they believed it not, and they loved Satan more than God. And men began from that time forth to be carnal, sensual, and devilish.

14 And the Lord God called upon men by the Holy Ghost everywhere and commanded them that they should repent;

15 And as many as believed in the Son, and repented of their sins, should be saved; and as many as believed not and repented not, should be damned; and the words went forth out of the mouth of God in a firm decree; wherefore they must be fulfilled.

16 And Adam and Eve, his wife, ceased not to call upon God. And Adam knew Eve his wife, and she conceived and bare Cain, and said: I have gotten a man from the Lord; wherefore he may not reject his words. But behold, Cain hearkened not, saying: Who is the Lord that I should know him?

APPENDIX C

ABRAHAM 4:1–5:21

CHAPTER 4

1 And then the Lord said: Let us go down. And they went down at the beginning, and they, that is the Gods, organized and formed the heavens and the earth.

2 And the earth, after it was formed, was empty and desolate, because they had not formed anything but the earth; and darkness reigned upon the face of the deep, and the Spirit of the Gods was brooding upon the face of the waters.

3 And they (the Gods) said: Let there be light; and there was light.

4 And they (the Gods) comprehended the light, for it was bright; and they divided the light, or caused it to be divided, from the darkness.

5 And the Gods called the light Day, and the darkness they called Night. And it came to pass that from the evening until morning they called night; and from the morning until the evening they called day; and this was the first, or the beginning, of that which they called day and night.

6 And the Gods also said: Let there be an expanse in the midst of the waters, and it shall divide the waters from the waters.

7 And the Gods ordered the expanse, so that it divided the waters which were under the expanse from the waters which were above the expanse; and it was so, even as they ordered.

8 And the Gods called the expanse, Heaven. And it came to pass that it was from evening until morning that they called night; and it came to pass that it was from morning until evening that they called day; and this was the second time that they called night and day.

9 And the Gods ordered, saying: Let the waters under the heaven be gathered together unto one place, and let the earth come up dry; and it was so as they ordered;

10 And the Gods pronounced the dry land, Earth; and the gathering together

of the waters, pronounced they, Great Waters; and the Gods saw that they were obeyed.

11 And the Gods said: Let us prepare the earth to bring forth grass; the herb yielding seed; the fruit tree yielding fruit, after his kind, whose seed in itself yieldeth its own likeness upon the earth; and it was so, even as they ordered.

12 And the Gods organized the earth to bring forth grass from its own seed, and the herb to bring forth herb from its own seed, yielding seed after his kind; and the earth to bring forth the tree from its own seed, yielding fruit, whose seed could only bring forth the same in itself, after his kind; and the Gods saw that they were obeyed.

13 And it came to pass that they numbered the days; from the evening until the morning they called night; and it came to pass, from the morning until the evening they called day; and it was the third time.

14 And the Gods organized the lights in the expanse of the heaven, and caused them to divide the day from the night; and organized them to be for signs and for seasons, and for days and for years;

15 And organized them to be for lights in the expanse of the heaven to give light upon the earth; and it was so.

16 And the Gods organized the two great lights, the greater light to rule the day, and the lesser light to rule the night; with the lesser light they set the stars also;

17 And the Gods set them in the expanse of the heavens, to give light upon the earth, and to rule over the day and over the night, and to cause to divide the light from the darkness.

18 And the Gods watched those things which they had ordered until they obeyed.

19 And it came to pass that it was from evening until morning that it was night; and it came to pass that it was from morning until evening that it was day; and it was the fourth time.

20 And the Gods said: Let us prepare the waters to bring forth abundantly the moving creatures that have life; and the fowl, that they may fly above the earth in the open expanse of heaven.

21 And the Gods prepared the waters that they might bring forth great whales, and every living creature that moveth, which the waters were to bring forth abundantly after their kind; and every winged fowl after their kind. And the Gods saw that they would be obeyed, and that their plan was good.

22 And the Gods said: We will bless them, and cause them to be fruitful and

multiply, and fill the waters in the seas or great waters; and cause the fowl to multiply in the earth.

23 And it came to pass that it was from evening until morning that they called night; and it came to pass that it was from morning until evening that they called day; and it was the fifth time.

24 And the Gods prepared the earth to bring forth the living creature after his kind, cattle and creeping things, and beasts of the earth after their kind; and it was so, as they had said.

25 And the Gods organized the earth to bring forth the beasts after their kind, and cattle after their kind, and every thing that creepeth upon the earth after its kind; and the Gods saw they would obey.

26 And the Gods took counsel among themselves and said: Let us go down and form man in our image, after our likeness; and we will give them dominion over the fish of the sea, and over the fowl of the air, and over the cattle, and over all the earth, and over every creeping thing that creepeth upon the earth.

27 So the Gods went down to organize man in their own image, in the image of the Gods to form they him, male and female to form they them.

28 And the Gods said: We will bless them. And the Gods said: We will cause them to be fruitful and multiply, and replenish the earth, and subdue it, and to have dominion over the fish of the sea, and over the fowl of the air, and over every living thing that moveth upon the earth.

29 And the Gods said: Behold, we will give them every herb bearing seed that shall come upon the face of all the earth, and every tree which shall have fruit upon it; yea, the fruit of the tree yielding seed to them we will give it; it shall be for their meat.

30 And to every beast of the earth, and to every fowl of the air, and to every thing that creepeth upon the earth, behold, we will give them life, and also we will give to them every green herb for meat, and all these things shall be thus organized.

31 And the Gods said: We will do everything that we have said, and organize them; and behold, they shall be very obedient. And it came to pass that it was from evening until morning they called night; and it came to pass that it was from morning until evening that they called day; and they numbered the sixth time.

CHAPTER 5

1 And thus we will finish the heavens and the earth, and all the hosts of them.

2 And the Gods said among themselves: On the seventh time we will end our

work, which we have counseled; and we will rest on the seventh time from all our work which we have counseled.

3 And the Gods concluded upon the seventh time, because that on the seventh time they would rest from all their works which they (the Gods) counseled among themselves to form; and sanctified it. And thus were their decisions at the time that they counseled among themselves to form the heavens and the earth.

4 And the Gods came down and formed these the generations of the heavens and of the earth, when they were formed in the day that the Gods formed the earth and the heavens,

5 According to all that which they had said concerning every plant of the field before it was in the earth, and every herb of the field before it grew; for the Gods had not caused it to rain upon the earth when they counseled to do them, and had not formed a man to till the ground.

6 But there went up a mist from the earth, and watered the whole face of the ground.

7 And the Gods formed man from the dust of the ground, and took his spirit (that is, the man's spirit), and put it into him; and breathed into his nostrils the breath of life, and man became a living soul.

8 And the Gods planted a garden, eastward in Eden, and there they put the man, whose spirit they had put into the body which they had formed.

9 And out of the ground made the Gods to grow every tree that is pleasant to the sight and good for food; the tree of life, also, in the midst of the garden, and the tree of knowledge of good and evil.

10 There was a river running out of Eden, to water the garden, and from thence it was parted and became into four heads.

11 And the Gods took the man and put him in the Garden of Eden, to dress it and to keep it.

12 And the Gods commanded the man, saying: Of every tree of the garden thou mayest freely eat,

13 But of the tree of knowledge of good and evil, thou shalt not eat of it; for in the time that thou eatest thereof, thou shalt surely die. Now I, Abraham, saw that it was after the Lord's time, which was after the time of Kolob; for as yet the Gods had not appointed unto Adam his reckoning.

14 And the Gods said: Let us make an help meet for the man, for it is not good that the man should be alone, therefore we will form an help meet for him.

15 And the Gods caused a deep sleep to fall upon Adam; and he slept, and they took one of his ribs, and closed up the flesh in the stead thereof;

16 And of the rib which the Gods had taken from man, formed they a woman, and brought her unto the man.

17 And Adam said: This was bone of my bones, and flesh of my flesh; now she shall be called Woman, because she was taken out of man;

18 Therefore shall a man leave his father and his mother, and shall cleave unto his wife, and they shall be one flesh.

19 And they were both naked, the man and his wife, and were not ashamed.

20 And out of the ground the Gods formed every beast of the field, and every fowl of the air, and brought them unto Adam to see what he would call them; and whatsoever Adam called every living creature, that should be the name thereof.

21 And Adam gave names to all cattle, to the fowl of the air, to every beast of the field; and for Adam, there was found an help meet for him.

BIBLIOGRAPHY

Andersen, Neil L. "A Compensatory Spiritual Power for the Righteous." BYU Devotional, 18 August 2015.

Aristotle. *Physics, Volume I: Books 1–4.* Translated by P. H. Wicksteed, F. M. Conford. Loeb Classical Library 228. Cambridge, MA: Harvard University Press, 1957.

Asay, Carlos E. "The Temple Garment: 'An Outward Expression of an Inward Commitment.'" *Ensign*, August 1997.

Aschkenasy, Nehama. *Eve's Journey: Feminine Images in Hebraic Literary Tradition.* Detroit, MI: Wayne State University Press, 1994.

Ashton, Brian K. "The Father." *Ensign*, November 2018.

Attridge, Harold W., ed. *The HarperCollins Study Bible: New Revised Standard Version.* San Francisco, CA: HarperOne, 2006.

Ball, Terry, and Nathan Winn. *Making Sense of Isaiah: Insights and Modern Applications.* Salt Lake City, UT: Deseret Book Company, 2009.

Ballard, M. Russell. "This Is My Work and Glory." *Ensign*, May 2013.

Ballard, M. Russell. "Women of Dedication, Faith, Determination, and Action." BYU Women's Conference address, 1 May 2015.

Ballard, Melvin J. "Struggle for the Soul." From an address delivered in the Salt Lake Tabernacle, 5 May 1928.

Beck, Julie B. "Mothers Who Know." *Ensign*, November 2007.

Beck, Julie B. "Teaching the Doctrine of the Family." Seminaries and Institutes of Religion Satellite Broadcast, 4 August 2009.

"Becoming Like God." Gospel Topics Essays, churchofjesuschrist.org.

Bednar, David A. "Seek Learning by Faith." CES Satellite Broadcast, 3 February 2006; reprinted in *Ensign*, September 2007.

Bednar, David A. "The Tender Mercies of the Lord." *Ensign*, May 2005.

Bednar, David A. "We Believe in Being Chaste." *Ensign*, May 2013.

Bennion, Francine R. "A Latter-day Saint Theology of Suffering." In *At the Pulpit: 185 Years of Discourses by Latter-day Saint Women.* Edited by Jennifer Reeder and Kate Holbrook. Salt Lake City, UT: The Church Historian's Press, 2017, 212–31.

Benson, Ezra Taft. "To the Elect Women of the Kingdom of God." In *Woman.* Salt Lake City, UT: Deseret Book Company, 1979, 69–76.

Bigelow, Claudine. "Creativity." BYU Devotional, 4 August 2015.

Brown, Francis, et al. *Brown-Driver-Briggs Hebrew and English Lexicon.* Snowball Publishing, 2010.

Brown, Matthew B. *The Gate of Heaven: Insights on the Doctrines and Symbols of the Temple.* American Fork, UT: Covenant Communications, 1999.

Brown, Peter C., Henry L. Roediger, III, and Mark A. McDaniel. *Make It Stick: The Science of Successful Learning.* Cambridge, MA: Belknap Press, 2014.

Browning, Elizabeth Barrett. "Aurora Leigh." New York, NY: Oxford University Press, 2008.

Busche, F. Enzio. "Do We All Believe in the Same God?" *Ensign,* May 1980.

Caine, Christine. *Unashamed: Drop the Baggage, Pick Up Your Freedom, Fulfill Your Destiny.* Grand Rapids, MI: Zondervan, 2016.

Callister, Tad R. *The Infinite Atonement.* Salt Lake City, UT: Deseret Book Company, 2000.

Callister, Tad R. "Our Identity and Our Destiny." BYU Devotional, 14 August 2012.

Campbell, Beverly. *Eve and the Choice Made in Eden.* Salt Lake City, UT: Deseret Book Company, 2003.

Cannon, Elaine. "Agency and Accountability." *Ensign,* November 1983.

Cannon, George Q. "Freedom of the Saints." In *Thy Servants Speak: Collected Discourses of George Q. Cannon, volume 2,* compiled by Jason Hansen. Salt Lake City, UT: 3rd Day Publishing, 2012, 221–28.

Carey, John. *The Essential Paradise Lost.* London, England: Faber and Faber, 2017.

Christofferson, D. Todd. "The Doctrine of Christ." *Ensign,* May 2012.

Christofferson, D. Todd. "Free Forever, to Act for Themselves." *Ensign,* November 2014.

Christofferson, D. Todd. "The Power of Covenants." *Ensign,* May 2009.

Collinge, William J. *The A to Z of Catholicism.* Lanham, MD: Scarecrow Press, 2001.

Cook, Quentin L. "The Eternal Everyday." *Ensign,* November 2017.

Cook, Quentin L. "Looking beyond the Mark." *Ensign,* March 2003.

Derr, Jill Mulvay, Carol Cornwall Madsen, Kate Holbrook, and Matthew J. Grow, eds. *The First Fifty Years of Relief Society: Key Documents in Latter-day Saint Women's History*. Salt Lake City, UT: Church Historian's Press, 2016.

Dew, Sheri L. "Are We Not All Mothers?" *Ensign*, November 2001.

Dew, Sheri L. "It Is Not Good for Man or Woman to Be Alone." *Ensign*, November 2001.

Dew, Sheri L. *Worth the Wrestle*. Salt Lake City, UT: Deseret Book Company, 2017.

Durham, G. Homer. "Woman's Responsibility to Learn." In *Woman*. Salt Lake City, UT: Deseret Book Company, 1979, 32–40.

Eubank, Sharon. "Eyes to See, Discipline to Create, Glue to Bind—Converted unto the Lord." BYU Women's Conference address, 4 May 2017.

Eubank, Sharon. "Turn On Your Light." *Ensign*, November 2017.

Evans, Rachel Held. *Inspired: Slaying Giants, Walking on Water, and Loving the Bible Again*. Nashville, TN: Nelson Books, 2018.

Eyring, Henry B. "Daughters in the Covenant." *Ensign*, May 2014.

Eyring, Henry B. "Renaissance of Marriage: To Become as One." An address given during *The Complementarity of Man and Woman: An International Interreligious Colloquium*, Vatican City, 18 November 2014. Full text available at churchof jesuschrist.org.

"The Family: A Proclamation to the World." *Ensign*, November 2010.

Farrelly, Maura Jane. "Freshman Women at Duke University Battle 'Effortless Perfection.'" *VoA News*, March 28, 2005. Available at IMdiversity.com.

Faulconer, James E. "Chaos and Order, Order and Chaos: The Creation Story as the Story of Human Community." In *Fleeing the Garden: Reading Genesis 2–3*. Edited by Adam S. Miller. Provo, UT: The Neal A. Maxwell Institute for Religious Scholarship, 2017, 48–67.

Faust, James E. "What It Means to Be a Daughter of God." *Ensign*, November 1999.

Gaskill, Alonzo L. *The Lost Language of Symbolism: An Essential Guide for Recognizing and Interpreting Symbols of the Gospel*. Salt Lake City, UT: Deseret Book Company, 2003.

Giocondo, Giovanni. "A Letter to the Most Illustrious the Contessina Allagia degli Aldobrandeschi, Written Christmas Eve Anno Domini 1513." The British Museum stated in 1970 that it had "proved impossible" to identify Fra Giovanni, the purported author of this letter. The letter was published, probably in the 1930s, "with Christmas Greetings" from Greville MacDonald, son of novelist George MacDonald and Mary MacDonald. More information about Fra Giovanni Giocondo is available at the *Catholic Encyclopedia*, www .newadvent.org.

Givens, Terryl, and Fiona Givens. *The Christ Who Heals: How God Restored the Truth That Saves Us.* Salt Lake City, UT: Deseret Book Company, 2017.

Givens, Terryl, and Fiona Givens. *The Crucible of Doubt: Reflections on the Quest for Faith.* Salt Lake City, UT: Deseret Book Company, 2014.

Givens, Terryl, and Fiona Givens. *The God Who Weeps: How Mormonism Makes Sense of Life.* Salt Lake City, UT: Ensign Peak, 2012.

Graham, William. www.patternsinnature.org.

Groberg, John H. "The Beauty and Importance of the Sacrament." *Ensign*, May 1989.

Hafen, Bruce C., and Marie K. Hafen. *The Contrite Spirit: How the Temple Helps Us Apply Christ's Atonement.* Salt Lake City, UT: Deseret Book Company, 2015.

Hafen, Bruce C., and Marie K. Hafen. "Crossing Thresholds and Becoming Equal Partners." *Ensign*, August 2007.

Hallett, Vicky. "A new study about what makes sports fun for kids finds that winning isn't everything." *The Washington Post*, 22 July 2014.

Holland, Jeffrey R. "Be Ye Therefore Perfect—Eventually." *Ensign*, November 2017.

Holland, Jeffrey R. "Behold Thy Mother." *Ensign*, November 2015.

Holland, Jeffrey R. *Christ and the New Covenant: The Messianic Message of the Book of Mormon.* Salt Lake City, UT: Deseret Book Company, 1997.

Holland, Jeffrey R. "For Times of Trouble." BYU Devotional, 18 March 1980.

Holland, Jeffrey R. "The Ministry of Angels." *Ensign*, November 2008.

Holland, Jeffrey R. "Tomorrow the Lord Will Do Wonders among You." *Ensign*, May 2016.

Holland, Jeffrey R. *Trusting Jesus.* Salt Lake City, UT: Deseret Book Company, 2003.

Holland, Jeffrey R. "Where Justice, Love, and Mercy Meet." *Ensign*, May 2015.

Holland, Patricia T. "Filling the Measure of Your Creation." BYU Devotional, 17 January 1989.

Holland, Patricia T. "'One Thing Needful': Becoming Women of Greater Faith in Christ." *Ensign*, October 1987.

Hudson, Valerie. "The Two Trees." FairMormon Conference address, August 2010. www.fairmormon.org/conference/august-2010/the-two-trees#en3.

Hudson, Valerie M., Bonnie Ballif-Spanvill, Mary Caprioli, and Chad F. Emmett. *Sex and World Peace.* New York, NY: Columbia University Press, 2012.

Hunter, Howard W. "Being a Righteous Husband and Father." *Ensign*, November 1994.

Hunter, Howard W. In Conference Report, April 1967, 115–16.

Hymns of The Church of Jesus Christ of Latter-day Saints. Salt Lake City, UT: The Church of Jesus Christ of Latter-day Saints, 1985.

Johnson, Sherrie. *Man, Woman, and Deity.* Salt Lake City, UT: Bookcraft, 1991.

Journal of Discourses, 26 vols. Los Angeles, CA: Gartner Printing & Litho Co., 1956.

Kendrick, L. Lionel. "Our Moral Agency," *Ensign*, March 1996.

Kimball, Spencer W. "The Blessings and Responsibilities of Womanhood." *Ensign*, March 1976.

Kimball, Spencer W. *Faith Precedes the Miracle.* Salt Lake City, UT: Deseret Book Company, 1972.

Kimball, Spencer W. "Marriage and Divorce." BYU Devotional, 7 September 1976.

Kimball, Spencer W. "Ocean Currents and Family Influences." *Ensign*, November 1974.

Kimball, Spencer W. "Privileges and Responsibilities of Sisters." *Ensign*, November 1978.

Kimball, Spencer W. "The Role of Righteous Women." *Ensign*, November 1979.

King James Version Apocrypha: Reader's Edition. Peabody, MA: Hendrickson Publishers, 2009.

Klebingat, Jörg. "Defending the Faith." *Ensign*, September 2017.

Koelliker, Paul E. "He Truly Loves Us." *Ensign*, May 2012.

Kolb, David A. *Experiential Learning: Experience as the Source of Learning and Development.* Englewood Cliffs, NJ: Prentice-Hall, 1984.

Kübler-Ross, Elisabeth, M.D. *Death: The Final Stage of Growth.* New York, NY: Simon and Schuster, 1975.

Lahey, Jessica. *The Gift of Failure: How the Best Parents Learn to Let Go So Their Children Can Succeed.* New York, NY: HarperCollins, 2015.

Lawrence, Larry R. "The War Goes On." *Ensign*, May 2017.

Lectures on Faith. Salt Lake City, UT: Deseret Book Company, 1985.

Lee, Harold B. *Decisions for Successful Living.* Salt Lake City, UT: Deseret Book Company, 1973.

Lee, Harold B. *Ye Are the Light of the World.* Salt Lake City, UT: Deseret Book Company, 1974.

Lewis, C. S. *The Letters of C. S. Lewis.* Edited by W. H. Lewis and Walter Hoopes. New York, NY: HarperCollins, 1966.

"The Living Christ: The Testimony of the Apostles." *Ensign*, April 2000.

Locke, John. *An Essay Concerning Human Understanding, Vol. I. The Gutenberg Project*, 23 August 2017, www.gutenberg.org/files/10615/10615-h/10615-h.htm.

Lyon, Jack M. *Understanding Temple Symbols through Scripture, History, and Art.* Salt Lake City, UT: Deseret Book Company, 2016.

Madsen, Truman. "House of Glory, House of Light, House of Love." BYU Women's Conference address, 1998.

Matthews, Robert J. "The Fall of Man." In *The Man Adam.* Edited by Joseph Fielding McConkie and Robert L. Millet. Salt Lake City, UT: Bookcraft, 1990, 37–64.

Maxwell, Neal A. *All These Things Shall Give Thee Experience.* Salt Lake City, UT: Deseret Book Company, 2007.

Maxwell, Neal A. "The Great Plan of the Eternal God." *Ensign,* May 1984.

Maxwell, Neal A. "The Inexhaustible Gospel." BYU Devotional, 18 August 1992.

Maxwell, Neal A. *Lord, Increase Our Faith.* Salt Lake City, UT: Bookcraft, 1994.

McBaine, Neylan. *Women at Church: Magnifying LDS Women's Local Impact.* Salt Lake City, UT: Greg Kofford Books, 2014.

McConkie, Bruce R. "Christ and the Creation." *Ensign,* June 1982.

McConkie, Bruce R. "Eve and the Fall." In *Woman.* Salt Lake City, UT: Deseret Book Company, 1979, 57–68.

McConkie, Bruce R. "Our Sisters from the Beginning." An address delivered at the dedication of the Nauvoo Monument to Women, 29 June 1978. *Ensign,* January 1979.

McConkie, Bruce R. *The Promised Messiah: The First Coming of Christ.* Salt Lake City, UT: Deseret Book, 1978.

McConkie, Bruce R. "What Think Ye of Salvation by Grace?" BYU Devotional, 10 January 1984.

McConkie, Joseph Fielding. "The Mystery of Eden." In *The Man Adam.* Edited by Joseph Fielding McConkie and Robert L. Millet. Salt Lake City, UT: Bookcraft, 1990, 25–35.

McKay, David O. In Conference Report, April 1950, 31–37.

McKay, David O. In Conference Report, April 1969, 4–10.

McKay, David O. *Gospel Ideals.* Salt Lake City, UT: The Improvement Era, 1953.

Merriam-Webster Online Dictionary. April 2019. Merriam-Webster Incorporated. https.//www.merriam-webster.com/.

Meservy, Keith. "The Four Accounts of the Creation." *Ensign,* January 1986.

Meyers, Carol. *Discovering Eve: Ancient Israelite Women in Context.* New York, NY: Oxford University Press, 1988.

Miller, Adam S. "Introduction: On Biblical Literalism." In *Fleeing the Garden:*

Reading Genesis 2–3. Edited by Adam S. Miller. Provo, UT: The Neal A. Maxwell Institute for Religious Scholarship, 2017, vii–xiii.

Miller, Adam S. "Theoscatology: On Dirt, Dung, and Digestion in God's Garden." In *Fleeing the Garden: Reading Genesis 2–3*. Edited by Adam S. Miller. Provo, UT: The Neal A. Maxwell Institute for Religious Scholarship, 2017, 82–95.

Monson, Thomas S. "Finding Joy in the Journey." *Ensign*, November 2008.

Monson, Thomas S. "The Race of Life." *Ensign*, May 2012.

Monson, Thomas S. "The Will Within." *Ensign*, May 1987.

Moore, Rebecca. *Women in Christian Traditions*. New York, NY: New York University Press, 2015.

Morris, George Q. In Conference Report, April 1958, 37–40.

Myer, David W. *Psychology*, 10th edition. New York, NY: Worth Publishers, 2014.

Nelson, Russell M. "The Atonement." *Ensign*, November 1996.

Nelson, Russell M. "The Creation." *Ensign*, May 2000.

Nelson, Russell M. "Faith in Jesus Christ." *Ensign*, March 2008.

Nelson, Russell M. "Lessons from Eve." *Ensign*, November 1987.

Nelson, Russell M. "Perfection Pending." *Ensign*, November 1995.

Nelson, Russell M. "Personal Preparation for Temple Blessings." *Ensign*, May 2001.

Nelson, Russell M. "A Plea to My Sisters." *Ensign*, November 2015.

Nelson, Russell M. "Salvation and Exaltation." *Ensign*, May 2008.

Nelson, Russell M. "Sisters' Participation in the Gathering of Israel." *Ensign*, November 2018.

Nibley, Hugh W. "The Atonement of Jesus Christ, Part I." *Ensign*, July 1990.

Nichols, Roy, and Jane Nichols. "Funerals: A Time for Grief and Growth." In Elisabeth Kübler-Ross, M.D., *Death: The Final Stage of Growth*. New York, NY: Simon and Schuster, 1975, 81–96.

Oaks, Dallin H. "Good, Better, Best." *Ensign*, November 2007.

Oaks, Dallin H. "The Great Plan of Happiness." *Ensign*, November 1993.

Oaks, Dallin H. "The Plan and the Proclamation." *Ensign*, November 2017.

Oaks, Dallin H. "Truth and the Plan." *Ensign*, November 2018.

Olson, Camille Fronk. *Women of the Old Testament*. Salt Lake City, UT: Deseret Book Company, 2009.

Oxford English Dictionary Online. March 2019. Oxford University Press. http://www.oed.com.

Packer, Boyd K. "Atonement, Agency, Accountability." *Ensign*, May 1988.

Packer, Boyd K. "The Mystery of Life." *Ensign*, November 1983.

Pearson, Kevin W. "Stay by the Tree." *Ensign*, May 2015.

Perry, L. Tom. “Fatherhood, an Eternal Calling.” *Ensign*, May 2004.

Personal Writings of Joseph Smith. Rev. ed. Compiled by Dean C. Jessee. Salt Lake City, UT: Deseret Book Company, 2002.

Petersen, Mark E. “Adam, the Archangel.” *Ensign*, November 1980.

Petersen, Mark E. *Adam: Who Is He?* Salt Lake City, UT: Deseret Book Company, 1976.

Peterson, Daniel C. “The Qur’anic Tree of Life.” In *The Tree of Life: From Eden to Eternity*. Edited by John W. Welch and Donald W. Parry. Provo, UT: Neal A. Maxwell Institute for Religious Scholarship, 2011, 193–216.

Pingree, John C., Jr. “I Have a Work for Thee.” *Ensign*, November 2017.

Pocket Oxford Latin Dictionary: English-Latin. Edited by James Morwood. Oxford University Press, 2005.

Pope Francis. “Pope Francis’s Homily at the Family Synod’s Opening Mass.” *Catholic Herald*, 4 October 2015. www.catholicherald.co.uk.

Pratt, Parley P. *Spirituality: The Key to the Science of Theology*. Springville, UT: Cedar Fort, 2007.

Rabelais, François. *Gargantua and Pantagruel*. Translated by Burton Raffel. New York, NY: Norton, 1990.

Renlund, Dale G. “Choose You This Day.” *Ensign*, November 2018.

Rey, H. A. *Curious George*. New York, NY: Houghton Mifflin Harcourt, 1941.

Richards, E. Randolph, and Brandon J. O’Brien. *Misreading Scripture with Western Eyes: Removing Cultural Blinders to Better Understand the Bible*. Downers Grove, IL: InterVarsity Press, 2012.

Roberts, B. H. *The Truth, The Way, The Life: An Elementary Treatise on Theology*. Edited by Stan Larson. San Francisco, CA: Smith Research Associates, 1994.

Rockwood, Jolene Edmunds. “The Redemption of Eve.” In *Sisters in Spirit: Mormon Women in Historical and Cultural Perspective*. Edited by Maureen Ursenbach Beecher and Lavina Fielding Anderson. Chicago, IL: University of Illinois Press, 1987, 3–36.

Rohr, Richard. *Falling Upward: A Spirituality for the Two Halves of Life*. San Francisco, CA: Jossey-Bass, 2011.

Romney, Marion G. In Conference Report, Mexico City Area Conference 1977.

Roosevelt, Theodore, III. *All in the Family*. New York, NY: G.P. Putnam’s Sons, 1929.

Saint Irenaeus of Lyon. *Against Heresies: The Complete English Translation from the First Volume of the Ante-Nicene Fathers*. Edited by Alexander Roberts and James Donaldson. San Bernardino, CA: Ex Fontibus Company, 2015.

Schulz, Kathryn. *Being Wrong: Adventures in the Margin of Error.* New York, NY: Ecco, 2010.

Scott, Richard G. "Honor the Priesthood and Use It Well." *Ensign*, November 2008.

Scott, Richard G. "Learning to Recognize Answers to Prayer." *Ensign*, November 1989.

Scott, Sam. "Should We Lose the Lecture?" *Stanford Magazine*, March/April 2017, 66–71.

Short, Kathy G. "Children Taking Action within Global Inquiries." *The Dragon Lode*, vol. 29, no. 2 (Spring 2011), 50–59.

Simmons, Rachel. *Enough As She Is: How to Help Girls Move Beyond Impossible Standards of Success to Live Healthy, Happy, and Fulfilling Lives.* New York, NY: HarperCollins, 2018.

Skousen, Eric N. *Earth: In the Beginning.* Orem, UT: Verity Publishing, 2006.

Smith, Joseph. *Joseph Smith Papers.* http://josephsmithpapers.org.

Smith, Joseph. *The Words of Joseph Smith: The Contemporary Accounts of the Nauvoo Discourses of the Prophet Joseph Smith.* Compiled and edited by Andrew F. Ehat and Lyndon W. Cook. Salt Lake City, UT: Bookcraft, 1980.

Smith, Joseph Fielding. In Conference Report, October 1967, 121–23.

Smith, Joseph Fielding. *Doctrines of Salvation*, 3 vols. Edited by Bruce R. McConkie. Salt Lake City, UT: Bookcraft, 1999.

Snow, Eliza R. "Let Us Cultivate Ourselves." In *At the Pulpit: 185 Years of Discourses by Latter-day Saint Women.* Edited by Jennifer Reeder and Kate Holbrook. Salt Lake City, UT: The Church Historian's Press, 2017, 41–45.

Sorensen, Alma Don, and Valerie Hudson Cassler. *Women in Eternity, Women of Zion.* Springville, UT: Cedar Fort, 2014.

Spackman, Ben. "'Adam, Where Art Thou?' Onomastics, Etymology, and Translation in Genesis 2–3." In *Fleeing the Garden: Reading Genesis 2–3.* Edited by Adam S. Miller. Provo, UT: The Neal A. Maxwell Institute for Religious Scholarship, 2017, 31–47.

Strong, James. *The New Strong's Exhaustive Concordance of the Bible.* Nashville, TN: Thomas Nelson Publishers, 2001.

Strong, Kristen. *Girl Meets Change: Truths to Carry You through Life's Transitions.* Grand Rapids, MI: Revell Books, 2015.

Talmage, James E. *The Articles of Faith.* Salt Lake City, UT: Deseret Book Company, 1984.

Talmage, James E. "The Earth and Man." Address delivered in the Tabernacle, Salt Lake City, UT, 9 August 1931.

Talmage, James E. *The House of the Lord.* Salt Lake City, UT: The Church of Jesus Christ of Latter-day Saints, 1912.

Talmage, James E. *Jesus the Christ.* American Fork, UT: Covenant Communications, 2006.

Tannen, Deborah. *You Just Don't Understand! Women and Men in Conversation.* New York, NY: HarperCollins, 1990.

Tanner, John S. "Making a Mormon of Milton." In *BYU Studies,* vol. 24, no. 2 (Spring 1984).

Tate, George S. "Obedience, Creation, and Freedom." BYU Devotional, 25 July 1995.

Taylor, John. *The Gospel Kingdom: Selections from the Writings and Discourses of John Taylor.* Edited by G. Homer Durham. Salt Lake City, UT: Deseret Book Company, 2002.

Teachings of Presidents of the Church: Brigham Young. Salt Lake City, UT: The Church of Jesus Christ of Latter-day Saints, 1997.

Teilhard de Chardin, Pierre. *The Divine Milieu: An Essay on the Interior Life.* New York, NY: Harper & Row, 1960.

Tingey, Mattie Horne. "The School of Experience." In *At the Pulpit: 185 Years of Discourses by Latter-day Saint Women.* Edited by Jennifer Reeder and Kate Holbrook. Salt Lake City, UT: The Church Historian's Press, 2017, 83–87.

Tonkin, Boyd. "Why Milton Still Matters." *The Spectator,* 18 March 2017. www.spectator.co.uk/2017/03/why-milton-still-matters/.

Trible, Phyllis. *God and the Rhetoric of Sexuality.* Philadelphia, PA: Fortress Press, 1978.

Uchtdorf, Dieter F. "The Gift of Grace." *Ensign,* May 2015.

Uchtdorf, Dieter F. "The Greatest Among You." *Ensign,* May 2017.

Uchtdorf, Dieter F. "Happiness, Your Heritage." *Ensign,* November 2008.

Wadyka, Sally. "Get the Health Benefits of Fruit." *Consumer Reports,* 19 May 2018. www.consumerreports.org.

Wagner, Danielle B. "Hilarious Misheard Hymn Lyrics That Will Make You Laugh Out Loud." *LDS Living,* 3 November 2018.

Walton, John H. *Ancient Near Eastern Thought and the Old Testament: Introducing the Conceptual World of the Hebrew Bible.* Grand Rapids, MI: Baker Academic, 2006.

Welch, John W. "The Tree of Life in the New Testament and Christian Tradition." In *The Tree of Life: From Eden to Eternity.* Edited by John W. Welch and

Donald W. Parry. Provo, UT: Neal A. Maxwell Institute for Religious Scholarship, 2011, 81–107.

Widtsoe, John A. *Gospel Interpretations: More Evidences and Reconciliations*. Salt Lake City, UT: Bookcraft, 1947.

Wilcox, Brad. *Changed through His Grace*. Salt Lake City, UT: Deseret Book Company, 2017.

Wilson, Lynne Hilton. *Christ's Emancipation of Women*. Palo Alto, CA: Good Sound Publishing, 2015.

Wordsworth, William. "Ode: Intimations of Immortality from Recollections of Early Childhood." www.poets.org.

Worthen, Kevin J. "In the Multitude of Counsellors There Is Safety." BYU Women's Conference address, 2016. In *One in Charity: Talks from the 2016 BYU Women's Conference*. Salt Lake City, UT: Deseret Book Company, 2017, 62–77.

Yarden, Leon. *The Tree of Light: A Study of the Menorah, the Seven-Branched Lampstand*. Ithaca, NY: Cornell University Press, 1971.

Young, Brigham. *The Complete Discourses of Brigham Young*. 5 vols. Edited by Richard S. Van Wagoner. Salt Lake City, UT: The Smith-Pettit Foundation, 2009.

Youngberg, Kjirstin. *Sacred Baby Names: Over 4,500 Names for Boys and Girls from Religions around the World*. Springville, UT: Plain Sight Publishing, 2012.

INDEX

Action, taking, 50–51. *See also* Effort

'Adam, 61, 63, 80n6, 81n19

Adam: interdependence between Eve and, xv; perversions of story of, 9–10; in premortality, 35–37, 41n33; as Michael, 36–37, 41n33; Edenic state of, 52n10; creation of, 61–62, 63, 71n15; evolution of name of, 62; marriage of, 68–69, 114n11; courage of, 79; partakes of fruit, 91–92, 96n39, 101. *See also* Complementarity; Eden; Fall

'Adamah, 61

Agency: in plan of salvation, 32–34; exaltation and, 40n25; in premortality, 40n28; as gift, 58–59; sin as by-product of, 70n10; knowledge as prerequisite of, 78, 81n22; choice and, 82, 83, 88; and conflicting alternatives facing Adam and Eve, 84; of Adam to partake of fruit, 91–92; repentance and, 152. *See also* Choice(s)

Alma, 115n27

Andersen, Neil L., 154

Antionah, 115n27

Apple, 20–21

Aquinas, Thomas, 63

Archangel, 36

Aristotle, 1

Asay, Carlos E., 116–17n51

Aschkenasy, Nehama, xiii–xiv

Ashton, Brian K., 39n16

Atonement, 6, 111–12, 116–17n51, 152–54

Ball, Terry, 127n5

Ballard, M. Russell, 8, 107–8

Banah, 62–63

Beck, Julie B., 3, 7n7, 141

Bednar, David A., 60, 79, 131, 151

Bennion, Francine R., 38

Ben Sira, 13

Benson, Ezra Taft, 137

Bible: challenges posed by stories of, 9–10; translations of, 12; interpretation of, 13, 18n16; redactions from, 13–14, 18n18, 45; tree of life in, 23; plan of salvation in, 41n45; compilation of Old Testament, 56

Birth: state of children at, 59–60, 70–71n10; of Adam and Eve, 61; giving, 90, 106. *See also* Childbirth

Bjork, Elizabeth and Robert, 127n7

Blessings: of trials, 147–48; contingent

on effort and commitment, 149–51; redeeming, 152–53; empowering, 153; compensatory, 153–54
Blood, 128, 134n1
Body / Bodies: changes to Adam and Eve's, 27n20, 128, 134n1; relationship between spirit and, 128–30; gifts of, 130–32; and self-compassion, 132–33; and compassion of Jesus Christ, 133–34; quickening of mortal and immortal, 134n1
"Bone of my bones, and flesh of my flesh," 68–69
Brown, Matthew, 94–95n29
Browning, Elizabeth Barrett, 42
Busche, F. Enzio, 2
Butterflies, 42–43

Caine, Christine, xvi n. 2
Callister, Tad R., xii, xvi n. 4, 30, 126, 155
Campbell, Beverly, 77
Cannon, Elaine, 81n22
Cannon, George Q., 40n2
Cassler, Valerie Hudson, 90–91, 96n42, 107
Change, 152–53
Childbirth, 90, 106. *See also* Birth
Children of God, 30–31
Choice(s): agency and, 82, 83; and competing demands, 82–83; facing Adam and Eve, 83–84. *See also* Agency
Christofferson, D. Todd, 15–16, 50, 146, 150, 152
Cleave, 69
Clothing, 99, 111–13
Coats of skins, 111–13
Comfort, 148–49
Commandment to multiply, 86, 92–93n7, 106
Compassion: for ourselves, 132–33; of Jesus Christ, 133–34
Compensatory blessings, 153–54
Complementarity, 54–55; scriptural accounts depicting Eve and Adam's, 54–55; in Genesis Creation Account A, 56–60, 70nn4–5; in Genesis Creation Account B, 60–69, 70nn4–5; and stewardships of men and women, 89–91, 96–97n43, 106–8. *See also* Marriage; Unity
Conable, Barber B., 7n11
Connotations, 14
Construction project, improvisation in, 28–29
Contrast, 48–49, 52n16
Cook, Quentin L., 30
Council in Heaven, 33–34, 37, 57
Courage, 79, 96n42, 156, 158–59
Creation(s): multiple scriptural accounts of, 18–19n21; awe at magnitude and magnificence of, 42–43; purpose of, 43; Restoration and understanding of, 43–46, 51–52nn6–7,9; phases of, 45–46; order as principle of, 46–47; differentiation as principle of, 47–49; participation in, 49–51, 53nn20,24, 71n15; complementarity in accounts of, 56–69, 70nn4–5
Cultural biases, 14, 89–90
Cursing, of ground, 109, 116n41

Death, 110–11
Desirable difficulties, 121–22, 127n7
Dew, Sheri L., 1, 6n1, 16, 124, 153
Differentiation, as principle of Creation, 47–49

Discernment, 95–96n36
Divine identity, 30–31
Divine potential, 32
Doctrinal understanding, holes in, 1–3, 7n6
"Dress and keep," 75–76
Dualism, 24–25, 27n18
Durham, G. Homer, 72n44
Dust, Adam's creation from, 61–62, 63

'Eden, 75
Eden: conditions in, 74–75; duties and qualifications in, 75–76, 80n6; transition and tutelage in, 76–77, 80n6, 81nn19,26
Effort, 149–51. *See also* Action, taking
Elohim, 58
Eloiheam, 57
Emotion, 130–31, 135n13, 158–59
Empowering blessings, 153
Endowment, 105
Eternal laws, 104
Eubank, Sharon, 16n5, 53nn20,24
Eve: misconceptions concerning, xii–xiv; interdependence between Adam and, xv; as example of womanhood, 1, 6n1; perversions of story of, 9–10; first recorded negative statements regarding, 13; in premortality, 35–37; Edenic state of, 52n10; creation of, 61, 62–64, 71n15; significance of name of, 64; as help meet, 65–68; marriage of, 68–69, 114n11; courage of, 79, 96n42; deception of, 87; partakes of fruit, 87–91, 96n39, 101–2; character of, 89; discernment of, 95–96n36. *See also* Complementarity; Eden; Fall
Everlasting covenant, 40–41n30, 108, 120, 127n5
Exaltation: as journey, 6; agency and, 40n25; and new and everlasting covenant, 108; marriage and, 138; as contingent on obedience, 140; versus salvation, 140; process of, 154–56. *See also* Salvation
Experiential learning, 118–20, 125–26, 131–32, 150–51
Eyring, Henry B., xvi, 143–44
'Ezer kenegdo, 65–68

Faith, demonstrating, 51, 149–51
Fall: lack of understanding regarding, xii–xiii, 2–3, 5–6, 9–10; fictional retellings of, 10–11, 17nn7–9; multiple scriptural accounts of, 15–16, 17–18n14; bodily changes following, 27n20, 128–30, 134n1; consequences of, 70n10, 80n8, 98–100; as transgression, 85–86, 93–94nn13,15, 95n33, 97n45; deception of Eve preceding, 87; Eve's decision to partake of fruit, 87–91, 96n39, 101–2; Adam's decision to partake of fruit, 91–92, 96n39, 101; Adam and Eve prepared for mortality following, 98–113
Fallenness, 60, 71n14
Family: importance of, 3, 7n7; Satan's attack on, 3–5; societal impact of, 5. *See also* Marriage
"Family: A Proclamation to the World, The," 86, 140
Fasting, 131
Faust, James E., 86
Fig leaves, 99
Fig tree, 113n3
Forgetfulness, veil of, 76, 80–81n15

Francis, Pope, 54
Fruit: misunderstanding of nature of, eaten by Eve, 20–21; as representation of doorway to mortality, 21–22; of tree of life, 24, 27n20; of tree of knowledge of good and evil, 25–26, 27n20; false ideas concerning Eve's consumption of, 26n5
Fruitfulness, 49–51, 53nn20,24, 86, 92–93n7, 106

Garments, 112–13
Generosity, 144
Giocondo, Fra Giovanni, 158
Givens, Terryl and Fiona, 92, 95–96n36, 98
God: and plan of salvation, 29–30; identity as children of, 30–31; character of, 31, 39nn16–17, 40n2, 84; trusting, 32, 40n2, 149; becoming like, 37–38, 120, 155; and everlasting covenant, 40–41n30; as God of law, 46; blesses Adam and Eve, 58–59; converses with Adam in Eden, 76–77; prepares Adam and Eve for mortality, 100–113; respect of, for eternal laws, 104; separation from, 126
Godly progress, 125–26
Goodness, God's commitment to, 31
Ground, cursing of, 109, 116n41
Guilt, 100

Hafen, Bruce C. and Marie K., 108, 111–12, 116n38
Happiness, 128–29
"Help meet," 65–68
Holland, Jeffrey R.: on reality of Adam and Eve, xiii; on fruit of tree of knowledge of good and evil, 26; on our divine potential, 32; on Adam and Eve's choice to transgress, 38, 97n45; on Adam and Eve's learning of gospel, 77–78, 81n26; on choice and agency, 82; on competing demands, 82; on mortality as gift, 91–92; on godly progress, 125; on challenges facing Adam and Eve, 126; on self-criticism, 132; on trying, 150; on repentance, 152–53
Holland, Patricia T., 51
Hudson, Valerie M., 4–5, 7n10. *See also* Cassler, Valerie Hudson
Human nature, 59–60, 71n14
Humility, 144
Hunter, Howard W., 33, 67–68

Identity, as children of Heavenly Parents, 30–31
Improvisation, 28–29
Innocence, versus knowledge, 77–78
Interdependence. *See* Complementarity; Marriage; Unity
Interpretation, 13, 18n16
Irenaeus, 102–3

Jaredites, 122–23
Jesus Christ: trusting, 32; becoming like, 120, 150; compassion of, 133–34; as gift, 146–47; comfort through, 148–49; effort in divine collaboration with, 149–51. *See also* Atonement
Johnson, Samuel, 17n7
Johnson, Sherrie, 63

Kafata, 117n51
Kendrick, L. Lionel, 81n22
Kenegdo, 67

Kimball, Spencer W.: on plan of salvation, 29, 41n44; on natural man, 60; on Eve's creation from rib, 61; on name *Adam*, 62, 80n6; on benefits of experiential learning, 120; on women's role in marriage, 138
Klebingat, Jörg, 40n28
Knowledge: of Adam and Eve, 77–78, 80n6, 81nn19,26, 84–85; as prerequisite of agency, 78, 81n22. *See also* Learning
Koelliker, Paul E., 133
Kolb, David, 118–19
Kübler-Ross, Elisabeth, 147

Labash, 112
Language, limitations of, 11–14, 89–90
Laws: physical, 47; eternal, 104; consequences of breaking, 116n41
Learning: in Eden, 76–77, 80n6, 81nn19,26; experiential, 118–20, 125–26, 131–32, 150–51; process for, 118–20; through desirable difficulties, 121–22; strengthened through practice, 122–23; persistence in, 123–25. *See also* Knowledge
Lee, Harold B., 73n45
"Let Us All Press On," 66
Lewis, C. S., 156
Life. *See* Mortality
Light of Christ, 103
Lisker, Donna, 135n18
"Living Christ: The Testimony of the Apostles, The," 23–24
Locke, John, 20
Lucifer, 87. *See also* Satan
Luther, Martin, 66
Madsen, Truman, 86
Marriage: of Adam and Eve, 68–69, 114n11; as eternal covenant, 73n47; celestial order of, 107–8; Adam and Eve as ideal pattern for, 136–38; harmonized voices in, 138–41; unity in, 141–43. *See also* Complementarity; Unity
Matthews, Robert J., 41n45
Maxwell, Neal A., 17–18n14, 41n46, 125, 150–51
McBaine, Neylan, 7n6
McConkie, Bruce R.: on Fall, 27n20, 80n8; on plan of salvation, 29–30, 37, 39n9; on premortal Adam and Eve, 35, 37; on Edenic state, 52n10; on name *Adam*, 62; on commandment against partaking of fruit, 86; on unity of Adam and Eve, 137, 157n8
McConkie, Joseph Fielding, 9
McKay, David O., 33
Men. *See* Complementarity; Marriage; Priesthood; Unity
Meservy, Keith, 18–19n21
Meyers, Carol, xiv, 93n13
Michael, 36–37, 41n33. *See also* Adam
"Mighty Fortress Is Our God, A," 66
Milton, John, 11, 17nn7–9
Mixed emotions, 158–59
Monson, Thomas S., 80–81n15, 94n19, 152
Moonlighting, 142–43
Morris, George Q., 110
Mortality: necessity of, 25–26, 27n23; purpose of, 33, 37–38, 105, 115n27, 120, 134n4, 147; in plan of salvation, 34–35, 84–85; suffering in, 41n46; as result of Fall, 70n10, 80n8; difficult decisions in, 82–83; as

gift, 91–92, 97n45; Adam and Eve prepared for, 98–113; experiential learning in, 118–19, 120, 126; perfection in, 124; courage in, 156, 158–59. *See also* Body / Bodies
Multiply, commandment to, 86, 92–93n7, 106

Nakedness, 98–101, 111–13
Natural man, 59–60, 71n14
Nelson, Russell M.: on plan of salvation, 39n10; on perfection, 39n17; on purpose of Creation, 43; on paradisiacal Creation, 45; on order in Creation, 46, 52n6; on Eve's creation from rib, 63; on garment, 112; on marriage, 138; on women's perspectives, 139; on salvation and exaltation, 140
Nephi, 116n41, 121–22
Nibley, Hugh, 117n51
Nichols, Roy and Jane, 147–48
Nutrition, 21–22

Oaks, Dallin H.: on Eve's transgression, xi, 89; on restored gospel's views on Eve, xiv; on Satan's tactics, 3; on Fall, 27n23, 85–86, 95n33; on competing demands, 82
Obedience, 83–84, 153–54
O'Brien, Brandon J., 14
Old Testament, compilation of, 56
Olson, Camille Fronk, xiii, 63, 106, 137
Order, as principle of Creation, 46–47
Ordinances, 132
Original sin, 59–60, 70–71n10
Origin story, 9

Packer, Boyd K., 38, 41n46, 84
Paradise Lost (Milton), 11, 17nn7–9
Paradisiacal Creation, 45–46
Perfection, 39n17, 123–25, 132–33, 151
Perry, L. Tom, 141
Persistence, 123–25
Petersen, Mark E., 74, 81n19
Physical laws, 47
Pingree, John C., 94n19
Plan of salvation: perfection of, 29–30; agency in, 32–33; acceptance of, 33–35, 40n29; Bruce R. McConkie on, 39n9; Russell M. Nelson on, 39n10; purpose of, 41n44; in Bible, 41n45; noncompliance to, 41n46; taught to Adam and Eve, 77–78, 80n6, 84–85; death as part of, 110–11
Practice, learning through, 122–23
Pratt, Parley P., 27n18
Premortality, 33–37, 40nn28–29, 41n33, 41n46, 57
Priesthood, 91, 96–97n43, 107
Priesthood blessing, given to Adam and Eve, 58–59
Progress: eternal, 1–6; through taking action, 50–51; versus perfection, 123–25; godly, 125–26

Rabelais, François, 1
Redaction, 13–14, 18n18, 45
Redeeming blessings, 152–53
Renlund, Dale G., 152
Repentance, 152
Rib, Eve's creation from, 61, 62–64
Richards, E. Randolph, 14
Roberts, B. H., 25
Rohr, Richard, 157n20
Romney, Marion G., 137
Roosevelt, Theodore, 52n16, 121

Sacred symbolism, understanding, 17n6
Salvation, 28, 140. *See also* Exaltation; Plan of salvation
Satan: falsehoods of, 2; attacks family, 3–5; portrayed as serpent, 87, 94n25; deception and uncertainty introduced by, 87–89, 94–95nn29,31–32, 102–3; Eve discerns deception of, 95–96n36, 101–2; as cause of wickedness, 95n32; and consequences of Fall, 99–100, 101; enmity between children of Eve and, 103; manipulates bodies into burden, 132–33
Schulz, Kathryn, 124
Scott, Richard G., 96–97n43
Self-compassion, 132–33
Self-criticism, 132
Selfishness, 143–44
Self-reliance, 98–100
Serpents, 87, 94n25
Shame, 100–101
Simmons, Rachel, 135n19
Sin, 70n10, 85
Smith, George Albert, 71n15
Smith, Joseph: on limitations of language, 11; on translation, 12; on understanding sacred symbolism, 17n6; on dualism, 27n18; on Christ and Adam, 36; on everlasting covenant, 40–41n30; on Creation, 44, 51–52nn6–7; on term *Eloiheam*, 57; on marriage, 68; on Adam and Eve's learning of gospel, 75, 80n6; on Eden, 76–77; on competing demands, 82; on Fall, 85; on Satan as cause of wickedness, 95n32; on happiness and body, 128; on unity, 143; on process of exaltation, 155–56
Smith, Joseph F., 71n15
Smith, Joseph Fielding: on necessity of mortality, 27n23; on premortal Adam, 36; on agency, 40n25; on plan of salvation, 40n29; on marriage, 73n47; on Eden, 77; on knowledge of Adam, 78; on Fall, 80n8, 93–94n15; on commandment to multiply, 92–93n7; on death, 111; on quickening of mortal and immortal bodies, 134n1; on purpose of mortality, 134n4, 147
Snow, Eliza R., 149
Sorensen, Alma D., 107
Sorrow, 105–6, 109–10
Soul, 128
Spirit, relationship between body and, 128–30
Spiritual Creation, 45
Spiritual experiences, pivotal, 42–43
Spiritual impressions: reception of, 15–16; physical manifestations of, 131; recognizing, 153
Stephens, Evan, 66
Stewardships, of men and women, 89–91, 96–97n43, 106–8
Suffering, 41n46. *See also* Trials
Sweetness, 21–22
Symbolism, understanding, 17n6

Talmage, James E., 26n5, 27n23, 35, 75, 86
Tannen, Deborah, 139
Tanner, John, 17n9
Tate, George S., 49–50
Teilhard de Chardin, Pierre, 53n26
Temptation, 95n32
Tender mercies, 151

Tingey, Martha Horne, 90, 96n41
Transgression, 85–86, 93–94nn13,15, 95n33, 97n45
Translation, 12, 13–14
Tree of knowledge of good and evil, 22, 24–26, 27n20, 90–91
Tree of life, 22–24, 26, 26–27n11, 27n20, 90–91, 102, 104–5
Trees, 22
Trials: facing Adam and Eve, 105–6, 109–10; purpose of, 119–20, 147; as desirable difficulties, 121–22; avoidance of, 124; and godly progress, 125–26; blessings of, 147–48. *See also* Suffering
Truth, God's commitment to, 31
Tsela, 62–63

Uchtdorf, Dieter F., 12, 28, 49
Uncertainty, 88–89
Unity: of Adam and Eve, 137, 157n8; in marriage, 141–43
Unselfishness, 143–44

Vacuum, filling of, 1–2
Van Gogh, Vincent, 118
Variety, 48
Veil of forgetfulness, 76, 80–81n15
Vitamins, 21–22
Vulnerability, 98–101

Welch, John W., 26–27n11
Widtsoe, John A., 86, 88
Wieman, Carl, 123
Wilson, Lynne Hilton, 115n34
Wilson, Mary Grace, 93n13
Women: hostility aimed at, xii; degradation of Eve and, xiii, 61; Eve as example for, 1, 6n1; societal devaluation of, 4–5, 7n11; in culture and belief of restored gospel, 7n6; childbirth as privilege reserved for, 90; as equal partners in marriage, 138; perspectives and communication styles of, 139. *See also* Complementarity; Marriage; Unity
Woodruff, Wilford, 25
Word associations, 20–21
Word of Wisdom, 131–32
Wordsworth, William, 59–60

Young, Brigham, 71nn14–15, 77, 93–94n15, 105, 134n7, 156n2

ABOUT THE AUTHOR

MELINDA WHEELWRIGHT BROWN earned a bachelor's degree in economics from Brigham Young University and is a respected teacher and public speaker. She has a passion for solving problems, particularly those faced by women. This has led to her involvement in and support of several nonprofit organizations, including Fight the New Drug, Days for Girls, Better Days 2020, Big Ocean Women, and the Elizabeth Smart Foundation, where she currently chairs the board. Melinda and her husband, Doug, are the parents of four children and have recently entered the delightful world of grandparenthood.

ABOUT THE COVER ART

For the Beauty of the Earth, by Lisa DeLong

The delicate balance of macrocosm and microcosm reveals a multi-layered, fractal pattern infused with the harmonies of the golden ratio. Drawn with compass and square, the geometry of this piece is an exploration of the fivefold proportions found in nature: the seeds of the apple, the dance of the planet Venus, and even human DNA.

LISA DELONG lives in London, where she works for the Prince's Foundation School of Traditional Arts. Visit lisadelong.com to see more of her work or to commission a painting.